B.R. Ambedkar
The Quest for Justice

Editorial Advisory Board

Anand Teltumbde
Annapurna Waughray
G. Haragopal
Kalpana Kannabiran
Laurence R. Simon
Meena Dhanda
Moses Seenarine
Rochana Bajpai
S. Japhet
Sukhadeo Thorat
Suraj Yengde
Valerian Rodrigues

B.R. Ambedkar

The Quest for Justice

VOLUME IV
Gender and Racial Justice

Edited by
Aakash Singh Rathore

OXFORD
UNIVERSITY PRESS

Oxford University Press is a department of the University of Oxford.
It furthers the University's objective of excellence in research, scholarship,
and education by publishing worldwide. Oxford is a registered trademark of
Oxford University Press in the UK and in certain other countries.

Published in India by
Oxford University Press
22 Workspace, 2nd Floor, 1/22 Asaf Ali Road, New Delhi 110002, India

© Oxford University Press 2021

The moral rights of the authors have been asserted.

First Edition published in 2021

All rights reserved. No part of this publication may be reproduced, stored in
a retrieval system, or transmitted, in any form or by any means, without the
prior permission in writing of Oxford University Press, or as expressly permitted
by law, by licence, or under terms agreed with the appropriate reprographics
rights organization. Enquiries concerning reproduction outside the scope of the
above should be sent to the Rights Department, Oxford University Press, at the
address above.

You must not circulate this work in any other form
and you must impose this same condition on any acquirer.

ISBN-13 (print edition): 978-0-19-012788-6
ISBN-10 (print edition): 0-19-012788-0

ISBN-13 (eBook): 978-0-19099201-9
ISBN-10 (eBook): 0-19-099201-8

Typeset in Trump Mediaeval LT Std 10/13
by Tranistics Data Technologies, Kolkata 700 091
Printed in India by Rakmo Press, New Delhi 110 020

Contents

List of Figures and Tables	vii
Foreword by Shailaja Paik	xi
Preface by S. Japhet	xix
List of Abbreviations	xxvii
Introduction by Aakash Singh Rathore	xxxi

PART ONE: GENDER JUSTICE

1. Double Disadvantage of Sanitation Workers and Government Responses — 3
   SANGHMITRA S. ACHARYA

2. The Shame of India: Stigma and Shame among Dalit Women in Rural Agricultural Relations — 40
   MUSHTAQ AHMAD MALLA

3. Gender Equality and Women's Empowerment: Ambedkar in Contemporary Context — 69
   RAJESH RAUSHAN

4. Ambedkar as a Feminist Philosopher — 91
   SUNAINA ARYA

5. Ambedkar on Women's Empowerment and the Status of Dalit Women in Karnataka — 116
   MALA MUKHERJEE

6. Constructing a New Female Subjectivity:
   Ambedkar's Perspective   137
   KOMAL RAJAK AND N. SUKUMAR

PART TWO: RACIAL JUSTICE

7. Organic Resistance: The Relevance of Ambedkar,
   Du Bois, and Garvey to Diaspora, Caste, Race,
   and Women's Liberation   157
   MOSES SEENARINE

8. Racelessness and Ambedkar's Idea of Annihilation:
   Post-apartheid South Africa   184
   GOOLAM VAHED AND ASHWIN DESAI

9. Common Struggles? Why There Has Not Been
   More Cooperation between African-Americans and Dalits   205
   KEVIN BROWN AND LALIT KHANDARE

10. Can Ambedkar Speak to Africa? Colour, Caste, and Class
    Struggles in Contemporary South Africa   230
    GOOLAM VAHED

Index   248
Editor and Contributors   256

Figures and Tables

Figures

1.1	Framework for Conducive Environment for Women Workers	9
2.1	Negative Effects of Bonded Labour Experience	51
2.2	Factors That Create Negativity	51
2.3	Bonded Labour Experience Affecting the Way Other People Treat You	52
2.4	Working Conditions in the Master's Farm or House	53
2.5	Personalized Shaming—I	54
2.6	Personalized Shaming—II	55
2.7	Importance of Masters in Family's Survival: Landless Families versus Landlord Families	64
2.8	Importance of Masters in Family's Survival: Families with Livestock versus Families without Livestock	65
3.1	Trend in Sex Ratio and Sex Ratio at Birth in India (per 1,000): 1961–2011	77
3.2	Sex Ratio at Birth in India: 2010–15	78
3.3	Index of Sex Preference for Male Children in India: 2015–16	79

5.1	Percentage and Growth of SC Population in Karnataka (2001–11)	122
5.2	Composition of SC Population in Karnataka (2011)	123
5.3	Social Group-wise Sex Ratio	124
5.4	Adult and Child Sex Ratio of SC Population in Karnataka	124
5.5	Percentage of Children Out of School in the Age Group of 7–14 Years	125
5.6	Literacy Rates and Gender Gap	126
5.7	Male and Female WPR	127
5.8	Gender Gap in WPR (SC Population), 2011	128
5.9	Educational Background of SC Female Main Workers in Karnataka (2011)	129
5.10	Educational Background of SC Male Main Workers in Karnataka (2011)	130
5.11	Percentage of Ever-Married Women in the SC Population	131

Tables

A1.1	Deaths among Sewer Workers in 14 Wards of the BMC	28
A1.2	Gender Differentials in the Nature of Work of Young Sanitation Workers	29
A1.3	Protective Gear/Equipment Used by Sanitation Workers in Different Cities	31
A1.4	Gender-wise Use of Protective Gear/Equipment in Different Cities	32
A1.5	Workers and Their Educational Attainment	34
A1.6	Gender Differentials in Facing Any Problem	35
A1.7	Workers and Their Health Conditions	36
A1.8	Gender Differentials in Illness and Treatment Seeking	37
A1.9	Awareness and Utilization of Benefits for Family	39
A1.10	Factors for Young People's Continuance in Sanitation Work	39

2.1	Daily Wage Rate Scenario of Female Dalit Agricultural Labourers	53
3.1	Varimax Rotation Factor Score of Sex Preferences and Female Mortality, Nutrition, and Literacy across States/Union Territories in India	81
3.2	Varimax Rotation Factor Score of Women's Autonomy and Empowerment in States/Union Territories in India	82
3.3	Varimax Rotation Factor Score of Gender Equality, Health, Nutrition, and Empowerment in States/Union Territories in India	84
A3.1	Missing Girls over Decades in Indian States: 1991–2011	88
A3.2	List of Variables Included in the Study	89
A5.1	Percentage of Male and Female SC Students Attending College and Higher Education Institutes, 2011	135
A5.2	Infant and Childhood Mortality Indicators for Social Groups	136
A5.3	Percentage of Underweight Women (BMI < 18.5) between Ages 15 and 49	136

Foreword

B.R.Ambedkar was particularly innovative and forceful in articulating and refashioning the Dalit agenda after the 1920s. He politicized, democratized, and nationalized the Dalit question and played a creative role in Dalit women's subject formation by emphasizing women's education, reducing gender inequalities, and refashioning Dalit women. He also sought to internationalize the caste and Dalit question by establishing connections between Dalits and African-Americans. This volume focuses on Ambedkar's initiatives in two areas: (*i*) women and gender justice; and (*ii*) parallels between caste and race discrimination.

In 1916, the 25-year-old Ambedkar argued that women seemed to be 'gateways to the caste system'.[1] By initiating this intellectual enquiry, he articulated a gendered analysis of caste. He critically intervened in the 'woman question' and deployed 'feminist technologies'[2] by analysing the interlocking operations of caste, gender, and sexuality that oppressed *all* women. As such, Ambedkar exposed the intimate working of Brahmanical patriarchy and contended with some powerful Brahmin men who had accumulated power and deprived women of their freedom.

---

[1] Available at http://www.columbia.edu/itc/mealac/pritchett/00ambedkar/txt_ambedkar_castes.html; last accessed on 11 October 2019.

[2] For details on this and the analysis given after, see Shailaja Paik. 2014. *Dalit Women's Education in Modern India: Double Discrimination*. London and New York: Routledge.

After coming on the national stage in the 1920s, he consistently attacked the social and sexual discrimination of Dalit women and strove, throughout his life, to create a new self-possessed personhood for Dalit women and men. The colonial government, social reform movements, and the feminist movement were little concerned with the Dalit question and denied Dalits a space to critique gender, caste, and untouchability. Moreover, unlike middle-class, upper-caste women, Dalit women never figured as *subjects* or *agents* in historical accounts of the anti-colonial nationalist struggle or women's reforms.

Ambedkar and Dalit women's political strategy then centred on the *radical remaking* of the self and construction of subjectivity. Ambedkar challenged the double patriarchy of dominant and privileged *savarnas*[3] as well as Dalit men to enhance women's autonomy within and outside the household. He attacked the dominant discourse of both the savarnas and the British that frequently characterized Dalit women as 'unruly' and with 'loose' morals. He exhorted women to fight their triple discrimination on the lines of caste, gender, and sexuality. He advised Dalit women to rethink their attitudes towards education, motherhood, public roles, and employment, and encouraged them to find a new voice through women's conferences and active involvement in politics. At the famous Mahad Satyagraha of 26–7 December 1927, Ambedkar specifically put the burden of social responsibility and ending untouchability on Dalit women:

> [T]he problems of annihilating caste and everyday life have to be tackled by men and women together.... If men alone undertake this work, I have no doubt that they will take a longer time to complete it. If women, however take this up, I believe that *compared to men, women would do a better job and will soon succeed*.[4]

Ambedkar, thus, pulled women into the political public sphere and looked upon them as 'equal partners' in the fight for social justice, equality, and emancipation.

---

[3] They are touchables from dominant castes.
[4] Ambedkar quoted in Paik, *Dalit Women's Education in Modern India: Double Discrimination*, p. 165; emphasis added.

By articulating a Dalit 'body politics',[5] Ambedkar enabled Dalit women's agency to repossess their bodies and create new voices for themselves. He radically rejected some detestable caste-specific identity markers that savarnas strictly policed—clothing, jewellery, naming, and housing. By giving up caste-specific stigmatized dressing styles, Dalit women asserted themselves against both Brahmanical (caste and gender codes) as well as intra-caste patriarchies. Dalit women were not merely imitating the savarna style of dressing; instead, they were intentionally performing their intimate physical desire that was hitherto a purview of savarnas and threatened the latter's historic identity. In the process, Dalit women resisted and destabilized Brahmanical norms to generate broad possibilities and power for themselves.

Women's education was at the core of social transformation. The fundamental task of education for most ordinary Dalit women and men was to build self-respect and self-reliance, and *remake*, not merely refine, their whole selves as savarna women did. Ambedkar emphasized the significance of knowledge and understanding for both girls and boys:

> Knowledge and learning are not for men alone, they are essential for women too. Our ancestors were aware of this or else the people serving in the platoons would not have educated their girls. As is the quarry so will be the stone. So, you must remember that if you want to improve future generations, education of girls is very important. You cannot afford to forget my speech or to fail to put it in to practice.[6]

Ambedkar thus emphasized women's cultivation of the intellect and self-development for personal freedom. Moreover, unlike many upper-caste leaders, he believed that Dalit women and men *had to enter schools together*. *Sudharna* or 'improvement' and 'progress' became a metaphor for regenerating the Dalit community. Ambedkar argued that without education and improvement, women would remain 'backward' and unable to provide intelligent

---

[5] Ambedkar quoted in Paik, *Dalit Women's Education in Modern India: Double Discrimination.*

[6] Ambedkar quoted in Paik, *Dalit Women's Education in Modern India: Double Discrimination*, p. 159.

training and discipline to their children. Most significantly, he wanted Dalit women to provide education and create a sense of self-respect and ambition in their children. He encouraged them to 'awaken [children's] aims and ambitions gradually. Emphasize on their minds that they will be *thor* [respectable]. Do away with their inferiority complex'.[7] He thus sought to link the emancipation of Dalit women through education with an internal transformation of the culture and ethos of the family.

These processes also led to other possibilities because education was a marker of respectable status, especially important for Dalit women. At times, Ambedkar's strategy for tackling the 'woman question' often echoed that of savarna Hindu nationalists. Women, by virtue of their care-taking functions and roles as transmitters of culture, were depicted as 'custodians' of the community, who were responsible for the upliftment and improvement of the community as a whole.

Yet, I must reiterate that we need to pay particular attention to Ambedkar's intentions—his politics needs to be located in a specific local, historical, and doubly colonial (British and Brahmanical) context, which required Dalit women to nurture confident children who could be recognized as fully human by the wider society and who could enjoy equal human rights. Dalit women were to educate, train, shape, and instil in children ambition, instead of servitude, and challenge disciplinary norms which created feelings of shame and low self-respect. Many women actively engaged and interpreted Ambedkar's political discourse not only to explicate their situation but also to construct a concrete strategy for change. Rejecting the lofty upper-caste, middle-class ideals of *soundarya* (beauty), *vaibhav* (wealth and prosperity), *streedharma* (moral codes for women), and the 'softer' virtues of beauty, compassion, and submission, Ambedkar and Dalit women emphasized the development of the inner resources of self-respect and self-reliance that had been denied to Dalits.

In the process, Ambedkar provided a motive force for Dalit women's subject formation. Women gained political consciousness due to their direct and indirect involvement in campaigns, protests,

---

[7] Ambedkar, B.R. 2002. *Dr. Babasaheb Ambedkar: Writings and Speeches*, Vol. 18 (compiled and edited by Vasant Moon), Part 2, p. 426. Mumbai: Government of Maharashtra.

demonstrations, *satyagrahas*;[8] listening to political debates; and participation in activities of the social reform movement, for example, via the Bahishkrit Hitakarini Sabha (Committee for the Beneficence of the Boycotted). Women at the 1942 Scheduled Caste Federation conference argued for the right to divorce and for a law against bigamy, and continued to fight for access to water and the responsibility of women and men with regard to contraception. They also supported the programme of reform of property, marriage, and divorce laws in the Hindu Code Bill of the 1950s. Women contested elections, participated in school committees, fought for landless labour, joined the Naamaantar Movement to change the name of Marathwada University to Dr Babasaheb Ambedkar University, and continuously challenged the hegemonic ruling communities and the state.

It was at this complicated conjunction of social, educational, and political battles that Dalit women emerged as historical subjects. In these emotionally contoured political and personal struggles, they were constituted as transgressive agents through discourses, power, and the efforts of upper-caste elites' exclusionary politics and caste differentiation, as well as repression of the truth of untouchability and the particular problems of Dalit 'womanhood'. The Dalit woman was produced by the processes of Dalit women's active critique of upper-caste (Brahmin) exceptionalism, direct and indirect involvement in the politically charged programme of education, remaking of the self, and founding of political organizations.

However, there were some contradictions. Like imperial feminists and savarna nationalists, Ambedkar emphasized that women were jewels of the community. His disciplinary rectitude was, to an extent, similar to the bourgeois values of Victorian and Brahmanical construction of ideal womanhood. This was the double bind: Dalit women's subjection was produced and restrained by the very structures of power through which women sought emancipation. Although Ambedkar was radical in carving out women's agency, his anxieties and contradictions affect(ed) many Dalit women and had serious consequences for them. Nevertheless, women have continued to carve spaces (even if small) for themselves. Ambedkar's movement and post-Ambedkar Dalit movement witnessed the increased prominence and participation of Dalit women in forging

---

[8] Non-violent civil disobedience campaigns.

a new Dalit consciousness and expanding the terrain of gender and sexuality in post-colonial times. Dalit women's politics has promoted the most inclusive and productive politics and possibilities for social action and change inside and beyond South Asia.

The timing of Dalit and African-American solidarity is most significant because the United States (US) Congress (like its British and European counterparts) has seriously begun to recognize the issue of caste in India and the US. Dialogue between the two marginalized communities would facilitate the development of broader and joint struggles between the subordinated populations of the world. Dalit and African-American women's collective ideas, comparisons, and learning and coping strategies will allow us to build some connections and solidarity between the two dispossessed communities. Third-World feminists have, theoretically, attempted to work across national borders but, in practice, we have yet to mobilize gender as a means to interrogate cultural boundaries between Dalits and African-Americans.[9]

There has been a long history of interconnections between Dalits and African-Americans. Especially from the middle of the nineteenth century, some non-Brahmin and Dalit leaders have attempted to connect with blacks in the US not only as victims but also in their political commitment to attack ideologies and practices of caste, race, gender, and sexuality discrimination. The non-Brahmin leader Jyotirao Phule (1827–1890) was aware of the American Revolution and the Civil War, as well as the atrocities committed against the African-Americans. He had read the life story of George Washington and works by Thomas Paine. Phule even gave the title *Gulamgiri*, or 'slavery', to his 1873 tract focusing on the plight of shudras and Dalits battling with Brahmanical hegemony. Similarly, Ambedkar and other Dalit leaders analysed slavery and subordination and often compared race with caste because to them slavery was a powerful metaphor for caste.

In the middle of the twentieth century, Ambedkar expressed solidarity with African-Americans by sending to the sociologist and public intellectual W.E.B. Du Bois a copy of a letter he had directed to the United Nations on the elimination of caste and

---

[9] For this information and details see Shailaja Paik. 2014. 'Building Bridges: Articulating Dalit and African-American Women's Solidarity', *Women's Studies Quarterly* 42(3–4): 74–96.

racial attitudes. Further, in 1972, Dalits founded the Dalit Panther Party, modelled on the Black Panther Party. Sociologists since the 1930s, anthropologists from the 1940s, and a few historians have explored theoretical and concrete aspects of comparison between Dalits and blacks. Social activists also began their 'historic collaboration' with African-Americans in 1987 to internationalize the Dalit problem and invite the attention of the 'whole black world'.

In a similar vein, in 2003, activists from the Dalit Freedom Network (DFN) spoke before the US House of Representatives on the topic, 'India's Unfinished Agenda: Equality and Justice for 200 Million Victims of the Caste System'. Activist Udit Raj had a major role to play in this initiative. Moreover, in 2007, the US Congress passed House Concurrent Resolution 139, 'expressing the sense of the Congress that the United States should address the ongoing problem of untouchability in India'.[10] Significantly, on 15 January 2014, some African-Americans engaged in a collaborative effort with DFN to commemorate what would have been the 85th birthday of Martin Luther King Jr with a historic event: They joined congressional members and staff to sign a 'Declaration of Empathy', which addressed the oppression of Dalits in India. Continuing these efforts in 2017, Martin Luther King III participated in the Bengaluru Ambedkar International Conference on which these volumes are based.

Learning from and teaching about Dalit and African-American movements provides the possibility of connecting these complex lives and allows a broad feminist, anti-patriarchal, anti-caste, anti-untouchability, and anti-racist analysis. Such an exercise of building bridges may allow African-Americans, Dalits, and other marginalized communities to effectively share their experiences and struggle together for an inclusive, deeply democratic, transnational politics.

Shailaja Paik
Associate Professor of History, Faculty Affiliate,
Women, Gender, and Sexuality Studies, and Asian Studies
University of Cincinnati, Ohio, USA

---

[10] 'African Americans to "Declare Empathy" with Dalits of India, Victims of Modern-Day Slavery, in Historic Commemoration of King Birthday.' *PRWeb*, 31 December 2013. Available at http://www.prweb.com/releases/2014/01/prweb11454166.htm.

Preface

This book forms part of a five-volume publication entitled *B.R. Ambedkar: The Quest for Justice*, an ambitious project that originated during the B.R. Ambedkar International Conference, 'Quest for Equity', held at Bengaluru, India, in July 2017, with some 350 speakers and thousands of participants. That conference took place keeping in view that the values of social, political, and economic justice that were so vigorously championed by Dr Ambedkar are now under attack at several levels: constitutional norms and public institutions created to fight against dominance and subservience have proved inadequate or have been subverted; norms and policy often merely pay lip service to egalitarian considerations; and the rise of social intolerance and exclusion tends to effectively whittle down and even sabotage an inclusive conception of polity and citizenship. The complexity of the social, political, and economic environment in which the value of social justice has to be envisaged too has undergone significant changes: we understand social inequality and diversity to be layered and multidimensional; and the State has to reckon with several competing centres of religious, communal, and cultural allegiances. Despite these serious challenges, new sites for social and political assertions have re-emerged, renewing the call for justice. These five volumes are very much part of that engagement.

Social activism in India today is inspired by Dr B.R. Ambedkar's insightful lifework analysing complex social and political challenges and proposing daring and radical policy measures in response. His approach to critical intellectual and policy challenges may inspire similar interventions elsewhere in the world, particularly throughout the Global South. Thus, in the light of the conference, this five-volume collection emerged as an invitation to scholars and policymakers to substantially rethink current political, social, legal, economic, gender, racial, religious, and cultural paradigms motivated by Dr B.R. Ambedkar's imaginative and creative work.

The project has succeeded in encouraging a wide interdisciplinary engagement among academics, scholars, activists, and policymakers on each of these themes, which are treated across the five volumes. This is apparent from a review of their tables of contents:

B.R. Ambedkar: The Quest for Justice
(in five volumes)

Volume I: *Political Justice*

1. Bhikhu Parekh *The Intellectual and Political Legacy of B.R. Ambedkar*
2. Cosimo Zene *B.R. Ambedkar and Antonio Gramsci: Justice for the Excluded, Education for Democracy*
3. Anand Teltumbde *Ambedkar and Democracy: Critical Reflections*
4. Neera Chandhoke *Repairing Complex Historical Injustice*
5. Pradeep Gokhale *Dr Ambedkar and the Trio of Principles: Liberty, Equality, and Fraternity*
6. Vidhu Verma *Discrimination, Colonial Injustice, and the Good Society*
7. Scott Stroud *Communication, Justice, and Reconstruction: Ambedkar as an Indian Pragmatist*
8. J. Daniel Elam *Of Castes and Crowds: B.R. Ambedkar's Anti-colonial Endosmosis*
9. Pushparaj Deshpande *A Constellation of Ideas: Revisiting Ambedkar and Gandhi*
10. Shaunna Rodrigues *Self-Respect as a Primary Political Ideal: Ambedkar's Challenge to Political Theory*

Volume II: *Social Justice*

1. Martin Fuchs *Ambedkar's Theory of the Social: The Universal Condition of Recognition*
2. James Manor *B.R. Ambedkar: Visionary and Realist*
3. G.C. Pal *Caste and Delivery of Social Justice: Revisiting Ambedkar*
4. Meena Dhanda *'Made to Think and Forced to Feel': The Power of Counter-Ritual*
5. David N. Gellner, Krishna P. Adhikari, Arjun Bahadur B.K. *Dalits in Search of Inclusion: Comparing Nepal with India*
6. Navyug Gill *Ambedkar, Labour, and the Political Economy of Dalit Conversion in Colonial Panjab*
7. Shailaja Menon *The Fractured Society of the Republic*
8. Karen Gabriel and Prem Kumar Vijayan *Whose State Is It Anyway? Reservation, Representation, Caste, and Power*
9. Jagannatham Begari *Reclaiming Social Justice and Deepening Democracy*
10. Suraj Yengde *Ambedkar's Internationalization of Social Justice*
11. Karthik Raja Karuppusamy *Foregrounding Social Justice in Indian Historiography: Interrogating the Poona Pact*
12. Ajay Verma *Ambedkar and the Metaphysics of Social Justice*

Volume III: *Legal and Economic Justice*

Part One: Legal Justice

1. Upendra Baxi *Lawless Law, Living Death, and the Insurgent Moral Reason of Babasaheb Ambedkar*
2. R. Sudarshan *B.R. Ambedkar's Exemplary Adherence to Constitutional Morality*
3. Arvind Narrain *Radical Constitutionalism: Towards an Ambedkarite Jurisprudence*
4. Antje Linkenbach *B.R. Ambedkar's Imaginations of Justice*
5. Umakant *The Significance of Rights and Rule of Law under the Indian Constitutional Framework*
6. Anupama Rao *B.R. Ambedkar and Indian Democracy*

Part Two: Economic Justice

7. Vijay Gudavarthy *Development through Informalization and Circulation of Labour: The Emerging Anatomy of an Uncivil Society*
8. Joseph Tharamangalam *India's Paradox of 'Hunger Amidst Plenty' Has a Name: Caste-Based Discrimination and Exclusion*
9. Aseem Prakash *Dalits Enter the Indian Markets as Owners of Capital: Adverse Inclusion, Social Networks, and Civil Society*
10. Pritam Singh *Ambedkar's Economic Methodology for Social Justice: The Centrality of Dalits*
11. Jawed Alam Khan *Economic Justice: Policy and Public Investment for Pasmanda Muslims*

Volume IV: *Gender and Racial Justice*

Part One: Gender Justice

1. Sanghmitra S. Acharya *Double Disadvantage of Sanitation Workers and Government Responses*
2. Mushtaq Ahmad Malla *The Shame of India: Stigma and Shame among Dalit Women in Rural Agricultural Relations*
3. Rajesh Raushan *Gender Equality and Women's Empowerment: Ambedkar in Contemporary Context*
4. Sunaina Arya *Ambedkar as a Feminist Philosopher*
5. Mala Mukherjee *Ambedkar on Women's Empowerment and the Status of Dalit Women in Karnataka*
6. Komal Rajak and N. Sukumar *Constructing a New Female Subjectivity: Ambedkar's Perspective*

Part Two: Racial Justice

7. Moses Seenarine *Organic Resistance: The Relevance of Ambedkar, Du Bois and Garvey to Diaspora, Caste, Race, and Women's Liberation*
8. Goolam Vahed and Ashwin Desai *Racelessness and Ambedkar's Idea of Annihilation: Post-apartheid South Africa*

9. Kevin Brown and Lalit Khandare *Common Struggles? Why There Has Not Been More Cooperation between African-Americans and Dalits*
10. Goolam Vahed *Can Ambedkar Speak to Africa? Colour, Caste, and Class Struggles in Contemporary South Africa*

Volume V: *Religious and Cultural Justice*

Part One: Religious Justice

1. Laurence R. Simon *Searching for a Theology of Liberation in India*
2. Kanchana Mahadevan *Ambedkar's Critical Hermeneutics of Religion*
3. Debora Spini *Civil Religion, Uncivil Society: A Reflection on Baba Sahib Dr B.R. Ambedkar's Conception of a 'Religion for Civil Society'*
4. Priyanka Jha *The Gaze on Justice: A Genealogy from Anagarika Dharmapala to B.R. Ambedkar*
5. Bansidhar Deep *B.R. Ambedkar's Philosophy of Religion*
6. Matthew H. Baxter *Two Concepts of Conversion at Meenakshipuram: Seeing through Ambedkar's Buddhism and Being Seen in EVR's Islam*

Part Two: Cultural Justice

7. Pramod K. Nayar *Marginality, Suffering, Justice: Questions of Dalit Dignity in Cultural Texts*
8. Y. Srinivasa Rao *Asura: Myth into Cultural Reality*
9. John Clammer *Cultural Rights in the Context of Ambedkarite Social Justice*
10. Raju Sakthivel *Education in a Hierarchical Culture*
11. Jadumani Mahanand *Ambedkar in/and Academic Space*

Despite the wide range of themes spread across these five volumes, the collection as a whole is oriented towards articulable specific aims and objectives. These aims and objectives are inspired by and fully consistent with the life and legacy of Dr Ambedkar, a man who was, on the one hand, a scholar of indubitable genius, and on the other hand, a dynamic agent of social and political action.

1. *B.R. Ambedkar: The Quest for Justice* seeks to explore the multifaceted idea of justice in dialogue with Ambedkar's *opus* for a society that encompasses manifold social inequalities, deep diversities, exclusion, and marginality.
2. In dialogue with Ambedkar's writings, the contributions to the collection aim in an overall way to suggest constitutional, institutional, and policy responses to the concerns of justice, and to reformulate the conceptual and policy linkages between social justice and other related norms and concerns.
3. Through high-level scholarship, this collection aims to help identify modes of thought and agency and social and political practices inimical to the pursuit of justice, and to delineate social and political agency and modes of action conducive to the furtherance of justice in line with Dr Ambedkar's own writings and mission.

Thus, in sum, Dr Ambedkar's conception of justice and his life's work shaping the idea of India offer this collection the vantage points for sustained reflection on concerns of justice and its relation to other human values. This is particularly relevant, indeed urgent, in our day, not only in India but also throughout the world.

As convener of the organizing committee of the Dr B.R. Ambedkar International Conference, 'Quest for Equity', held at Bengaluru, India, in July 2017, where many of the chapters included in this volume were originally presented, I would like to gratefully acknowledge the people and institutions that made the conference a success and helped to make these volumes possible.

First and foremost, I must acknowledge the Government of Karnataka with Chief Minister Siddaramaiah at the helm, which hosted and funded the conference. Many put in extraordinary time and effort: Dr H.C. Mahadevappa, convenor and hon'ble minister for Public Works Department (PWD); H. Anjaneya, hon'ble minister for Social Welfare Department; Dr G. Parameshwara, hon'ble minister for home affairs; Shri T.B. Jayachandra, hon'ble minister for law and minor irrigation; Shri R. Roshan Baig, hon'ble minister for infrastructure development and information; Shri Basavaraj Rayareddy, hon'ble minister for higher education; Shrimati Umashree, hon'ble minister for women and child welfare development; Priyank M. Kharge, publicity convener and hon'ble minister for information technology and biotechnology; Krishna Byre Gowda, logistics convener and hon'ble minister for agriculture;

and Captain Manivannan, secretary, Social Welfare Department. Thanks also to Dr M.C. Srinivasa, joint director, Social Welfare Department, and Dr H. Nataraj, secretary, State Safai Karmachari Commission, both nodal officers attached to Captain Manivannan, for taking care of the logistics of the conference organization. I would also like to thank Dr Nagalakshmi and Mehroz Khan, who were coordinators for the conference; Shri Srinivasulu, managing director, Ambedkar Development Corporation, attached to Krishna Byre Gowda; and Dr Nandan Kumar, officer on special duty to Priyank Kharge. I must also thank Luthfulla Atheeq, principal secretary to the chief minister; Shri Venkataiah, special advisor to Social Welfare Department; M.V. Savithri, commissioner, Social Welfare Department; and numerous other officials and staff of the Social Welfare Department, who worked so diligently.

Special thanks are due to the Scheduled Castes Department team of the All India Congress Committee: Shri K. Raju, head of the Congress President's Office, for his ideation and immense political support, and Pushparaj Deshpande, in-charge of the Quest for Equity website and other logistical support. I cannot fail to mention Oum, Navil, Deepika, and the rest of the Phase I team, who worked tirelessly.

I would like to express my profound thanks to the members of the various committees, specially members of the academic committee, Professors Sukhadeo Thorat, Valerian Rodrigues, G. Haragopal, Aakash Singh Rathore, and Dr Rochana Bajpai, Sudhir Krishnaswamy, S.G. Siddaramaiah, K. Marulasiddappa, Siddalingaiah, L. Hanumanthaiah, Mallika Ganti, and K.B. Siddaiah. Special thanks are also due to the editorial advisory board for their invaluable advice and assistance throughout, including those members from the academic committee mentioned earlier, as well as Dr Suraj Yengde and Professors Anand Teltumbde, Kalpana Kannabiran, Lawrence R. Simon, and Meena Dhanda. My heartful thanks to Professor Aakash Singh Rathore for taking the responsibility of editing these volumes.

Of course, I cannot fail to mention the support of Shabin John and Chandrashekar for their office and logistics support and Dr Ramkhok Raikhan for research assistance to the editor.

S. Japhet
Professor and Vice Chancellor,
Bengaluru Central University, India

Abbreviations

AAP	Aam Aadmi Party
ACL	African Communities League
ANC	African National Congress
BCM	Black Consciousness Movement
BEE	Black Economic Empowerment
BJP	Bharatiya Janata Party
BMC	Brihanmumbai Municipal Corporation
BMI	body mass index
CAB	Citizenship Amendment Bill
CEC	Centre for Education and Communication
CORE	Congress of Racial Equality
COSATU	Congress of South African Trade Unions
CSR	child sex ratio
CSWE	Council on Social Work Education
DFN	Dalit Freedom Network
DMK	Dravida Munnetra Kazhagam
DSS	Dalit Sangharsha Samiti
EEA	Employment Equity Act
EFF	Economic Freedom Fighters
FGDs	focus group discussions
FIRs	first information reports
GoI	Government of India
HRW	Human Rights Watch
HSA	Hindu Succession Act
ICPD	International Conference on Population and Development

ICSSR	Indian Council for Social Sciences Research
IIDS	Indian Institute of Dalit Studies
IEC	Information, Education, and Communication
IIPS	International Institute for Population Sciences
ILO	International Labour Organization
IMR	infant mortality rate
INC	Indian National Congress
JMI	Jamia Millia Islamia
JNU	Jawaharlal Nehru University
MHA	Ministry of Home Affairs
MMA	mixed-methods approach
MoJS	Ministry of Jal Shakti
MSK	Mahila Samakhya Karnataka
NAACP	National Association for the Advancement of Colored People
NCDHR	National Campaign on Dalit Human Rights
NFDW	National Federation of Dalit Women
NFHS	National Family Health Survey
NMR	neonatal mortality rate
NP	National Party
NREGA	National Rural Employment Guarantee Act
NRIs	non-resident Indians
OBC	Other Backward Class
PSR	person sex ratio
RG&CCI	Registrar General and Census Commissioner, India
RSBY	Rashtriya Swasthya Bima Yojana
RTI	Right to Information
SAD	Shiromani Akali Dal
SBA	Swachh Bharat Abhiyan
SC	Scheduled Caste
SECC	Socio-economic Caste Census
SACP	South African Communist Party
SHGs	self-help groups
SKA	Safai Karamchari Andolan
SKVS	Safai Kamgar Vikas Sangh
ST	Scheduled Tribe
TDP	Telugu Desam Party
TRC	Truth and Reconciliation Commission
UAE	United Arab Emirates
UCT	University of Cape Town

UDF	United Democratic Front (South Africa)
U5MR	under-five mortality rate
UK	United Kingdom
UKZN	University of KwaZulu-Natal
UN	United Nations
UNCHR	United Nations Commission on Human Rights
UNDP	United Nations Development Programme
UNIA	Universal Negro Improvement Association
US	United States
WHO	World Health Organization
WPR	work participation rate

Introduction

AAKASH SINGH RATHORE

Gender Justice

This volume includes two themes, namely, gender justice and racial justice, treated in two different parts of the book. Here, it is possible to introduce gender justice with more background than racial justice because it is only now that the critical study of race has begun to interface with the life and work of Ambedkar. At present, there is precious little background research material in the emerging but unquestionably important field of intersection between race and caste. The excellent 'Foreword' by Shailaja Paik has signalled to some of it, as well as to its importance. Issues of gender justice, however, have long been a staple of Ambedkar studies, and very fittingly too, as gender justice was a central and quintessential component of Ambedkar's own lifelong quest for justice.

The anthology *Dalit Feminist Theory* (Arya and Rathore 2020) has brought much of this to the forefront. As pointed out there, Ambedkar underlines the inadequacy of understanding the caste system in terms of the 'idea of pollution' (Ambedkar 2014[2003]: 7) and argues instead that its fundamental characteristic is its tie up with gender, specifically with the practice of *endogamy*—the absence of intermarriage—which he has called its *essence* (Ambedkar 2014[2003]: 9). Patriarchy in India has long been enforced and sustained through inhumane rituals like sati, enforced widowhood, and child marriage. Controlling women's sexuality has been and remains an essential way to sustain the caste system. Ambedkar, thus, regards patriarchy as Brahmanism's twin sister. Ambedkar's analysis of caste reveals the inbuilt connection between caste and gender, and consequently results in the innumerable social expressions with which we are all familiar: the prevention of Dalit women's entry into Hindu temples; the phenomena of *devadasi*s (ritual prostitutes); and so on.

The Brahmanical Nature of Patriarchy

Patriarchy operating in India today is influenced by 'Brahmanical patriarchy', as exposited by Ambedkar (see Ambedkar 2014[2003]: 150–1). This is a structural concept—also known as 'graded inequality'—which explains a specific modality of patriarchy by explicating a set of discriminatory levels constituting a hierarchical organization of society based on caste, which is quite unique to the Indian subcontinent. Within this structure—implicit, insidious, and seemingly impossible to challenge—'upper'-caste men are at the top, followed by 'upper'-caste women; 'lower'-caste men are at the bottom and 'lower'-caste women are further disadvantaged among the disadvantaged. The middle-caste men and women have their place accordingly. This hierarchical system allocates everyone a status of privilege or deprivation, ranking them on the basis of caste first and then gender. As we shall see in Chapter 4, 'lower'-caste women are most vulnerable to discrimination, violence, and exploitation. They face multiple kinds of oppression corresponding to their many identities: (*i*) caste-based oppression at the hands of 'upper' castes; (*ii*) class-based at the hands of 'upper' classes; and (*iii*) gender-based oppression at the hands of all men, including 'lower'-caste ones.

In her chapter 'Ambedkar as a Feminist Philosopher', Sunaina Arya argues that Dalit women face double discrimination in the caste–gender matrix. Caste-based discrimination in the vertical structure of society and gender-based discrimination in the horizontal structure of society. Sharmila Rege (2000), a pioneer of Ambedkarite feminism, argues, therefore, that the gender issue cannot be comprehended without bringing in the caste question within the Indian social structure. The logic behind this claim can be better discerned by considering the example of 'honour killing'. There are generally two reasons for a couple/lovers getting murdered by their parents or elders or local authorities: one reason is that the lovers defied norms by marrying partners of their choice without parental/societal approval; the second, usually the catalyst, is that they chose partners outside of their caste. Caste is generally crucial in such murder cases.

It is important to observe that the concept of Brahmanical patriarchy does not refer to the patriarchal practices followed by Brahmin men; instead, it represents the multiform nature of patriarchy against women in India. Anyone, regardless of their caste or gender, who believes, practices, preaches, or encourages any kind of discrimination based on this hierarchical structure, would be considered a follower of Brahmanism by definition. Just as it does not require a man to practice misogyny, it is not necessarily Brahmins who practice Brahmanism.

In the article, 'Intersections of Gender and Caste', Rege et al. (2013: 36) argue: '[I]n analysing the caste and gender matrix in Indian society, merely pluralising the term patriarchy is not enough. The task is to map the ways in which the category "women" is being differently reconstituted within regionally diverse patriarchal relations cross-hatched by graded caste inequalities.'

As further covered in Chapter 4, the experience of a Dalit woman cannot be understood as simply either patriarchal or casteist. An 'either–or' approach to Brahmanical patriarchy is not useful in comprehending the cases like Bhanwari Devi (1992), a Dalit *saathin* (meaning 'friend', a ground-level worker). As part of the Women's Development Project, Devi was campaigning against child marriage. As a punishment for her campaign to prevent an infant girl's marriage, she was gang-raped by five 'upper'-caste men who were related to one other (three brothers, their uncle, and their brother-in-law) in her husband's presence. Those 'upper'-caste men intended to punish Devi for 'interfering' in their household, where child marriage was customary, and to instil fear in the Dalit community about their assertion. This brutal rape was a consequence of Devi's social identity at the intersection of caste and gender. An 'upper'-caste woman would not have been regarded as *sexually available* by those men. A Dalit man might have suffered violence differently than rape. One not belonging to a lower class would have availed better options than working as a *saathin*. Ambedkarite feminist thought draws on this. No single aspect of her identity would help us comprehend the frame. There is a 'difference' of experience at the juncture of a Dalit woman's multiple marginalization that is unique. In our caste-stratified society, this difference is not of degree but of kind. Therefore, only by adequately capturing this 'difference' we can hope to work for legislative and social justice.

To put this in another way, a case such as that of Bhanwari Devi exemplifies that mainstream Indian feminists fail to recognize that 'something unique is produced at the intersection point of different types of discrimination' (Symington 2004: 3).

For this reason, Ambedkarite feminist thought draws on this interconnected web of caste, gender, and class together to challenge Brahmanical patriarchy with a multi-axis approach. This is crucial, as Rege et al. (2013: 35–6) argue: In order to have a 'real feminism', there is a need to deal with gender-based issues keeping the caste question at the centre.

Was Ambedkar Feminist Enough?

On the topic of Ambedkarite feminism, especially the frequent ad hominem critiques forwarded by mainstream feminists, Rege (2013: 23) responds to accusations that Ambedkar was not *feminist enough* as he neglected to bring his wife into the forefront of his pursuit of justice, in contrast to Mahatma Phule, for example. According to Rege (2013: 24), these critics fail to appreciate the depth of his commitment for an overall just society and criticize his contributions based on a 'selective and erroneous understanding of his personal sphere'.

Along the same lines, Shailaja Paik, who also addressed this issue in her 'Foreword' to this volume, has written:

> Phule, Ambedkar and Dalit women pushed caste out of the confines of the social, religious, and personal into the political. They debated it in public, in the spheres of constitutional law in state legislatures, and at national and international levels.... Dalit narratives turned rhetoric into powerful discourse that shaped Dalit woman's affect, behaviour, and subjectivity through their participation in collective action for education and empowerment. (Paik 2016: 33)

Paik (2016: 35) concludes that though Phule seems more radical in this respect, Ambedkar has undeniably deeply influenced feminist progress in India. The present volume on gender justice and racial justice stands as a clear testament to this influence.

Ambedkarite Approaches to Gender Justice

This volume launches by homing in on a specific empirical circumstance that has paradigmatic significance. Sanghmitra S. Acharya, in her chapter 'Double Disadvantage of Sanitation Workers and Government Responses', points out that Dalits who are predominantly engaged in sanitation work have not drawn much attention from the required sectors. Sanitation work is still associated with caste. This work passes on to the progeny and is considered guaranteed employment and thus a source of regular income. This serves to strengthen caste identity and consolidate entrenchment of youth in this sort of 'polluted work'. The chapter aims to examine the factors which perpetuate the engagement of Dalits in sanitation work. Along the way, the central role that gender plays in this regard is uncovered, making the connection between social justice and gender justice explicit.

Mushtaq Ahmad Malla, in his chapter 'The Shame of India: Stigma and Shame among Dalit Women in Rural Agricultural Relations', pushes along a similar line of thinking as Sanghmitra S. Acharya. In this case, Malla argues that caste, class, and gender intersectionality continue to create stigma and shame for female Dalit agricultural labourers who used to be bonded labourers in Karnataka. When survival dependence on 'higher'-caste landlords intersects with gender subordination and patriarchal collective-cultural norm preferences, these women end up experiencing and internalizing the cruellest forms of stigma and shame in production relations. The author suggests that even though India has moved from autocracy to democracy, from feudal to neoliberal, production relations for rural Dalit women nevertheless continue to be semi-feudal and monopolistic. Thus, Malla asserts, in order to fight against oppression and stigma, a collective livelihood approach is a more resilient, powerful, and sustainable alternative.

Rajesh Raushan, in his chapter 'Gender Equality and Women's Empowerment: Ambedkar in Contemporary Context', indicates that the current state is not as progressive as we are often led to assume. Ambedkar had observed decades ago that women were victim to an oppressive, caste-based, rigid hierarchical social system in India. Raushan suggests that this is still true today, despite the fact that India has reached a milestone in eradicating such discrimination. Discriminatory behaviour and the threat of gender inequality hinder the notion of women's economic and social development and degrade the process of social justice. As Ambedkar had argued, social awareness and social responsiveness are the basic ingredients of gender equality and women's empowerment. According to the author, this can be achieved through a bottom-up approach and community-based sensitization and awareness to stop hazardous and discriminating behaviour. This would be a big step towards strengthening and achieving social justice in India.

Sunaina Arya, in her chapter 'Ambedkar as a Feminist Philosopher', addresses Ambedkar's endeavours to lay the groundwork for a gender-just society by uplifting the conditions of women. In particular, Arya seeks to establish that Ambedkar's theoretical analysis and advocated principles (liberty, equality, and fraternity) qualify his approach as a bona fide feminist philosophy. According to the author, Ambedkar scrutinizes the conditions, causes, and practices of women's deprivation in order to advocate their achievement of a dignified humane life. His aim, she posits, is to lay the foundation for a society which may be just for *all* of its members.

Chapter 5, though also articulating Ambedkar's own position, zooms in from theory at large down to a local case. Mala Mukherjee, in 'Ambedkar on Women's Empowerment and the Status of Dalit Women in Karnataka', reminds us, once again, that Ambedkar had said that the degree of women's progress indicates the progress of a community overall. However, in India, women face not only patriarchy but caste-embedded patriarchy, in which they are used for maintaining the purity of caste through endogamy. Looking at a particular empirical instance, Mukherjee points to various sources that reveal that although Karnataka records a high urbanization rate as well as per capita income for all social groups, there are some sectors in which women, especially those who are from the Dalit community, face far more gaps or deprivation as compared to their non-Dalit counterparts. The author thus advances Ambedkar's conceptual framework, as well as operationalizes it through an empirical case—she seeks thereby to help redefine caste, class, and identity in terms of gender.

In Chapter 6, 'Constructing a New Female Subjectivity: Ambedkar's Perspective', Komal Rajak and N. Sukumar go in the direction of philosophy to interrogate the emergence of a new female subjectivity in colonial India based on the philosophical contributions of Ambedkar. Ambedkar, they argue, developed a unique feminist epistemology. The authors attempt to delineate the practices, nature, process, outcomes, and ideals of such an endeavour. Ambedkar never failed to exhort women to shed their cultural veil of purity and participate in the public sphere. Indeed, building upon the efforts of Phule, Periyar, and others, Ambedkar, through innovate ways—the authors attempt to show—strove to completely dismantle the structural roots of female oppression in Indian society.

From Gender Justice to Racial Justice: The Intersection

Since academic writings on feminism have historically, preponderantly, originated from white, First-World feminists—largely on account of their privileged institutional locations—the mainstream articulation of gender-based issues tended to neglect the deeper afflictions of black women. Black women's day-to-day resistance against race and gender discrimination gradually helped them to enter into the field of articulation. During this long process, black women realized that their social reality was not captured or reflected in mainstream feminism, from which they were marginalized—mainstream feminism thus took on the character of a 'white' feminism from the point of view of the racially marginalized. For mainstream feminists, patriarchy, not race, was *their* problem. Consequently, black feminists forwarded strong critiques of mainstream feminism for its failure to address the issues of *all* women.

Black feminist thought has emerged as an established discipline in contemporary academia. Kimberle Crenshaw (1989) introduced the concept of intersectionality based on black women's 'difference' from race-privileged women, filling the lacuna of First-World feminist discourse which had failed to address the issues of *all* (First World) women. Although the concept of intersectionality originated in black feminist history and theory, it certainly bears universal applicability for its deep philosophical relevance and insight. Intersection denotes a junctional point where two or more elements meet. In the context of the First World, race, gender, and class constitute the crucial intersection for black feminism; in the Indian context, caste, gender, and class seem to constitute the crucial intersection for Ambedkarite feminism. In both contexts, intersectionality operates as a tool to observe and address the patriarchal injustices faced by the most marginalized and vulnerable women of the world.

Patricia Hill Collins (1989) has theorized this 'difference', placing it at the crux of feminist philosophy in order to resolve the race biases of First-World feminists. Through the lens of this 'difference', this race aspect, Collins democratizes feminist thought because gender justice bears no meaning if it does not entail gender justice for *all* women of all races.

The so-called Third-World feminists have adopted the idea of 'difference', as well as that of intersectionality, based on their differences grounded in location. However, the very idea of intersectionality, which is the theoretical ground for 'difference', has long been rejected in the works of mainstream feminists, who reject internal differences between Third-World women even as they assert their own difference from First-World feminists (see Stephens 1994).

Rege (1998) offers a critique of 'difference' from a Dalit feminist standpoint and argues that feminist 'difference' is incomplete unless the difference from a caste perspective, that is, Dalit difference, is added to it. Or, as Smita M. Patil (2013: 43) has neatly captured it: 'Dalit feminist thought has the epistemic vantage location to challenge the authenticity of knowledge that is generated for the emancipation of the oppressed through pointing out the caste-cum-class privilege of the dominant intelligentsia and institutional histories.'

The mutual support and solidarity that may be forged between Ambedkarite feminists and black feminists should, by now, have become fairly clear for readers to appreciate. Questions of gender justice and racial justice are not, as mentioned earlier, mutually exclusive—Ambedkar's quest for justice was total, not piecemeal. Let us now consider elements of racial justice in the light of race-related scholarship directly inspired by Ambedkar's life and work.

Racial Justice

The mention of Du Bois and Garvey by Moses Seenarine in 'Organic Resistance: The Relevance of Ambedkar, Du Bois, and Garvey to Diaspora, Caste, Race, and Women's Liberation' nicely transitions us to Part Two on racial justice in the present volume. This part compares race and caste, and explores the ways in which the movements for racial justice and caste equality can learn from one another and seek strategies of synergy. The chapter, thus, bridges the first and second parts of this volume, as it straddles themes of both gender justice and racial justice. The author enters into a fascinating discussion on culture among diasporic Hindus, which is often phrased in terms of a 'retention' versus 'change' hypothesis. The author, largely autoethnographically, explores Indian migration, caste and race relations, and their dynamics in the Caribbean and North America. The chapter also looks at similarities in caste oppression and race oppression, and the solutions offered by Ambedkar, W.E.B. Du Bois, and Marcus Garvey.

Not widely known, but of special significance, W.E.B. Du Bois, the great black intellectual activist and liberator, had a correspondence with Ambedkar. Ambedkar wrote to Du Bois: 'I know you by name as everyone does who is working in the cause of securing liberty to the oppressed people' (Yengde and Teltumbde 2018: xix). In turn, Du Bois wrote: 'I have often heard of your name and work and of course have every sympathy with the Untouchables of India' (Yengde and Teltumbde 2018: xx). The full extent of Ambedkar's influence on the Civil Rights Movement is as yet unexplored in literature, but a very promising start is made in this volume.

In the chapter 'Racelessness and Ambedkar's Idea of Annihilation: Post-apartheid South Africa', Goolam Vahed and Ashwin Desai examine the concept of non-racialism and racelessness. They argue that it is not the fact of categorization that is creating race tensions in the post-apartheid period, but the continuation of apartheid geography and economic inequality. The authors further argue that race-based redress is necessary, but affirmative action based on race only is a misnomer. It is in this context that they use Ambedkar's notion of annihilation, which they understand as a programme to destroy race and, in the process, attack the conditions that allow these identities to be used as anchors and catapults of privilege.

If the previous chapter nicely illustrates the possibility of fruitfully juxtaposing the twin struggles for racial justice and caste justice, the question naturally arises: Why has there not been more cooperation between African-Americans and Dalits? This is precisely what is asked and answered in the chapter 'Common Struggles? Why There Has Not Been More Cooperation between African-Americans and Dalits', by Kevin Brown and Lalit Khandare. Both African-American and Indian nationalists drew upon the analogy of the black struggle against white supremacy in the United States (US) in the form of segregation and Indian struggle against white supremacy in the form of its independence movement. These comparisons led to the creation of an African-American perspective of viewing its struggle in the international arena as one of people of colour against white supremacy. However, such a focus significantly lessens the attention that they pay to the intra-national struggles against oppression by groups such as Dalits in India. As the authors show, since the end of colonialism, these intra-national struggles are better analogies to the continuing African-American struggle in the US than the former analogies made to colonial struggles for independence.

In the final chapter of this volume, 'Can Ambedkar Speak to Africa? Colour, Caste, and Class Struggles in Contemporary South Africa', Goolam Vahed trenchantly argues that Ambedkar's social location as a Dalit, his prescient critique of the Indian National Congress, and his refusal to countenance any compromise with regard to caste spoke both to the historical evolution of Indians in South Africa and to the contemporary politics of those who seek to smash the icons of colonialism, challenge the gods of liberation, and prosecute a radical anti-imperial struggle out of the dung-heap (to borrow Ambedkar's poignant phrase) of post-colonial dead-ends. According to Vahed, Ambedkar's ideas of caste continue to have relevance because new forms of social inclusion and exclusion, based around class, caste, religion, and language, are emerging amongst Indians, both within India and across the diaspora.

More work could have been featured within Part Two of the present volume, tying together the race question with gender and not only caste. There has been an attempt to fill this lacuna in another book, *Dalit Feminist Theory: A Reader*, that calls attention to these synergies and their utility towards achieving solidarity on issues of caste, race, class, and gender (Arya and Rathore 2020). In the current volume, Ambedkar's role as a pioneer and paradigm for the quest for justice is the primary focus. In this respect, the book takes a big stride forward by exhibiting his inspiration and relevance at the international level.

References

Ambedkar, B.R. 2014[2003]. *Dr. Babasaheb Ambedkar: Writings and Speeches* (edited by Vasant Moon). Vol. 17. New Delhi: Dr Ambedkar Foundation.

Arya, Sunaina and Aakash Singh Rathore. 2020. *Dalit Feminist Theory: A Reader*. Oxon, New York and New Delhi: Routledge.

Collins, Patricia Hill. 1989. 'The Social Construction of Black Feminist Thought', *Signs: Journal of Women in Culture and Society* 14(4): 745–73.
Crenshaw, Kimberle. 1989. 'Demarginalizing the Intersection of Race and Sex: A Black Feminist Critique of Antidiscrimination Doctrine, Feminist Theory and Antiracist Politics', *University of Chicago Legal Forum*, Issue I, Article 8: 140–67.
Paik, Shailaja. 2016. 'Forging a New Dalit Womanhood in Colonial India: Discourse on Modernity, Rights, Education, and Emancipation', *Journal of Women's History* 28(4): 14–40.
Patil, Smita M. 2013. 'Revitalising Dalit Feminism: Towards Reflexive Anti-caste Agency of Mang and Mahar Women in Maharashtra', *Economic and Political Weekly* 48(18): 37–43.
Rege, Sharmila. 1998. 'Dalit Women Talk Differently: A Critique of "Difference" and towards a Dalit Feminist Standpoint Position', *Economic and Political Weekly* 33(4): WS39–46.
———. 2000. 'Real Feminism and Dalit Women'. *Economic and Political Weekly* 35(6): 493.
———. 2013. *Against the Madness of Manu: B. R. Ambedkar's Writings on Brahmanical Patriarchy*. New Delhi: Navayana.
Rege, Sharmila, J. Devika, Kalpana Kannabiran, Mary E. John, Padmini Swaminathan, Samita Sen. 2013. 'Intersections of Gender and Caste', *Economic and Political Weekly* 48(18): 35–6.
Stephens, Julie. 1994. 'Feminist Fictions: A Critique of the Category "Non-Western Woman" in Feminist Writings on India', in Ranajit Guha (ed.), *Subaltern Studies VI: Writings on South Asian History and Society*, pp. 92–125. New Delhi: Oxford University Press.
Symington, Alison. 2004. 'Intersectionality: A Tool for Gender and Economic Justice', *Women's Rights and Economic Change* 9: 3.
Yengde, Suraj and Anand Teltumbde. 2018. *The Radical in Ambedkar: Critical Reflections*. Delhi: Penguin Random House.

ONE
Gender Justice

1

Double Disadvantage of Sanitation Workers and Government Responses

SANGHMITRA S. ACHARYA

The year 2019 marked the 128th birth anniversary of B.R. Ambedkar, the principal architect of the Indian Constitution, who also made significant efforts for the political rights and social freedom of the Dalits. It was his concern for the downtrodden engaged in the cleaning of human excreta and the consequent efforts that resulted in the passing of the Employment of Manual Scavengers and Construction of Dry Latrines (Prohibition) Act, 1993 (Government of India [GoI] 1993) and, subsequently, the Prohibition of Employment as Manual Scavengers and Their Rehabilitation Act, 2013, under Entry 24 (Welfare of Labour) in the Concurrent List by the union government (GoI 2013). Though the legislative measure was enacted, the social efforts to execute it remain wanting till date. The sanitation workers clean sewers, drains, and toilets; collect the waste, including night soil, with minimum supporting tools; and transport it for disposal. Brooms, scraping tools, and bare hands are used to collect the waste, which is then loaded into buckets, baskets, or containers before being disposed of at designated drains or dumping areas called *ghura* (PACS India et al. 2016). Most of these sanitation workers are Dalits. Ambedkar said: '[I]n India a man is not a scavenger because of his work. He is a scavenger because of his birth irrespective of the question whether he does scavenging or not' (Moon 1989: 292–3). The United Nations Commission on Human Rights (UNCHR 2002) has also noted: 'By reason of their birth, Dalits are considered to be "polluted" and the removal of human and animal waste by members of the "sweeper" community is allocated to them and strictly enforced.' In addition to social apathy and stigma, they are at risk of illness and diseases, like dysentery, malaria, typhoid, skin infections, and tuberculosis, as well as exposure to toxic gases in sewers (Centre for Education and Communication [CEC] 2007).

The workers engaged in cleaning works are protected under the 2013 Act as it prohibits employment of manual scavengers, manual cleaning of sewers and septic tanks without protective equipment, and construction of insanitary latrines. It seeks rehabilitation of manual scavengers in alternative employment. Section 2(g)(b) of the Act mentions that 'a person engaged or employed to clean excreta with the help of such devices and using such protective gear, as the central government may notify in this behalf, shall not be deemed to be a manual scavenger' (GoI 2013). This clause is self-defeating as it suggests the continuance of manual scavenging, without using protective gears, in order to avail any benefits provided under this Act.

Dignity of Sanitation Workers

At this point of time, when the country has made a mark on the global landscape, it is rather shameful to have the persons engaged in conservancy, sanitation, sewerage, and allied works continue in their woeful state. Contextualizing Ambedkar to understand sanitation workers, especially women, is the endeavour of this chapter. Indeed, despite the Act banning manual scavenging, the country still has more than 700,000 persons engaged in it. As evident from the Census 2011 data on availability and types of latrine facilities, only 12 per cent households had piped sewer system while 22 per cent had septic tanks which needed periodic cleaning either manually or with machines. It is noteworthy that 2 per cent households had latrines without slab or open pits; 0.5 per cent disposed night soil in the open; 0.3 per cent households got the night soil removed by humans and 0.2 per cent by animals. Thus, out of a total of 246,692,667 households enumerated, those engaging manual cleaners amounted to 7,400,780 (Registrar General and Census Commissioner, India [RG&CCI] 2011). On an average, if one cleaner is assumed to be able to clean latrines in 10 households, then approximately 740,078 persons are required for scavenging purposes.[1] The *Socio-economic Caste Census* (SECC) 2011 states that 180,657 households are engaged in manual scavenging for a livelihood. The state of Maharashtra tops the list with the largest number of households (63,713) working as manual scavengers, followed by Madhya Pradesh, Uttar Pradesh, Tripura, and Karnataka (RG&CCI 2015). Manual scavenging still survives in parts of India that do not have proper sewage systems or safe faecal sludge management practices (*The Economist* 2008). It is thought to be most prevalent in Maharashtra, Gujarat, Madhya Pradesh, Uttar Pradesh, and Rajasthan (Human Rights Watch [HRW] 2014).

In nations where caste does not exist, such caste-based entrenchment into unclean jobs is also absent. The West generates more garbage than us, but they treat their cleaners with dignity. Also, their cleaning brigade does not need to be freed from the dehumanizing, obnoxious, abhorrent, and disgusting practice of caste-based discrimination. They enjoy the dignity of being human as much the others do. The state also cares for them by providing them with safety equipment (Acharya 2017). In comparison to rest of the world, more accidents and deaths at work have occurred among persons engaged in sanitation, sewerage, and allied services in India (Pepper 2007; Singh and Dasgupta 2019). A study has shown that the official deaths of manhole workers reported in Ahmedabad city alone was about nine every year on an average, in the last ten years (Manav Garima and Safai Karamchari Andolan [SKA] 2013; see also Desai 2014; Dutta 2016; Mishra et al. 2012). The Safai Kamgar Vikas Sangh (SKVS), workers of the Brihanmumbai Municipal Corporation (BMC), also sought information under the Right to Information (RTI) Act in 2006 (Anand 2007; Dadawala 2014). It was revealed that while the number of deaths had decreased between 2002–3 and 2004–5, it still remained high at around 300 (Table A1.1) in just 14 of the 24 wards of the BMC; in other words, about 26 deaths every month. These figures do not include civic hospital workers, gutter cleaners, or sanitation workers on contract (Dadawala 2014).

---

[1] That is, 2 per cent households with latrines without slab or open pits (4,933,853), plus 0.5 per cent disposing night soil in open (1,233,463), plus 0.3 per cent households which get the night soil removed by human beings (740,078), plus 0.2 per cent by animals (493,385), all add up to 7,400,780 households.

If all the BMC wards and the municipal wards of the other cities are included, then the number is likely to rise to tens of thousands. Even if we extrapolate the average deaths per month in only 14 BMC wards of Mumbai to the total number of districts in the country—725, as per Census 2011—the average number of deaths add up to about 18,608 per month by a very conservative count. As per the National Commission of Safai Karamchari data for 2019, 817 sewer workers' deaths have occurred since 1993, the year when the practice was outlawed in India through a legislation. This data, however, is only for 20 states, until 30 June 2019. The difference between the data produced by the state and non-state agencies reflect on the gross under reporting by state agencies. Compare this with the 5,100 soldiers—army, police, paramilitary—who have died between 1990 and 2007 combating militancy in Jammu and Kashmir (Ministry of Home Affairs [MHA] 2017)! The media coverage and state attention for the two have no parallel.

Invisible Vulnerability of Persons Engaged in Sanitation Work: The Problem

It is a disgrace that successive governments have remained insensitive till now to the recommendations made way back in the 1950s (Barve Committee Report) and reiterated during the 1960s (Malkani Committees Reports).[2] The protective gears provided to persons engaged in sanitation works include gumboots and masks. Other gears like bunny suits, helmets, and gloves are rarely provided, and if provided, they are often left unused because they are ill-fitting (Acharya 2016, 2017). Sanitation workers in countries like the United States (US), Hong Kong, and China need to undergo training and obtain a number of licences before they can work in this field. The workers there are well paid and respected for the hazardous work they do (Pepper 2007). In comparison, in India, a permanent sanitation worker with 20 years of experience is likely to make only US$ 150–200 a month.

[2] The Scavenging Conditions Enquiry Committee, under the chairmanship of N.R. Malkani, was constituted in 1957 and submitted its report in 1960; and the Abolition of Customary Rights of the Scavengers Committee was appointed by the Central Department of Social Welfare in 1965, again under the chairmanship of N.R. Malkani.

Women are observed to often begin working as sanitation workers after marriage, while about one-third of them are forced into it during childhood. They are also paid less than men. A vast majority of them neither have any other source of income nor agricultural land (Jan Sahas 2015).

Social exclusion of vulnerable populations has existed historically. Inclusive measures, therefore, have been the concern of affected communities, advocacy groups, and individuals, forcing governments to create an inclusive policy environment. This can be traced back to the drafting of the Constitution with Ambedkar in the chair. Factors contributing to the social divide across an array of axes—identity, caste, religion, region, language, nation, to name a few—have been continuously examined through academic and advocacy initiatives and addressed by the state and communities. However, relegation and disregard of persons who engage in scavenging and cleaning, due to little or no alternative available, is fairly well recognized in South Asia. Caste is a unique determinant of social discrimination in the Indian subcontinent—an evil against which Ambedkar crusaded; he experienced the menace himself but secured instruments to ensure safeguards for others. The process of caste-based social discrimination is embedded in religion and history, and thus accentuates the deprivation and denial among those engaged in cleaning.

As mentioned earlier, almost all persons engaged in sanitation, sewerage, and allied works are Dalits. They are known by a variety of names, such as, *bhangi, chuhra, mazhabi, lal begi,* and *halalkhor* in the north; *har, hadi, hela, dom,* and *sanei* in the east; *mukhiyar, thoti, chachati, pakay,* and *relli* in the south; and *mehtar, bhangi, halalkhor, ghasi, olgana, zadmalli, barvanshia, metariya, jamphoda,* and *mela* in the west and central India (Srivastava 1997). Manual scavenging is a caste-based practice and most manual scavengers come from the Hindu Valmiki community or the Muslim Haila (or Helas) community. Hailas are categorized as Other Backward Classes (OBCs), whereas the Valmikis belong to the Scheduled Caste (SC) category. It is estimated that 95 per cent of manual scavengers are women (PACS India et al. 2016).

Given the deep-rooted social inequalities entrenched in the Indian subcontinent, their vulnerability is exploited by the people as well as the state. While environment and its conservation has caught everyone's attention, and there is evident concern for the users of sanitation, sewerage, and allied work through provisioning of toilets under the Total Sanitation Campaign (TSC), Nirmal Bharat Abhiyan, and now the Swachh Bharat Abhiyan (SBA), the concern for sewerage and allied service providers is absent, despite the Malkani Committee Report pointing to it way back in the 1960s (Acharya and Patra 2019). Unlike the other parts of the world, in India, this work passes on to the progeny, and thus strengthens caste identity and consolidates entrenchment in the work which others will not even contemplate to engage with.

Deprivation and Disadvantage of Women Sanitation Workers

Women and development paradigm rests on the coordinates of health, education; skills and potential; facilities, providers, policies, programmes; and access to resources. Thus, the double disadvantage is embedded in social identity and its intersection with state vis-à-vis safeguards and opportunities. Women as workers, especially in low-paid jobs, have remained at the back-burner of the economy. Those engaged in cleaning are worst off (Isalkar 2013). As per the SECC 2011 estimate, 50 per cent of sanitation workers are women (RG&CCI 2015). Another estimate puts the figure at 1 million manual scavengers, stating that the actual number is 'unknown and declining' and 90 per cent of them are women (Ray and Prasad 2018). This lack of information on numbers requires interface between the individual, family, community, and policy environment through various agencies in order to enable data collection. Policy environment evolves a system in which resources, services, and facilities can be accessed and utilized by the women to enhance their work propensity, albeit in the backdrop of their own self-image. Their propensities are governed by the image they perceive of themselves through the lens of others, superimposed over their own (Acharya 2013). Inclusive policy necessitates creation of a conducive environment by generating opportunities and addressing the need to change the mindset which promotes hierarchical social system. Such hierarchies influence the environment for access, which may be enabling for some and disabling for the others. For instance, access to education is restricted for girls and women, which impacts their employability. Perceptions gear towards taking on the 'traditional work', all the more in the absence of education and/or training. Therefore, active implementation of the policies and programmes for enhancing education and skills, including those of high order, becomes imperative. Agencies, both state and non-state, play a pertinent role, given the gender dynamics that come into play in the already existing realm of caste-induced social hierarchy. Thus, not only inclusive measures are required in the sphere of work, but education and capacity building, rather than skill, also become relevant. In underprivileged conditions, health, both physical and mental, is affected. Therefore, nutritional support, counselling, and regular care services need to be infused in the general healthcare services for women engaging in cleaning occupations. Work-induced health hazards will require special management, both on-site and in the long term. The improved capacity is likely to enhance self-perception and can be brought about by community-based organizations, state agencies, and the community itself to engage with the issue of mindset and related prejudices on the one hand, and the execution of policies and programmes on the other. This will call for connecting with governance and systemic issues for sustainable solutions (Figure 1.1).

The critical issue in connecting women workers and their health requires locating them outside the frame of reproductive health. Women cleaners and scavengers hail predominantly from marginalized Dalit communities. The Dalit women constitute almost half of India's 160 million Dalits and comprise about 16 per cent of India's total female population and 8 per cent of the total population (RG&CCI 2011). Despite this, they are marginalized

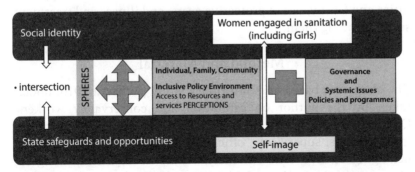

Figure 1.1 Framework for Conducive Environment for Women Workers

Source: Adapted from Acharya (2017).

on various axes, such as economic, religious, political, and ideological. The women sanitation workers comprise the manual scavengers and sewer, drain, and toilet cleaners. They manually clean dry latrines used by others. Amongst those involved in head-loading, 98 per cent are women (RG&CCI 2015). They are forced to do this work under social pressure. This work is caste based and is considered compulsory for a particular caste within the 'Dalit' community. It has not remained merely an occupation but has continued as a practice and custom (HRW 2014). Similar has been the observation of the National Advisory Council Resolution (2010): 'Manual scavenging is the worst surviving symbol of untouchability.' Most sanitation work in urban public spaces is outsourced to private contractors/organizations. In a study in 2017, it was found that there were nearly 5 million sanitation workers in India. About 45 per cent of sanitation workers worked in urban areas and nearly 50 per cent of them were women, mostly engaged in school toilet cleaning (Dalberg Advisors 2017).

Women who engage in cleaning jobs have remained backward in education, livelihood opportunities, and access to services, schemes, and opportunities to live a life with dignity. The most grievous situation is their forced retention in caste-based and hereditary occupations. They are not free to select occupations of their choice (Acharya 2017; Ray and Prasad 2018; Srivastava 1997). In order to address the arguments raised in this chapter, a profile of the workers engaged in sanitation, sewerage, and allied works has been drawn to understand the work conditions, problems faced, and discrimination experienced by them. The chapter examines: their access to resources and how it influences their work opportunities and family, use of protective gears, and illness and treatment seeking among them.

Method and Material

The chapter is based on a multi-city study (Acharya 2016) undertaken by the author on sanitation and conservancy workers. Qualitative and quantitative methods were used to collect data from workers, supervisors, officials, and other relevant personnel belonging to five cities, namely, Ahmedabad, Delhi, Gangtok, Nagpur, and Surat. A total of 1,143 individuals were part of the study. For the purpose of the present chapter, 963 young workers aged 15–35 years were analysed.

Composition of the Sanitation Workers

With regard to the composition of sanitation workers, it is noteworthy that, across the cities, there were more women engaged in surface cleaning—roads, streets, and so on—and garbage collection as compared to men. In contrast to this, cleaning drains, septic tanks, and sewers, as well as fumigation and removal of carcass, were done only by the male workers. Men and women in Bhubaneswar, Delhi, and Nagpur almost equally shared the job of cleaning the toilets. While loading and unloading of garbage trucks was done almost solely by men, in Gangtok, one female worker was engaged in this work. With regard to biomedical waste, the collection, storage, transportation, and disposal was done largely by men (Table A1.2).

Safety at Workplace and Safe Working Conditions

With exposure to dust, hazardous gases, and biomedical waste, there were evidences of accidents and illnesses reported by these workers. The government had made the provision for safety gears as per the policy regime, but the use of this equipment to safeguard the workers from exposure to health risks was not very encouraging.

> At various steps across our sanitation value chain—from toilets to the treatment plants—worker[s] must interact with faecal matter in extremely unsafe ways. They are often offered inadequate safety equipment and training; and are socially and culturally ostracised. An overwhelming majority of them are from [the] lowest Dalit sub castes—representational of India's traditional caste hierarchies and the manner in which these function. (Bhatnagar and Srivastava 2018)

Surat, with its post-plague consciousness and World Health Organization's (WHO) declaration as the cleanest city, had close to 90 per cent workers reporting access to protective gears, with only a quarter of them reporting any problems arising out of their use. Bhubaneswar and Nagpur, however, had only around 40 per cent workers reporting access and only about half of them reported problems while using these gears. Most of the problems reported were related to the improper fitting of gears such as uniforms, boots, gloves, and so on (Table A1.3).

Thus, it is observed that 87.4 per cent sanitation workers in Surat reported that they use protective gear and equipment while working, followed by Delhi (51 per cent), Gangtok (49.8 per cent), Nagpur (40.5 per cent), and Bhubaneswar (39.7 per cent). It is also observed that maximum percentage of workers used uniforms as protective gear equipment in all the states/cities under study. Boots and helmets were less used as protective gear equipment. Across cities, Bhubaneswar has the most number of workers (88.2 per cent) using uniforms as protective gear and Surat has the least (27.8 per cent).

It has been reported that sanitation workers in India do not use any protective equipment—boots, gloves, masks, or other equipment—while cleaning the drains or collecting solid and liquid waste (Mittal and Goswami 2006; Thekaekare 2013) In Chitradurga, Karnataka, the contract workers said that they were not provided any safety equipment (Society for Community Health Awareness Research and Action 2011). The health and safety of sanitation workers is not explicitly guaranteed by legislations such as those for workers in plantations, factories, mines, dock, and construction sector. Also, unlike the Factories Act, 1948, there is no legal mandate for reporting injuries. Furthermore, these workers are not covered by the Employees' State Insurance Scheme to safeguard them from occupational diseases or injuries. Thus, there are very few instances of compensation, and those too are largely due to the efforts of advocacy groups. The legislation of 2013 pertaining to manual scavenging fails to address health risks and is problematic as it does not define workers using protective gear or devices to clean faecal matter as manual scavengers. This definition and provision of safety equipment may only serve to legitimize manual scavenging and other forms of septic or sewage cleaning. It also fails to address long-term disability and medical rehabilitation of these workers. On the contrary, it seemingly perpetuates the caste-based engagement in the cleaning jobs (Acharya 2016; Acharya and Patra 2019).

It is also important to examine which protective gears were given to the workers and were used by them. Most of them had uniforms and masks. Some of them had gloves and boots too. About 80 per cent used uniforms across the five selected cities where the study was conducted. Gloves were only used by 44 per cent in Delhi, 46 per cent in Gangtok, and 49 per cent in Surat. Among the five cities, Nagpur had the most (80 per cent) workers using gloves. Boots were used least by the workers in Bhubaneswar (45 per cent) and most by those in Gangtok (73 per cent) (Table A1.4).

With regard to the gender differentials in use of protective gears across the cities selected for the present study, a mixed pattern was observed. Since most women were engaged for surface cleaning, use of brooms to sweep and masks to protect them from dust while sweeping was higher among them than men. Surat, however, showed a reverse pattern. Similarly, men were engaged in drain and sewer cleaning, therefore, use of boots was more among them as compared to women.

Educational Attainment

With respect to educational attainment, the level of education among the youth was higher than all workers'. About 22 per cent (Bhubaneswar) to 30 per cent (Gangtok) of all workers were uneducated. The share of illiterate young workers across the study cities was less (than all workers) and varied from 8.3 per cent in Delhi to 18.1 per cent in Gangtok. There was a gap of about 10–12 percentage points between the youth and all workers with regard to the attainment of primary education. This gap was in favour of youth, although it reduced at the secondary level of education (Table A1.5). This indicates that despite engaging with the dehumanizing work, younger people are geared towards improving their educational status. It is possible that the availability of scholarships for education have enabled this trend.

Problems and Experience of Discrimination

The young workers face various problems while working. It is observed that most workers in all the states/cities faced problems related to equipment. If the gender differentials are considered in the problems experienced, it is evident that more women faced problems as compared to men. Delhi, however, had more men than women who reported to have experienced problems in using protective gears. The equipment was reported to be unwieldy and ill-fitting. In case of women, most of the time, using the equipment over their 'sari'—their usual attire—made it very difficult. Masks, boots, and helmets were reported to be very uncomfortable to wear during work. Their subservient position too made them vulnerable and exposed them to unkind behaviour from service users. The users of the cleaning services—household members who interact with the cleaners—often refused to give them water to drink, and even if they did, it was in a separate vessel/container. They did not let the workers take shelter in their verandas in case of rain or heat. They spoke to them harshly and in a crude way. Across the cities, Nagpur reported the most problems faced by young female (55) and male (41) workers, while least number of workers (7) reported problems in Surat, but the number of women (6) was more than men (1) (Table A1.6).

Such attitude of the users of sanitation, sewerage, and allied services necessitates a functional restroom facility urgently. It also reiterates the need to work on the mindset of the people to eradicate the stigma associated with caste-based occupations and the consequent discrimination, which was proposed by Ambedkar decades ago and subsequently recommended by various committees[3] set up by the government for the welfare of people engaged in cleaning occupations. It is noteworthy that it was about 25 years later that the Government of India constituted a National Commission for Safai Karmacharis under the National Commission for Safai Karmacharis Act, 1993, in August 1994. Subsequently, National Safai Karamcharis Finance and Development Corporation was incorporated on 24 January 1997 under Section 25 of the Companies Act, 1956, as an apex institution for all-round socio-economic uplifting of the *safai karamcharis* and their dependents, and to extend concessional financial assistance to the safai karamcharis for the establishment of income-generating projects.

Apart from this, young women workers experienced two additional problems related to menstrual health and hygiene and sexual harassment. There were no toilet facilities, particularly for women. They had to hold their urge to ease themselves till they reached home or any other community toilet. This is medically known to cause adverse effects on health (National Kidney and Urologic Diseases

---

[3] The Scavengers' Living Conditions Enquiry Committee (B.N. Barve), Government of Bombay, 1949; Backward Classes Commission (Kaka Kalelkar), Government of India, 1953; Report of the Scavenging Conditions Enquiry Committee (N.R. Malkani), Ministry of Home Affairs, Central Advisory Board for Harijan Welfare, New Delhi, 1960; The Committee on Customary Rights to Scavengers (N.R. Malkani) Government of India, Ministry of Home Affairs, New Delhi, 1969; Committee on Conditions of Sweepers and Scavengers (B.P. Pandya) National Commission on Labor, Government of India, New Delhi, 1969.

Information Clearinghouse 2010). They could not use or change their sanitary pads, since there were no toilets in the beat offices (units in the municipal wards from where the safai karamcharis collect their daily work and are supposed to have space to rest, use the toilet, etc.). They were often harassed while working and using toilets. The following narratives endorse their concern and plight:

> Most of us usually come to work after using the toilet ... and perhaps praying that we do not have to go during the work hours. We try to drink less water.... Yes, I know we should drink lots of water. In fact, I do feel thirsty while working ... [there are] no toilets in the people's house and in the housing complexes where we work, toilets are restricted for our use. We also avoid using them because the watchmen often make lewd comments.[4]

Kalawati further corroborated this concern and the problems faced by the young women workers. She reflected on the gender dynamics at work and probable exposure to insecure spaces. She said:

> Sometimes the watchmen of the housing societies allow you to use the toilets which are meant for the Resident Welfare Association Office bearers and caretakers, albeit at a cost—which may range from a sexist comment to brushing across so that the body is touched 'accidentally', often followed by profuse 'apologies' with a sneer on the face, telling loud and clear that it was a purposefully created accident to ensure that the bodies touch! So sometimes, it gets difficult for us to figure out the real intent ... sometimes I feel maybe I am too sensitive ... do not know ... but certainly feel uncomfortable when I have to use the toilet in the 'X' housing society in Zone 13.[5]

Similar experiences were reported from the garbage-dumping site in Gangtok. Rani had been working at the site for the last seven years. She came from Cooch Behar to Siliguri, and then one of the labour contractors' middlemen brought her to this site for work. She did not know how much salary she got. She had been 'depositing' her salary with Sakharam who had brought her here.

---

[4] Personal interview with Srimanta (pseudonym), 31, *safai kamgar*, Surat Municipal Corporation, SMC Office Central Courtyard, Gujarat, India, 17 January 2015.
[5] Personal interview with Kalawati (pseudonym), Nagpur, 7 February 2015. Identifiers withheld for ethical reasons.

She had 'married' him. He took care of her and her money. Her marriage to Sakharam was a live example of perceiving marriage as a solution for sexual harassment. Seven years ago, Rani was young and innocent, with a robust built. Everyone around her appeared to be gauging her physical appearance. Men saw her as an object of desire, while women considered her a 'threat' to the integrity of their respective marriages. Some feared for her safety and almost dreaded the day she would be harassed and sexually assaulted. Their seasoned eyes had got the sense of what most men were thinking about her. All workers had been given housing space near the site along the Teesta River. Most of them had constructed temporary units to live in. When Rani had arrived unaccompanied by a man, with her two daughters in tow—the elder one 2 years old and the younger one about 7 months old—her character assassination had begun even before she could unload her meagre belongings from the truck in which she had arrived. Her illusion of escaping hunger and a violent husband in her native place was soon shattered when she found herself amidst her male coworkers who cast their eyes upon her with lust and desire and perceived her differently—not as their 'coworker'. Despite her small build, she was strong in many ways and gave a 'no-nonsense' signal to all undue advances towards her. Some older women sensed her vulnerability and advised her to get married. She took about a year before she plunged into yet another marriage. In the words of Rani, we get a glimpse of a lone woman trying to seek her rightful space in society and at workplace: 'I ran away from my violent husband, taking my little girls with me. I reached here, accepted the shelter provided to me by Sakharam [shyly pronounced the name], and married him to avoid the unpleasant advances from others.' Her experiences of sexual harassment at workplace were as follows:

> We load, unload and disaggregate the waste material that the trucks bring here. Some men tend to brush against us, touch us, or sing a song! Most of them are 'harmless', but some follow us till the toilet ... lonely and secluded ... it is scary! Most older men (and women), however, are very protective. We avoid going to the toilet alone. But I am happy here because I earn money and hope to see my girls go to a 'good school' someday.[6]

[6] Personal interview with Rani (pseudonym), Gangtok, Sikkim, India, 21 May 2015.

Thus, in addition to equipment-related problems and experiences of discrimination, women feel insecure too. Therefore, security, in addition to safety, is imperative for women workers.

Health Conditions

Sanitation work is considered to be one of the most hazardous jobs. Those engaged in these jobs are vulnerable to various kinds of illnesses (CEC 2007; Pepper 2007; Ramasamy 2005). An analysis of the illnesses reported by the young workers across the cities selected for the study suggests that more than half of them were suffering from respiratory ailments. The share of such diseases among the young workers varied from 33.24 per cent in Bhubaneswar to about 60 per cent in Surat. About 8–12 per cent of workers reported body aches—back, legs, and head. Nagpur (8.3 per cent) reported the lowest, while Delhi (17.29 per cent) reported the highest. Injuries were one of the most commonly occurring 'illnesses'. While respiratory ailments were lesser among the youth as compared to the older workers, the reverse was evident in case of injuries. Incidents of injuries were about 3–10 per cent higher among the youth across the cities as compared to the older workers (Table A1.7).

Nature of Illness and Treatment Seeking: Gender Differentials

An analysis of the nature of the illness, including injuries suffered, and treatment sought across genders brings out certain stark realities. On the basis of the discussion, the reported illness was disaggregated as:

- injuries
- recent illness—occurred in the last three months
- continuing illness—suffering from it for over three months

While most men continued working after preliminary dressing when an injury occurred, and went to both public and private healthcare providers or facilities, women usually preferred self-medication and, at most, went to the public hospital. Men also reported getting time to rest if injured, while women remained quiet on this aspect. Men reported chest pain, while women reported pain in different parts of the body, ranging from the head to the back, lower back, neck, and legs. Menstrual cramps were not 'recognized' as illness by any of the participating women. They also did not report the discomfort of not being able to use the washroom. Men reported pain in lower abdomen, while women reported fever, cough, and cold as continuing illnesses (Table A1.8)

The young sanitation workers are energetic and full of aspirations. However, the circumstances fail to support the realization of their dreams. Most of them are migrants, remain at low levels of education, and have poor health. Poor propensities and poor work conditions act as a hindrance in their access to healthcare. If they do avail treatment, most of the time it is from public sector facilities and providers (Acharya 2016).

Awareness and Utilization of Benefits

An analysis of the benefits which the workers were aware of and could manage to use suggests that out of all the workers across different cities selected for the study, only around 18 per cent were aware of the benefits they could avail for their families. They knew that there are schemes for welfare of workers like them but had never used these. This awareness was slightly higher (20.49 per cent) among the young workers.

Around half of them (48.54 per cent) did not clearly mention how they used these benefits. They gave vague responses about 'some' benefits being availed, ranging from school fees, books, and uniform to healthcare. Some (about 3.88 per cent) could recall that they got soap, oil, and uniform (Table A1.9). Therefore, there is a need to disseminate information through specific targeted modules of Information, Education, and Communication (IEC).

Factors for Continuance in Sanitation Work

It is evident that the sanitation workers live in appalling conditions and aspire to switch to other jobs. However, there are many compulsions, over and above caste identity, which hinder their exit from such occupations. Their socio-economic conditions and educational attainment emerge as the important factors which contribute to their continuance in the conservancy works. About 64.50 per cent workers considered their low level of education (34.98 per cent) and poverty (29.50 per cent) as the main factors preventing them from becoming eligible for alternative occupations. This is associated with the historical deprivation which most of them have experienced and been unable to rid themselves off due to societal norms of caste-based graded inequality. It is noteworthy that less than 2 per cent continued to believe that this was their traditional job and therefore, there was nothing wrong in continuing with it (Table A1.10).

Delhi Jal Board employee, Ramadhin opined:

> Yes of course, there is no question that I should not do this work. My ancestors have done it and I am doing it. I know my job very well ... and do it better than the daily wager whom the Municipality brings ... Yes, it is tiring ... but someone has to do it ... and I do it better than everyone around me ... I have learned it from my forefathers ... no training can teach you the intuition which is needed to understand the lethal gases of a sewer ... before you plunge into it.[7]

It is also noteworthy that nearly 3 per cent said that they do not have to face any competition to get this work and are therefore continuing with it. This also reflects on the complacency which tends to set in because there are no other options or at the most, minimal alternatives available. Acceptance of the circumstances which are difficult to change—poor socio-economic conditions, low educational attainments, no alternative training, lack of social capital, no or extremely few avenues to change the profession—consolidate the continuance in conservancy work. While there are notions of some vertical mobility visible, absence of opportunities compels them to believe that the current work obtained with less competition is worth doing, especially when unemployment has been an issue in the country.

> You see no one except the Bhangis will come to do this job. So the competition is less ... if I have to apply for other jobs, I will face competition with far too many people—who will be better educated—educated in better institutions ... who know how to speak in English.... I cannot even spell my name in English [despondent laughter]. Let me continue with this work. At least I will earn my daily bread regularly.... Risk? Who is not at the risk of dying? So why

---

[7] Personal interview with Ramadhin (pseudonym), 34, Delhi Jal Board, Vikas Puri, New Delhi, 12 August 2015. Ramadhin looked much older than his age.

worry? Perhaps this is my destiny ... and if I die, my son will get the job ... he will be allotted a house too ... which other job can provide you all this ... no ... I am happy.[8]

Ambedkar's Concern for Health and the State's Response

As chairman of the Satyagraha Committee of Dalit movement in 1927, Ambedkar addressed the Dalits (Mahars), then labelled as untouchables, in Chavdar Tank in Mahad taluka of Maharashtra. This initiated the quest for the right to have access to drinking water from the tank which was denied to the Dalits. It also echoed the beginning of Ambedkar's concern for people's health—much before the constitution of the Bhore Committee in 1943. Access to safe drinking water was important, especially for the underprivileged populations. His ideas on women's health were reflected in the Bombay Legislative Council meeting held on 10 November 1938, in which disability of the parents was acknowledged as the prime reason for impacting children physically, mentally, and financially. He saw that the reproductive rights of women were important for their development and proposed limiting the number of births for health of the women and children, instead of the conventional stand of promoting family planning for reducing fertility levels and thereby population size. He also saw this as a measure to prevent maternal and infant deaths and reduce morbidity among them. Thus, he was undoubtedly among the first few who favoured medical termination of pregnancy to prevent unwanted births, in order to safeguard the mother's health. Mica Mines Labour Welfare Fund Bill[9] led to availability of maternity benefits for women mine workers initially, and subsequently laid the basis for extending it to all working women.

Decades later, as a signatory to the Alma-Ata Declaration in 1978, the world, including India, professed all that was envisioned by Ambedkar, albeit without acknowledging his efforts. Ambedkar's

---

[8] Personal interview with Mehram Chand (pseudonym), 35, All India Institute of Medical Sciences, New Delhi, India, 17 October 2015.

[9] See https://labour.gov.in/acts/mica-mines-labour-welfare-fund-act-1946 and http://www.ilo.org/dyn/natlex/natlex4.detail?p_lang=en&p_isn=51965&p_count=96150&p_classification=22.02&p_classcount=846; last accessed on 12 March 2020.

concern had a strong connection with the downtrodden communities and underprivileged workers, evident through the fundamental rights in the drafting of the Constitution. This laid the grounds for subsequent tabling and enactment of the legislative provision to stop manual cleaning of human excreta, which is expected, encouraged, and sanctioned to be done by specific communities only, through the enactment of the Employment of Manual Scavengers and Construction of Dry Latrines (Prohibition) Act in 1993. This Act provided for punishment and fine on employment of scavengers or on the construction of dry toilets. This was made possible only in 1993, although the committees set up to review the conditions of the persons engaged in cleaning occupations recommended their upliftment and drafted a road map for the purpose way back in the 1940s and 1950s. The Joseph Bhore Committee Report (1946) pointed towards the equitable need to address the health of the people of India, particularly the poor and disadvantaged, and this led to the setting up of subsequent committees like the Barve and Malkani committees. The N.R. Malkani Committee Report of the Scavenging Conditions Enquiry Committee (1960) and the Committee on Customary Rights to Scavengers (1969) further reiterated the necessity to address the needs of the groups engaged in such works. However, it took nearly three decades for the taskforce to be set up in 1991.

Manual scavengers continue to be employed by the municipalities, Indian Railways, defence establishments, and local authorities in rural and urban areas. Continuance of manual scavenging casts doubts on the government's intent to overcome caste barriers and project itself as an economic growth engine. The government's efforts to address this problem have to be multidimensional. There is a need to expand the ambit of manual scavenging to include workers who clean the sewers, septic tanks, and drains where human excreta is washed. It is also necessary to provide a mechanism to implement the rehabilitation programme for persons engaged in cleaning occupations and their immediate family members. The purview of the programme could include training in other professions and technical education. Arming the sanitation workers with state-of-the-art technology tools is also important. Developed nations have tools and equipment which protect sanitation workers from direct exposure to sewage water and waste. Also, extending the benefits of Rashtriya Swasthya Bima Yojana (RSBY) to scavengers and their family members, with provisions of free health check-ups on a regular basis, will be a positive step. Finally, a functional financial safety net can be provided to them by giving them subsidized loans for starting new ventures.

The cleanliness drive SBA was implemented in October 2014; more appropriately, the then existing scheme was relaunched. Over a five-year period, about Rs 62,009 crores were allocated to this programme. The centre was to pitch in Rs 14,623 crores. The mission aimed to cover 1.04 crore households, provide 2.5 lakh community toilets, 2.6 lakh public toilets, and a solid waste-management facility in each town (DoDW&S 2014). Despite these efforts, India still has the longest queues for toilets in the world (Mukherjee 2015; WaterAid Report 2017). Eradicating open defecation was the core objective of the SBA. It aimed to build 12 crore toilets in rural India by 2019, at a cost of 1.96 lakh crores. India has made some progress in providing sanitation by building toilets to desist people from defecating in the open. More than 1 crore toilets have been built as part of the SBA since the launch of the mission (DoDW&S 2019). However, less than 50 per cent of these toilets are in use due to lack of water (RG&CCI 2015). The other important reason for not using these toilets is the availability of persons to clean the excreta from dry latrines (Dalberg Advisors 2017). Lack of water pushes the people to continue using the dry latrines, which are cleaned by humans. This will continue to perpetuate the engagement of humans for cleaning the dry latrines.

Sensitivity towards Social Identity-Based Disparities

The issue of manual scavenging goes beyond poverty, indifference, lack of awareness, or reluctance to switch from traditional work. Manual scavenging 'is rooted in caste as surely as caste is rooted in Indian psyche' (Zaidi 2006). There is need to introspect and reconsider the perceptions about these people whose contribution towards the upkeep of the environment is second to none. There is also a need to resolve to give them what is due to them since long—dignity and social inclusion.

It is also important for persons currently engaged in cleaning occupations to be able to switch to alternative occupations, and work towards restricting the engagement of young people in cleaning occupations. The journey towards this goal will not be easy. For this, the following needs to be done by individuals and communities: reconstruction of self-image; completion of education against all odds; look for alternatives to enhance skills; increase vocational propensity; and above all, overcome the trap of 'government job' in the name of sewerage cleaning and assured risk to life. Correspondingly, the state too has the responsibility to mechanize all cleaning works; ensure adequate allocation of funds for the safety and health of the current workers and education of their children; and revisit the legislative safeguards to adequately include the excluded categories of cleaners. Urban planners, public health specialists, and civil engineers need to practise and evolve courses to sensitize human-friendly management of waste. Poor access to resources has perpetuated low levels of development for a long time. There is a need for generating data on socio-economic characteristics, health status, and housing conditions of specific groups engaged in cleaning occupations in order to plan positive programmes for them. Lack of basic data has also contributed in the failure to yield an expected outcome from the policy measures.

The humiliation experienced by those engaged in scavenging and cleaning in their daily life and in rendering their services needs to be documented. Their access to healthcare, housing, education, basic infrastructure, provisions for work-related safety, safeguards against health hazards, information on various schemes oriented towards their welfare, and the utilization of such schemes, have all largely remained confined as 'outcome' figures. The 'process' which precedes these outcomes has never, or rarely, been given any importance. It is for this reason that despite government measures towards affirmative action during the last few decades, the episodes of death due to humiliation and attack on the dignity of these persons continue. A true tribute to Ambedkar would be to continue with his efforts of empowering the lives of the persons engaged in cleaning occupations and to enable them to overcome the vicious cycle of caste and culture barrier, and use their potential; rather than washing their feet and co-dining with them. Otherwise, offering flowers on his statue on his birth anniversary every year will remain a futile tokenism.

References

Acharya, Sanghmitra S. 2013. 'Universal Health Care: Pathways from Access to Utilization among Vulnerable Populations', *Indian Journal of Public Health* 57(4): 242–7.

———. 2016. 'Engaging with Conservancy Work and Experience of Social Discrimination with Special Reference to Young People'. Unpublished project report, Indian Council for Social Sciences Research (ICSSR), New Delhi.

———. 2017. 'Historically Excluded Groups in India: Sanitation Workers and Realities of Livelihoods, Health and Safety', *The Indian Journal of Social Work* 78(1): 113–31.

Acharya, Sanghmitra S. and Golak B. Patra. 2019. 'Constitutional Provisions and Legal Safeguards for the Sanitation and Allied Workers in India', in S. Panneer, S.S. Acharya, and N. Sivakami (eds), *Health Safety and Well-Being of Workers in the Informal Sector in India: Lessons for Emerging Economies*, pp. 131–46. New Delhi: Springer.

Anand, S. 2007. 'Life Inside a Black Hole', *Tehelka Magazine* 4(47), 8 December. Available at http://www.tehelka.com/story_main36.asp?filename=Ne081207LIFE_INSIDE.asp; last accessed on 4 September 2018.

Bhatnagar, Niret and Kartik Srivastava. 2018. 'Not so Swachh Bharat: The Harsh Reality of Life for India's 5 Million Sanitation Workers'. *Quartz India*, 19 April. Available at https://qz.com/1254258/sanitation-workers-a-five-million-people-large-blind-spot-in-india/; last accessed on 2 March 2019.

Centre for Education and Communication (CEC). 2007. *Hole to Hell: A Study on Health & Safety of Sewage Workers in Delhi*. New Delhi: CEC. Available at http://www.thedailybeast.com/newsweek/2007/10/31/the-world-s-worst-job.html; last accessed on 2 December 2017.

Dadawala, Vikrant. 2014. 'Spare a Thought for Workers Who Keep Cities Clean', *Mumbai Mirror*. Available at https://mumbaimirror.indiatimes.com/mumbai/other/spare-a-thought-for-workers-who-keep-cities-clean/articleshow/44030214.cms?utm_source=contentofinterest&utm_medium=text&utm_campaign=cppst; last accessed on 20 February 2020.

Dalberg Advisors. 2017. 'The Sanitation Workers Project', Supported by Bill and Melinda Gates Foundation. Available at http://sanitationworkers.org/about/; last accessed on 23 December 2018.

Department of Drinking Water and Sanitation (DoDW&S). 2014. *Annual Report*. Ministry of Jal Shakti, Government of India. Available at https://sbm.gov.in/sbmReport/home.aspx; last accessed on 12 February 2019.

———. 2019. *Three Years of Good Governance*. SBM& NRDWP, Ministry of Jal Shakti, Government of India. Available at https://swachhbharatmission.gov.in/sbmcms/index.htm; last accessed on 12 February 2019.

Desai, D. 2014. 'Manual Scavenging Still Continues in Gujarat'. *The Hindu*, 24 May. Available at http://www.thehindu.com/todays-paper/tp-national/manual-scavenging-stillcontinues-in-gujarat/article4744632.ece; last accessed on 12 August 2018.

Dutta, Geetanjali. 2016. 'Socio-economic Challenges of Urban Sanitation Workers in Gujarat: An Analysis of Ahmedabad City', *Liberal Studies* 1(2): 267–81.
Economist, The. 2008. 'India's Manual Scavengers Clean-up—How to Abolish a Dirty, Low-Status Job', 10 July 2008. Available at https://www.economist.com/asia/2008/07/10/clean-up; last accessed on 28 October 2019.
Government of India (GoI). 1993. 'The Employment of Manual Scavengers and Construction of Dry Latrines (Prohibition) Act, 1993'. New Delhi: Ministry of Housing and Urban Poverty Alleviation.
———. 2013. 'The Prohibition of Employment as Manual Scavengers and Their Rehabilitation Act, 2013'. Available at http://legislative.gov.in/sites/default/files/A2013-25.pdf; last accessed on 13 June 2019.
Human Rights Watch (HRW). 2014. 'Cleaning Human Waste: "Manual Scavenging", Caste and Discrimination in India'. Available at https://www.hrw.org/report/2014/08/25/cleaning-human-waste/manual-scavenging-caste-and-discrimination-india; last accessed on 13 June 2019.
Isalkar, Umesh. 2013. 'Census Raises Stink over Manual Scavenging'. *The Times of India*, 30 April. Available at https://timesofindia.indiatimes.com/city/pune/Census-raises-stink-over-manual-scavenging/articleshow/19794299.cms; last accessed on 7 May 2020.
Jan Sahas. 2015. 'Dignity Campaign: Action for Liberation of Dalit Manual Scavenger Women in India', Social Development Society and Fund for Gender Equality, United Nations Entity for Gender Equality and the Empowerment of Women (UN Women).
Manav Garima and Safai Karamchari Andolan (SKA). 2013. 'Jan Vikas Survey by Ahmedabad Civil Rights Group', in collaboration with Manav Garima and SKA. Available at https://counterview.org/2013/07/17/posh-ahmedabad-is-still-not-free-from-manual-scavenging-described-national-shame-decades-ago-by-the-father-of-the-nation/; last accessed on 12 May 2019.
Ministry of Home Affairs (MHA). 2017. 'Fatalities in Jammu and Kashmir: 1990–2017'. Available at https://www.satp.org/satporgtp/countries/india/states/jandk/data_sheets/Fatalities_mha.htm; last accessed on 21 January 2018.
Mishra, A., I. Dodiya, and N. Mathur. 2012. 'An Assessment of Livelihood and Educational Status of Sanitation Workers in Ahmedabad'. IIMA Working Paper WP2012-10-01, Indian Institute of Management Ahmedabad, p. 4.
Mittal, Ashish and Goswami, P.J. 2006. *Hole to Hell: A Study on Health & Safety Status of Sewage Workers in Delhi*. New Delhi: Centre of Education and Communication.
Moon, Vasant (ed.). 1989. *Dr. Babasaheb Ambedkar's Writings and Speeches*, Vol. 9. Education Department. Bombay: Government of Maharashtra.

Mukherjee, Sanjeeb. 2015. 'India has World's Longest Queues for Toilets'. *Business Standard*, 20 November 2015. Available at https://www.business-standard.com/article/economy-policy/india-has-world-s-longest-queues-for-toilets-115111900137_1.html; last accessed on 2 March 2018.

National Advisory Council Resolution. 2010. Available at https://www.hrw.org/report/2014/08/25/cleaning-human-waste/manual-scavenging-caste-and-discrimination-india; last accessed on 22 March 2018.

National Kidney and Urologic Diseases Information Clearinghouse. 2010. 'Urinary Incontinence in Women'. Available at http://kidney.niddk.nih.gov/kudiseases/pubs/uiwomen/; last accessed on 6 August 2018.

PACS India, UK AID, and ifirst Consortium. 2016. 'What Is Manual Scavenging?' Available at http://www.pacsindia.org/projects/advocacy-and-campaigning/breaking-margins-campaign/what-is-manual-scavenging; last accessed on 12 March 2020.

Pepper, Daniel. 2007. 'The World's Worst Job?: India's Sewage Workers Are Certainly in the Running'. *Newsweek* (Web exclusive), 1 November. Available at https://www.thedailybeast.com/newsweek/2007/10/31/the-world-s-worst-job.html; last accessed on 5 April 2017.

Ramasamy, G. 2005. *India Stinking*. Chennai: Navayana.

Ray, I. and C.S.S. Prasad. 2018. 'Where There Are No Sewers: Photoessays on Sanitation Work in Urban India'. Sustainable Sanitation Alliance (SuSanA) Secretariat at GIZ, Eschborn, Germany.

Registrar General and Census Commissioner, India (RG&CCI). 2011. *Availability and Type of Latrine Facilities 2001–2011, Census of India 2011*. New Delhi: Ministry of Home Affairs, Government of India.

———. 2015. *Socio-economic Caste Census 2011*. New Delhi: Census of India, Ministry of Home Affairs.

Singh, Arkaja and Shubhagato Dasgupta. 2019. 'Safe and Dignified Sanitation Work: India's Foremost Sanitation Challenge—As Part of "Policy Challenges, 2019–2024: The Big Policy Questions for the New Government and Possible Pathways"'. Centre for Policy Research, 20 June. Available at https://www.cprindia.org/news/7910; last accessed on 23 January 2020.

Society for Community Health Awareness Research and Action. 2011. 'Invisible Guardians, Silent Victims: A Study on the Health Status of the *Pourakarmika*s of Chitradurga Town'. Bangalore: Community Health Cell, 28 April. Available at http://mfcindia.org/main/bgpapers/ bgpapers2013/am/bgpap2013w.pdf; last accessed on 12 January 2017.

Srivastava, B.N. 1997. *Manual Scavenging: A Disgrace to the Country*. New Delhi: Concept Publishing Company.

Thekaekare, M.M. 2013. 'Dying for a Living'. *Infochange India*. Available at http://infochangeindia.org/livelihoods/sidelines/dying-for-a-living.html; last accessed on 4 March 2019.

United Nations Commission on Human Rights (UNCHR). 2002. 'UN Sub-commission on the Promotion and Protection of Human Rights', Working Group on Contemporary Forms of Slavery, 27th Session, Geneva, 27–31 May.

WaterAid Report. 2017. 'Out of Order—The State of World's Toilets'. Available at https://washmatters.wateraid.org/publications/out-of-order-the-state-of-the-worlds-toilets-2017; last accessed on 21 August 2019.

Zaidi, Annie. 2006. 'India's Shame' (cover story), *Frontline: The Hindu*, Delhi, Vol. 23, no. 18, 9–22 September.

Appendix

Table A1.1 Deaths among Sewer Workers in 14 Wards of the BMC

Year	Number of Deaths	Average Death per Month
2002–3	320	27
2003–4	316	26
2004–5	288	24
Total/Average	924	26

Source: SKVS, 2006 Annual Report, data sought under RTI, cited in Dadawala (2014).

Table A1.2 Gender Differentials in the Nature of Work of Young Sanitation Workers

Nature of Work	Bhubaneswar No. (%)	Delhi No. (%)	Gangtok No. (%)	Nagpur No. (%)	Surat No. (%)
Garbage collection (Total)	39 (26.37)	42 (23.5)	41 (25.3)	60 (50.8)	7 (8.1)
Female	29	32	29	34	5
Male	10	10	12	26	2
Cleaning road/streets (Total)	20 (13.51)	52 (29.05)	48 (29.7)	28 (23.7)	63 (73.3)
Female	15	34	32	15	41
Male	5	18	16	13	22
Cleaning drains, septic tanks, and sewers (Total)	35 (23.65)	22 (12.29)	25 (15.4)	7 (5.9)	10 (11.6)
Female	0	0	0	0	0
Male	35	22	25	7	10
Cleaning toilets* (Total)	44 (29.73)	23 (12.8)	17 (10.5)	7 (5.9)	3 (3.5)
Female	23	10	12	4	3
Male	21	13	5	3	0
Cleaning/removing dead bodies (Total)	6 (4.05)	4 (2.3)	5 (3.1)	1 (0.8)	1 (1.2)
Female	0	0	0	0	0
Male	6	4	5	1	1
Fumigation/spraying (Total)	3 (2.03)	6 (3.3)	4 (2.5)	1 (0.8)	1 (1.2)
Female	0	0	0	0	0
Male	3	6	4	1	1

(Cont'd)

Table A1.2 (Cont'd)

Nature of Work	Bhubaneswar No. (%)	Delhi No. (%)	Gangtok No. (%)	Nagpur No. (%)	Surat No. (%)
Biomedical waste collection/storage, disposal (Total)	4 (2.7)	7 (3.9)	8 (4.9)	9 (7.6)	1 (1.2)
Female	1	1	2	1	0
Male	3	6	6	8	1
Loading/unloading garbage trucks (Total)	2 (2.03)	11 (6.1)	6 (3.8)	2 (1.7)	2 (2.3)
Female	0	0	1	0	0
Male	2	11	5	1	1
Any others (Total)	3 (2.03)	6 (3.4)	7 (4.3)	2 (1.7)	1 (1.2)
Female	0	2	1	1	1
Male	3	4	6	1	0
Youth (Total)	148 (63.79)	179 (62.15)	162 (60.22)	118 (51.98)	86 (67.72)
Female	78	81	88	63	51
Male	70	98	74	55	35

Notes: (i) The share of young workers in each category of work is to the total young workers, for example, the percentage of young garbage collectors equals 26.37 per cent (number of young garbage collectors divided by total number of young workers).
(ii) Workers reported doing more than one type of work.
*Community and personal.
Source: Acharya (2016).

Table A1.3 Protective Gear/Equipment Used by Sanitation Workers in Different Cities

Protective Gear/Equipment	Delhi		Surat		Nagpur		Gangtok		Bhubaneswar	
	No.	(%)	No.	(%)	No.	(%)	No.	(%)	No.	(%)
Have Used Any	147	51.0	111	87.4	92	40.5	134	49.8	92	39.7
Type										
Helmet	8	2.8	4	2.0	1	0.5	4	1.5	0	0.0
Mask	53	18.4	65	31.7	29	13.4	49	18.2	18	4.7
Uniform	129	44.8	57	27.8	75	34.6	114	42.4	149	88.2
Gloves	64	22.2	54	26.3	74	34.1	61	22.7	16	3.6
Boot	12	4.2	8	3.9	6	2.8	8	3.0	11	0.6
Brooms	22	7.6	10	4.9	21	9.7	20	7.4	15	3.0
Mops	0	0.0	7	3.4	11	5.1	13	4.8	0	0.0
Problems Related to Protective Gear/Equipment										
Workers Reporting Problems	60	41.0	26	23.42	52	85.4	54	77.1	35	43.9
Total	288	100	127	100	227	100	269	100	232	100

Note: Workers possessed/used multiple gears.
Source: Acharya (2016).

Table A1.4 Gender-wise Use of Protective Gear/Equipment in Different Cities

Any Protective Gear (PG)/Equipment (E)	Bhubaneswar No. (%)	Delhi No. (%)	Gangtok No. (%)	Nagpur No. (%)	Surat No. (%)
Helmet (Total)	0 (0)	8 (5.44)	4 (2.99)	1 (0.81)	4 (3.60)
Female	0	2	1	0	2
Male	0	6	3	1	2
Mask (Total)	49 (53.26)	63 (42.85)	69 (51.49)	49 (53.26)	65 (58.56)
Female	28	37	39	25	32
Male	21	26	30	24	33
Uniform (Total)	79 (85.87)	129 (87.76)	114 (85.07)	75 (81.52)	87 (78.38)
Female	35	67	54	42	45
Male	44	62	60	33	42
Gloves (Total)	69 (75.0)	64 (43.54)	61 (45.52)	74 (80.43)	54 (48.65)
Female	23	21	19	24	21
Male	46	43	42	50	33
Boot (Total)	41 (44.57)	82 (55.78)	98 (73.13)	66 (71.74)	58 (52.25)
Female	12	23	35	27	24
Male	29	59	63	39	34
Brooms (Total)	75 (81.52)	122 (82.99)	120 (89.55)	61 (66.30)	90 (81.08)
Female	49	73	69	39	51
Male	26	49	51	22	39

Any others* (Total)	0 (0)	02 (1.36)	01 (0.75)	11 (11.96)	7 (6.31)
Female	0	1	1	7	5
Male	0	1	0	4	2
Have/Use PGs (Total)	92 (39.7)	147 (51.0)	134 (49.8)	92 (40.5)	111 (87.4)
Female	42	62	58	41	54
Male	50	85	76	52	57
Total Workers	232 (100.0)	288 (100.0)	269 (100.0)	227 (100.0)	127 (100.0)

Note: Figures in parentheses denote the percentage of young workers who have used 'x' protective gear to the total young workers who have used any protective gear. These are multiple-response answers. A worker is likely to have used more than one PG/E. Therefore, sum of all the workers using different PG/E will not be equal to the total number of young workers who have used any PG/E.

* Torch, ladder, rope, mop, and so on.

Source: Acharya (2016).

Table A1.5 Workers and Their Educational Attainment

Workers	Bhubaneswar No. (%)	Delhi No. (%)	Gangtok No. (%)	Nagpur No. (%)	Surat No. (%)
No Education (%)					
All	21.5	24.7	29.9	26.6	23.3
Youth	11.4	8.4	18.1	12.4	11.6
Primary (I–V) (%)					
All	46.4	44.6	47.7	51.5	52.94
Youth	51.86	56.59	56.17	62.54	54.61
Secondary (VI–VIII) (%)					
All	31.2	16.8	17.7	20.4	21.4
Youth	34.22	19.51	20.21	22.78	26.23
Higher Secondary (IX–XII) (%)					
All	0.9	13.96	4.7	1.5	2.36
Youth	2.68	15.67	5.56	1.9	7.56
Total Youth	148 (63.79)	179 (62.15)	162 (60.22)	118 (51.98)	86 (67.72)
Total All	232 (100.0)	288 (100.0)	269 (100.0)	227 (100.0)	127 (100.0)

Note: Percentage of youth have been calculated as the share of youth at a given educational level with respect to the total youth, and percentage of 'all' at each educational level with respect to total all. Youth includes both men and women. 'All' includes all workers.
Source: Acharya (2016).

Table A1.6 Gender Differentials in Facing Any Problem

Facing Problem in Services	Bhubaneswar	Delhi	Gangtok	Nagpur	Surat
Related to Equipment (Total)					
Young Workers	16	49	42	87	1
Female	9	23	24	49	1
Male	7	26	18	38	0
Social Discrimination (Caste Names; Delay in Getting Work Done Due to Caste Identity)					
Young Workers	9	0	1	3	4
Female	5	0	0	2	3
Male	4	0	1	1	1
Verbal Abuse					
Young Workers	0	1	3	5	1
Female	0	0	2	3	1
Male	0	1	1	2	0
Inhuman Treatment*					
Young Workers	6	4	2	1	1
Female	3	2	1	1	1
Male	3	2	1	0	0
Total					
Young Workers	31	54	48	96	7
Female	17	25	27	55	6
Male	14	29	21	41	1

Note: Workers who reported problems in the one year preceding the survey. The categories are not mutually exclusive.
* Users of the cleaning services refuse to give the workers water to drink, do not let them take shelter in their veranda in case of rain or heat, and speak to them harshly and in a derogatory manner.
Source: Acharya (2016).

Table A1.7 Workers and Their Health Conditions

Workers	Bhubaneswar No. (%)	Delhi No. (%)	Gangtok No. (%)	Nagpur No. (%)	Surat No. (%)
Respiratory Illness (%)					
All	52.23	54.2	51.9	54.7	68.17
Young Men and Women	33.24	44.3	47.12	46.22	59.76
Body Aches (%)					
All	10.4	15.4	9.2	8.3	12.44
Young Men and Women	26.16	17.29	11.14	8.54	14.61
Injuries (%)					
All	35.2	24.1	27.7	26.7	10.3
Young Men and Women	39.22	25.71	32.11	35.21	17.23
Any others (eyes, skin, etc.) (%)					
All	2.2	6.16	11.2	10.3	9.8
Young Men and Women	1.68	12.27	10.56	9.54	8.41
All Injuries (%)					
Total Young Men and Women	148 (63.79)	179 (62.15)	162 (60.22)	118 (51.98)	86 (68.25)
Total All	232 (100.0)	288 (100.0)	269 (100.0)	227 (100.0)	126 (100.0)

Note: The percentages of 'All' have been calculated with 'Total All Workers' as the denominator and percentages of 'Young Men and Women' have been calculated with 'Total Young Men and Women' as the denominator.

Source: Acharya (2016).

Table A1.8 Gender Differentials in Illness and Treatment Seeking

Men		Women	
Nature of Illness	**Treatment Seeking**	**Nature of Illness**	**Treatment Seeking**
Injuries			
• Glass pieces bruising the foot and legs	• Continue working	• Bruises due to vehicles hitting against them	Self-medication; government hospital
• Bruises in hands and fingers by hurting against stone slabs	• Getting medicines or dressing the injury at a pharmacy after work hours	• Cuts on hands and feet from glass pieces	
• Bruises/cuts/ swelling in legs			
• Fall from garbage tractor/truck	• Allowed to rest at workplace and got medicines from the pharmacy		
• Bruises and cuts on hands and legs and other parts of the body due to hitting against the garbage-collecting tractor/truck	• Visited government/ private hospital		
• Burns while handling acid solutions thrown in waste-bins			
• Eye irritation, eye watering due to dust			
• Bruises, cuts on hands and legs including feet, while removing sewage debris from drains and sewers			

(Cont'd)

Table A1.8 (Cont'd)

Men		Women	
Nature of Illness	**Treatment Seeking**	**Nature of Illness**	**Treatment Seeking**
Recent Illness			
• Chest Pain • Body ache/ headache • Tiredness/ lethargy • Cough and cold • Leg pain • Redness in the eyes • Giddiness	• Over the counter medicines • Drink alcohol before work to prevent the onset of illness • Drink alcohol after work for chest pain, tiredness, and aches • Wash minor wounds with alcohol	• Swelling in the legs • Backache • Cramps in the legs and stomach • Chest pain • Body ache • Fever • Sneezing	• Pharmacy • Private doctor • Home remedies
Continuing Illness			
• Injuries at workplace • Repetitive episodes of chest pain, back ache/ neck ache • Lingering pain in legs • Discomfort in the lower abdomen • Persistent cough, sneezing, and cold • Fever	• Public hospitals/ healthcare facilities • Private hospitals/ healthcare facilities (occasionally)	• Repetitive episodes of cough and cold, sneezing, aches, fever, and headache	• Home remedies • Public hospitals/ healthcare facilities

Source: Acharya (2016).

Table A1.9 Awareness and Utilization of Benefits for Family

Aware of Benefits Available for the Family	No. of Workers	Percentage
Total number of workers	1,143	100
Workers who were aware	204	17.85
Total number of young workers	693	100
Total number of young workers who were aware	142	20.49
Young male workers who were aware	88	61.97
Young female workers who were aware	54	38.03
Total number of young workers who were aware and have used the benefits	103	100
For medical check-up	25	24.27
For providing notebooks	12	11.65
For providing uniform	12	11.65
For soap, etc.	4	3.88
Those who did not reply clearly	50	48.54

Source: Acharya (2016).

Table A1.10 Factors for Young People's Continuance in Sanitation Work

Reasons	No. of Workers	Percentage
Low educational attainment	268	34.98
No training	48	6.27
Poor awareness about existing opportunity	94	12.27
Poor economic conditions to get better training/education	226	29.50
Got the job as compensation for a kin's death at work	13	1.68
Consider it traditional work	14	1.83
No or less competition faced to get this job	20	2.61
Do not know*	83	10.84
Total response	766	100.00

Note: * 83 respondents selected the 'don't know' option, and out of 586 respondents, 207 chose multiple responses for this question.
Source: Acharya (2016).

2

The Shame of India

Stigma and Shame among Dalit Women in Rural Agricultural Relations

MUSHTAQ AHMAD MALLA*

Dalits, also called the untouchables or Scheduled Castes (SCs), have historically been involved in dirty and low-paying jobs of different kinds, with majority of them being manual scavengers or agricultural labourers or both. Since the origin of the caste-based class system, Indian society has moved through different phases of political economy and modes of production. Politically, the regimes have moved from feudal system to Mughal rule to Imperial occupation; and economically, from feudalism, semi-feudalism, and semi-capitalism to neoliberal India. These political-economic changes have changed the lives, livelihoods, and socio-economic status of many people. However, when we look at the Dalits—with the exception of a minuscule group of people who got mobility due to new urbanism and new occupations during Mughal and British India and affirmative action policies and so-called Dalit capitalism in Independent India (Mendelsohn and

---

* I am grateful to the research team of Poverty and Dignity Project, especially Professor Robert Walker (Oxford University, UK), Professor Sony Pellissery (NLSIU, Bangalore, India), and Professor Elaine Chase (SOAS University of London, UK) for their initial comments on the first draft of this chapter.

Vicziany 1998: 265)—most of them continue to be concentrated in their traditional occupations. Dalit women, particularly the rural Dalit women, are the ones who have experienced either no or very marginal mobility. The Dalit women question continues to be the question of agricultural labourers (Omvedt 1978: 380) and the problem of agricultural labourers continues to be a problem of Dalit women; in addition to being a Dalit (caste) and the problem of male chauvinism (Omvedt 1977, 1978).

It is well established that Dalits are among the most downtrodden in India, and untouchability—a pan-India phenomenon—is almost always associated with economic exploitation, in addition to being ritualistic/social (Shah et al. 2006: 21). However, when we look at Indian history, not much is documented about the economic history of Dalit women in agricultural labour and their experience of shame. One of the reasons for the lack of full information about them, especially up to 1869 (Hjejle 1967), is that slavery was key in socio-political institutions and the political economy, and hence was erased from the historical record (Chatterjee 1999). Even after 1869, until about two decades ago, the Dalit question, as a whole, was considered mainly a sociological subject that did little to counter the tendency for caste/class-based stigma and associated shame (Rege 2006). With the rise of Dalit literature since the 1970s and Dalit feminism since the 1990s, there has been an increased awareness about the life of Dalit women and the challenges that they face in the caste-ridden society of India (Mendelsohn and Vicziany 1998: 263). However, not much of direct encounters of the experience of shame faced by them in agricultural production relations are documented. Even the growing literature on the shame of poverty, since the first decade of the twenty-first century, has not dealt with this research area in much detail. Some of the earliest writers on the shame of poverty in India, such as Guru (2009), Pellissery and Mathew (2012, 2014a, 2014b), and Walker (2014), have highlighted that shaming/humiliation in India is institutionalized in the caste system. Shame of poverty, irrespective of the era considered, stems from caste; and caste-based interaction is both a setting in which shame occurs and a vector of its transmission. However, little has been said about the changing nature of rural agricultural production relations of Dalit women and their experience of stigma and shame, as well as the current state of Dalit women in these production relations and their experience of stigma and shame.

This chapter uses data from a field study to give an encyclopaedic explanation of the changing nature of stigma and shame and how they operate in the current production relations of Dalit women. The chapter is divided into different sections: conceptual framework; methodology; a retrospect of the shame of Dalit women in agriculture; their current experience and responses to shame; the link between shame and the lack of access to alternate livelihoods; and the way forward (collective livelihoods) to overcoming shame.

Conceptual Framework (Stigma–Shame Nexus)

The two main concepts of social psychology that this chapter is emphasizing are: stigma and shame. These two concepts are inherently different from each other in their intent and structural processes (Walker 2014). Shame as an attitude and belief aims to control the behaviour of an individual for a positive change, a collective good, and social inclusivity. It aims to ensure an individual's conformity to group attitudes and behavioural norms by threatening those who might threaten the group as a whole. In contrast, stigma as an attitude and belief aims for differentiation behaviour—us versus them, inferior versus superior—with discrimination, non-acceptance, and power differentials being the basic intent (Goffman 1963: 15; Walker 2014).

Unlike shame, a stigmatized individual or group is often not an aspirant of becoming like the stigmatized individual or group (s/he can be a proud black, gay, or migrant). However, if she or her group is not proud of whatever it is that distinguishes them from the other, then stigma is likely to be experienced as shame. In poverty, a woman might not want to be rich, but she certainly does not want to be poor. Therefore, a woman stigmatized for being poor or a Dalit poor, in any setting, is likely to experience stigma as shame. Further, shaming imposed by the power structures (state or local) is also likely to feel indistinguishable from stigma (Walker 2014). Moreover, instead of a positive intent in shaming, the consequence of both shame and stigma are overwhelmingly negative and the individual's reactions to both are remarkably similar (Walker 2014). When all these factors intersect, namely, lower social identities (Dalit and women), poverty, and the existence of autocratic local power structures (feudal landlord), the boundaries between stigma and shame become much more blurred. Hence, using this poverty–shame or stigma–shame nexus (Walker 2014) allows us to capture and present a comprehensive picture of the differential and degrading experiences that Dalit women undergo while working for their basic survival on a farm or in homes of upper-caste landlords.

Methodology

This chapter is part of the initial findings (not published anywhere yet) of a larger study on poverty and dignity, which was funded by the Economic and Social Research Council, United Kingdom (UK), and was conducted simultaneously in India, Uganda, and China. The Indian study brings together participatory action and experimental (randomized controlled trials) research designs to examine the theory of change. This chapter is based on findings from the first phase of this study, which was conducted with 16 women self-help groups (SHGs) from four districts (Mysore, Chikkaballapur, Yadgir/Gulbarga, and Bailhongal) and two provinces (south and north) of Karnataka state. These SHGs belong to women who have a personal and/or family history of being in bonded labour. It would be fair to say that the study captured the experience of two states because most of the sample groups in the northern border share the culture, language, and living style of Andhra Pradesh. This study used the mixed-methods approach (MMA) comprising 179 surveys, 32 in-depth interviews, and 16 focus group discussions (FGDs). Out of 32 in-depth interviews, saturation was reached after 14 and, therefore, only 16 were transcribed. Similarly, out of 16 FGDs, only 9 were transcribed and used in the analysis. The use of MMA helped to enhance the internal validity and broader geographic coverage enhanced the external validity of results. Therefore, this scale of the study is large enough for the study of these groups.

Dalit Women in Agriculture and Shame: A Retrospect

The later story of social classes, poverty, and shame is the story of the early disparity in asset distribution (Choudhry 2014). Therefore, before looking into the current experience of stigma and shame, it becomes important to get a sense of the origin and changing nature of shame for Dalit women in agricultural relations, their responses, and state action. This will not give a background but will help to draw a line of comparison between the past and present practices and policy response.

Experience of Shame

The origins of shame for women in agricultural production relations can be traced to the tribal mode of production and hoe culture (Iyer 1988, Vol. 1: 388–9). For Dalit women in particular, it could be argued that stigma and shame became an integral part of their life during the late Vedic period (1000 BCE onwards) when the economic division of labour was mixed with caste hierarchy, and caste-based untouchability in production relations came into origin (Bhowmik 1992; Mukherjee 1999). This developed in a full and more stringent form with the rise of Buddhism in 500 BCE to the Gupta age (CE 4 and 5) (Habib 1995), and travelled through in new forms and at new levels during the Mughal, colonial, and post-Independence India. Tracing from the personal diaries and letters of British visitors, official statements, revenue surveys, and reports, especially from south India, Hjejle (1967) and Chatterjee (1999) give three of the earliest first-hand accounts of the experience of stigma and shame by Dalit women in agricultural slavery. Such records about the period before this are more assumed, based on their later conditions rather than factually examined (Habib 1995).

One of the cruellest and probably the earliest form of shame and stigma documented is from the masters/landlords of these untouchable slave women. The nature of stigma and shame orchestrated by them had intergenerational, material, social, and personal components. Slaves were seen as measures of power and dignity by masters and therefore, there was a demand for lineage slavery on slave families, which especially included the acquisition of female and infant slaves (Chatterjee 1999). This *intergenerational* commitment to slavery or selling of generations was shameful in itself and it led to many other forms of stigmatization and shame from masters. In *material* terms, their labour was extracted from sunrise to sunset, with no signs of welfare, that perpetuated hopelessness and rising poverty. While the overall wage rate for these untouchable slaves was exploitative, for untouchable women it was much more stigmatizing (Hjejle 1967). Further, in most of the cases they were given house sites outside the village with no property rights, and were sold with both their labour and house sites. Destroying the *kinship system* was another form of stigmatization, with huge social costs for untouchable families and communities. Since slaves were the personal property of the master, they could be sold, mortgaged, and rented. This separated husbands from wives, families from communities, discouraged slaves from marrying, prevented slave parents from caring for their children, thereby dissolving tender ties of parental, filial, and fraternal affections, ultimately resulting in promiscuity and demoralization of slaves (Forbes 1813 in Chatterjee 1999: 14). Attacking the modesty of women through physical and sexual abuse was the cruellest form of *personal stigma* and *shame* which untouchable women had to undergo. They were neither allowed to wear fashionable jewellery nor upper garments to cover their chest (Shah et al. 2006: 32).[1] Besides physical labour in agriculture, they were forced into sexual labour as prostitutes or slave wives (Chatterjee 1999). All these intergenerational, material, kinship, and personal aspects of slavery were not only expressions of poverty but also of stigma and shame.

The second form of documented stigma and shame orchestrated on untouchable women is from their own family and community, by gifting them to masters to negotiate economic, social, and political favours. This was a well-established aspect of the political economy of the nineteenth century (Chatterjee 1999) and before (Buchanan 1809). When depressed castes were pressed to pay fines or debts or redeem mortgages, or were unable to cover dependents during floods or famines, they used to enter into this system of human gifting. These transacted daughters and wives were called slave wives by their masters. Moreover, sending women for permanent agricultural slavery in case of moral infringement was also a common practice. According to Chatterjee (1999), while external master's shaming exposed the Dalit woman to external enslavement, her own community's shaming exposed her to internal enslavement.

The third form of stigma and shame came from other low castes, and this was typically a feature of the colonial economy. On the one hand, the local weavers and associated workers lost their livelihoods due to the influx of foreign clothes; on the other hand, the growth of private property and monetization eliminated the old barter system. With increased labour supply and competition, while this

---

[1] Particularly referring to the case of Nadars and the Ezhavas of south India.

newly emerged agricultural labour class could enter into an agreement of tenancy, sharecropping, and agricultural labour, untouchables remained the least preferred and excluded, almost left to die of starvation (Dubois and Beauchamp 1905; Dutt 1927b; Kotovskii 1950). Their struggle for survival forced them to enter into new forms of slavery, such as debt slavery or bonded labour (Breman 1974). These economic changes shaped untouchability quite visibly and powerfully (Mendelsohn and Vicziany 1998). Untouchables, especially women, started facing new forms of stigma and shame not only from the higher classes (bonded labour led to the beginning of a new era whose remnants continue and are now called the shame of the twenty-first century), but also from a newly emerged peasant and ex-weaver agricultural labour class.

Response to Shame

Since the influence of high-caste feudal lords and Brahmins, with a strong religious explanation (theory of karma) of the division of labour, was paramount and there was also a lack of alternate survival options, the majority response to their exploitative occupation and the experience of stigma and shame was silence. In addition, there are also reports of some agricultural slaves trying to escape or decrease the starkness of shame by running away from bondage, changing their caste, and giving a less shameful name to slavery. However, some of them ended up in much more adverse conditions than before.

First, the runaway slaves (men and women) were caught and returned by force; if someone escaped, they could not find alliance without changing their village (Hjejle 1967). Earning the displeasure of masters, by running away or in other ways, led to: severe shame and stigma in the form of a beating, with no right to complain or obtain another form of redress (Dubois and Beauchamp 1905);[2] decree of eviction, which meant loss of livelihood forever (Aiyer 1925 cited in Dutt 1927b); murder of slaves; and strict punishment to fellow slaves who helped them escape (Chatterjee 1999). Slavery

---

[2] These slaves belonged to the inferior castes and were either called 'Sudra' or 'Panchum Bundum'. Till the *tehsil* (an administrative area in India) level, the courtiers were controlled by Brahmins and it was only at the district level that an English judge was sitting, where hardly any slave could reach (Hjejle 1967: 86).

was what Patterson (1982) called an alternative to death, and this was the moral legitimization even provided by their masters. Second, wherever there was a possibility, untouchable slave women always tried to change their 'ritual ranking' (that is, being labelled as untouchables, low caste, Dalit, because of which they had to get engaged in demeaning occupations and rituals) to avoid the shame and atrocities of being low caste, and in order to gain some self-respect (Iyer 1988; Shah et al. 2006). Hjejle (1967) refers to a case of mid-nineteenth century in which an English official mentions about 160 migrant women slaves, who were originally low castes (Chamars, Dosadhs, and Domes) and took the identity of belonging to higher castes (Koornies, Asheers, and Dhanooks) so that they could be treated better.[3] Third, the slave families as well as some masters used to soften the starkness of alienation experienced by slaves by changing the nomenclature of social relationships. For example, some Marathas referred to enslaved women as daughters of the state (*rajbetis*). Similarly, the son of an old slave man or woman in Sylhet (now a part of Bangladesh) would refuse to accept his father/mother as a slave and styled him/her as the high priest's dependent (Chatterjee 1999: 18). However, both these responses were either not accepted or took a long time to mitigate the stigma of birth, especially in places where the origin was known to others (Iyer 1988).

State Action

Since the origin of the caste system, the twelfth century was the first time when some untouchable agricultural labourers saw a change in their economic condition and their experience of shame. The new technology demands of the Mughals, such as paper making and lime mixing, led to the creation of what is known as indigenous capitalism (Kosambi 1956; Mukherjee 1999) in which the deprived castes (men and women) were traded from rural areas to urban settlements, which created a class of Dalit artisans (Habib 1995). However, this was a demand of a new mode of production, rather than deliberate efforts by the Mughals towards the removal of slavery. In fact, due to their strong economic interest in slavery

---

[3] Similarly, another record of 1897 Bengal shows that two untouchable caste girls were disposed of under fringe name as Brahman girls and an Ahir woman was sold for Rs 60 as a Rajputin girl (Chatterjee 1999: 8).

(cheap labour and revenue generation), they never touched this question and as a consequence, the caste system continued to be an important pillar of class exploitation (Habib 1995).

British imperialists too, just like their feudal predecessors had an economic interest in slavery as the core motivation, and were never committed towards any big change in the caste system or agricultural production relations (Dutt 1927b; Hjejle 1967). It was only with the direct intervention of the British government that the Slavery Abolition Act was enacted in 1843 and the Penal Code in 1861. However, both of them had so many loopholes that slave owners had no reason to be worried. One of the primary reasons for their failure, according to Hjejle (1967) and Dutt (1927a) was that they were not coupled with opportunities of alternative employment. One of the breakthroughs in some parts of India during the later part of the nineteenth century was the development of railways, modern industry, and public works programmes, as well as coffee plantations in Ceylon and Kerala (Habib 1995; Hjejle 1967; Kumar 2013: 128–43). These created a considerable number of alternate livelihood opportunities which, among others, helped some of the Dalit agricultural slaves to escape the economic shame and stigma in production relations.

In post-Independence India, while a lot of changes took place in the country, the most significant one for Dalits was the movement for socio-economic equality led by Dalit leaders—started by Ambedkar in the 1920s (Mendelsohn and Vicziany 1998: 80).[4] They negotiated for various constitutional provisions and policies

---

[4] A macro-level development that took place about 30 years before the end of this era was the political collectivization of Dalits across India. While the consciousness of oppression is as old as untouchability, it developed into the condition of military with the 1857 uprising, which led to the fight for gaining acceptance on equal basis within Hindu society (Mendelsohn and Vicziany 1998: 78). Dissatisfied with the Hindu religion, Ambedkar transformed this movement to represent secular politics and institutional advantage rather than religion and social reforms. Shah et al. (2006: 33) call it a move away from a religious fight to a class fight of depressed classes. This athleticism of Ambedkar vaulted untouchables to the centre stage, a position they had never occupied before (Mendelsohn and Vicziany 1998: 80). Though it did not have any direct impact on the experience of shame by female Dalit agricultural labourers, it shaped the late colonial and post-colonial socio-economic and policy environment for the emancipation of Dalits as a whole.

for overcoming the shame of Dalits, including the abolition of forced labour, prohibition of human trafficking, Bonded Labour System (Abolition) Act of 1976, political reservation, and affirmative action policies. During the initial years, there was a lot of zeal (Prasad 2008); however, all of this did not carry forward and the female Dalit agricultural labourers especially did not see any significant change in their production relations. This was mainly due to the semi-feudal and semi-colonial nature of the Indian political economy (Ray 1988), in which all the policies conformed to benefit the Dalits but none was widely transformative (Mendelsohn and Vicziany 1998: 268). The national survey on bonded labour in India, carried out between 1977 and 1978, highlighted 10 states having 2.617 million bonded labourers (Marla 1981). At an all-India level, 63 per cent of the SCs were landless and 80 per cent were agricultural workers; and in both cases, Dalit women were predominant. Their average monthly wage was Rs 60, of which Rs 20 was deducted towards interest or debt payment (Marla 1981). According to Mendelsohn and Vicziany (1998: 269), in contrast to the hopes of the mid-twentieth century, by the end of the century, the state was in an ambivalent mood and full of cynicism about its capacities as an instrument of social reform.

In the post-1990s, the Indian state was caught in a new form of imperialism—neoliberalism. In this state, the Dalits experienced three types of changes in their traditional production relations, which included a unique set of challenges: migration of some male and female Dalit agricultural labourers to urban settlements; the emergence of some Dalit entrepreneurs (Dalit capitalism) in private industries; and some job creation in the public sphere through affirmative action policies. The migrant Dalit workers now acquired the right to work with a fair wage, but continued to work in menial jobs and with lack of dignity due to the practice of purity and pollution and the monopoly of the upper caste (Mendelsohn and Vicziany 1998: 89–90; Shah et al. 2006: 103). Both Dalit capitalism and affirmative action policies led to economic mobility with the elimination of traditional economic aspects of shame in production relations (Guru 2016), but the interpersonal, cultural, and religious sphere of untouchability continued to haunt them to a great extent (Shah et al. 2006). Moreover, the real issue with the outcome of both these policy measures has been their minuscule nature—too little to be called a Dalit middle class (Mendelsohn and Vicziany 1998: 265). More importantly, irrespective of the size, there is a very marginal participation of Dalit women in general, and rural Dalit women in particular. Their dominant occupation continued, and still continues, to be as manual labourers in rural agriculture and other production systems (Shah et al. 2006: 171). This demands a fresh look not only at the nature of work but also the experience of stigma and shame in it.

Dalit Women in Agriculture and Shame: Current Relations

Experience of Shame

The nature and practice of shame that rural female Dalit agricultural labourers are facing currently is two-dimensional: one, the manifestations of past social shame; and two, the shame of current production relations.

Manifestations of Past Social Shame

The marks of past social stigma and shame are evident in two forms. First, the experience of repeated stigmatization during bonded labour, such as physical beating, sexual harassment, being called by caste name, forced to stay hungry for a long duration, forced to clean cowsheds and toilets, and not being able or allowed to attend a family emergency (birth of a child or death in family), has been internalized and is negatively influencing their current decision-making in personal and family life and interactions with others (Figure 2.1). The factors of the experience of bonded labour that are creating such negativity mainly include mental stress, lack of confidence, shyness, inferiority complex, and continued fear of masters (Figure 2.2).

Second, it also affects the way other people treat them (Figure 2.3). Particularly, this past identity of bonded labour is also used as a weapon of stigmatization by masters (upper-caste landlords) to demonize them, whenever they come in contact with these women. As reported by a few respondents, the most common spheres of this stigmatization while accessing public or private services and workplace include:

> When we go to the bank people will look down upon us (Dodmani, Temapur) ... treat us like *badavaru, athelpa, cooligara, jetadadu*

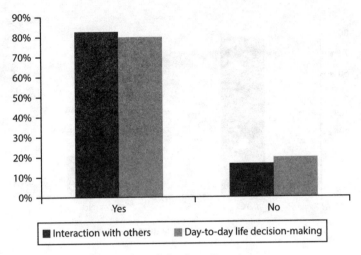

Figure 2.1 Negative Effects of Bonded Labour Experience
Source: Primary field study.

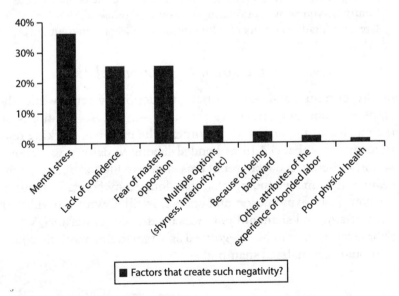

Figure 2.2 Factors That Create Negativity
Source: Primary field study.

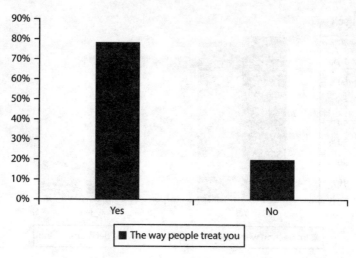

Figure 2.3 Bonded Labour Experience Affecting the Way Other People Treat You
Source: Primary field study.

[you are poor, worker, bonded labour, and low category] (Hava, Chivtgunday) ... make us feel like *medi milegay* [untouchable] and *kelu mata dali nodtara* [see us as downtrodden] (Laksha, Chivtgunday).... Give a feeling that you belong to the bonded labour family ... you were working in our home ... (Bhagya, HD-Kote).... Create difficulties for my children in school (Geeta, Chivtgunday).[5]

Shame from Current Production Relations

In the current rural agricultural production system, while the employers and employees are the same—high-caste landlords on the one hand, and Dalits on the other—the nature of working relationships has changed from bonded labour to daily wage labourers or/and contract labourers. This new production relationship, against the understanding that freedom from bonded labour is freedom from exploitation and shame, is filled with a number of stigmatizing and shameful practices on the part of masters, which in broader terms can be categorized as stigmatizing working conditions and personalized shaming.

---

[5] The names of research participants mentioned in the chapter have been changed in order to maintain anonymity.

Table 2.1 Daily Wage Rate Scenario of Female Dalit Agricultural Labourers

Wage Rate	Average Daily Wage Received (Rs)	Highest Daily Wage Received (Rs)
Mean	99.19	126.66
Std Deviation	32.804	44.292
Real difference	30–200	30–350

Source: Primary field study.

Stigmatizing Conditions: According to the International Labour Organization (ILO 2017), working conditions are at the core of paid work and employment relations, which include working time, rest period, work schedule, remuneration, as well as physical conditions and mental demands that exist at the workplace. The nature of these conditions for Dalit women in agricultural labour reflects the extreme form of stigmatization from authoritarian masters through discrimination, rejection, and exploitation. They are made to work for 6–11 hours daily (average of 9 hours) and are paid an average wage of Rs 99.19, which is well below the minimum wage of Rs 300 set by the Government of Karnataka for a daily agricultural labourer. The highest mean wage received in the last 12 months (Rs 126.66) is also nowhere close to the minimum wage supposed to be given to a daily wage labourer (Table 2.1). In case of worksite conditions/facilities, such as provision of drinking water, food, tea, break for lunch and the length of the break, and shade to rest and eat food, about 82 per cent reported it as being either bad or very bad (Figure 2.4). Surprisingly, due to lack of exposure to any other better production relations, the first-hand response to the question, 'How would you rate the

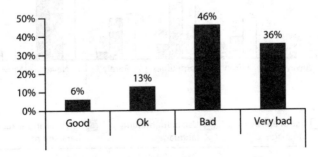

Figure 2.4 Working Conditions in the Master's Farm or House

Source: Primary field study.

worksite condition in your master's farm?', was 'good'. However, an overwhelming shift occurred when we unpacked the worksite condition/facilities by asking about each condition one by one, and then their overall assessment of these conditions. Similar was the case with freedom and flexibility at work, as it was hard for them to understand what freedom really means. However, when we asked about related conditions, such as would you be free to go home if you are not feeling well at work or if there is an emergency at home, the responses were overwhelmingly negative.

Personalized Shaming: The personal attacks on the modesty of a woman in the form of personalized stigmatization—using abusive and frightening language and physical harassment—and making them internalize shame—that is, making these women feel embarrassed, small, ignored, and helpless about themselves, their work, and where they belong, are also very common. The use of abusive and frightening language was reported by about 60 per cent (always, often, sometimes, and rarely) and physical and sexual harassment by 10 per cent of the respondents (Figure 2.5),

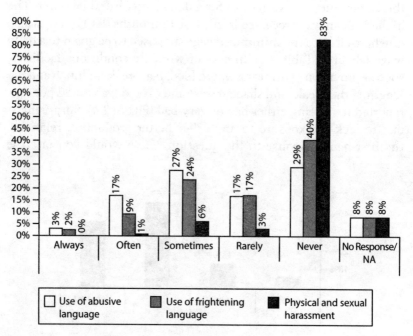

Figure 2.5 Personalized Shaming—I
Source: Primary field study.

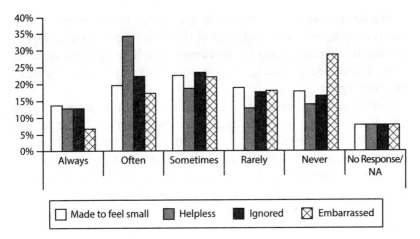

Figure 2.6 Personalized Shaming—II
Source: Primary field study.

while the incidents of being made to feel small, helpless, ignored, and embarrassed are reported by majority of the respondents (89 per cent, 77 per cent, 64 per cent, and 63 per cent, respectively) (Figure 2.6). The spheres of this personalized shaming in production relations are widespread. However, there are some common patterns across respondents, which highlight the incidences where one form is used more than the other.

'Abusive and frightening language' is mostly used when the masters feel that the labourers are working slowly or incorrectly. They scold them by saying *madigaru kammi jathi* (you are a low caste); or attack their modesty: *nimmamma akka* (abusive words targeting their mother or sister), *sulei makkale, boli makkale* (children of prostitutes), and in rare cases, *sulle munde* (prostitute). Physical and sexual harassment mostly takes place during the working hours, when women are outside the house. What is interesting in this case is that while reports of such incidents are less, there appears to be under-reporting due to a narrow understanding of what harassment actually constitutes. This is reflected in the following narrative: 'they do this ... like bad things, like they lust on us, they look with bad looks.... [But] no physical harassment like touching hands or legs' (Lakshi, Belgaum). Shah et al. (2006: 125) have also cautioned about this under-reporting, saying that landlords pass comments such as 'you are wearing exciting clothes or you will go with me to the sugarcane fields for cutting grass', but the women seem to have accepted it as a normal part of their life. Notwithstanding, an astonishing paradox that Dalit women face here is being regarded as polluted and untouchable and yet being exploited in a more intimate sphere.

'Embarrassment' is most strongly felt when these women have to ask for a loan and also, when the master comes to their home seeking payment in case they have not repaid the loan on time. Hence, taking credit is not only a shame in itself (Pellissery and Mathew 2014a) but also a shame multiplier, and this was directly felt by 50 per cent of the respondents who are currently indebted to masters. The 'feeling of being small' is felt mainly when masters reinforce themselves as being the only source of survival for labourers: 'feel small and inferior when masters say you are working under me' (Puttama, HD-Kote); and also, when they tease them by their caste and status in the labour market: '[they] use language like *dalita, kedu, kulihadu* [Dalits, low castes, and cooli workers]' (Mallav, Belgaum). 'Feeling of being ignored' comes when the masters do not listen to them and/or they are exposed to extremely differential treatment: 'when we were made to sit near *chappals* [slippers] ... I felt very ignored and pained' (Kanya, Heriballakatty). Finally, 'helplessness' is felt in its extreme form when masters destroy or restrict Dalit's access to their own or common assets, and this form of hostility is age old because these assets have the potential to give Dalits a modicum of economic security and prosperity (Shah et al. 2006: 99).[6] As reported by Lakshmi (Chikkaballapur), due to her land being adjacent to her master's land, there is a constant tendency of land grabbing, which results in fighting, as well as filing of first information reports (FIRs) and sometimes, the destruction of crops by the master.[7]

Control Over Work System and Susceptibility to Exposure of Shame

A worker's control over the work system (hours, wage rate, and worksite facilities) determines her susceptibility to the exposure of

---

[6] This denial of productive assets also extends to the leasing of agricultural land (Shah et al. 2006: 99).

[7] The issues of non-availability of money, mental stress, and feeling of not being born in a high caste also create a feeling of helplessness.

stigma and shame to a great extent. When questioned about this, all the respondents reported that the master's decision was final. With regards to timing, they have to go to work when they are asked. Similarly, in the case of worksite facilities, the majority corroborated with what Lakshi (Belgaum) said: 'We don't get anything ... we bring our own food, no tea, they provide only drinking water, we don't even have a proper place to sit and eat food. I feel bad about these conditions.' While some reported getting lunch and tea occasionally, its distribution system reinforces the traditional caste-based exclusion (Shah et al. 2006). As narrated by Gowra from Chikkaballapur: '[At certain places] ... the other caste people will also come for work ... and sometimes masters serve us food ... but they don't eat with us, because we are Madhiga, we are a different caste than the Reddy.' The other forms of such exclusion at workplace include wage payment at a respectable distance and non-engagement of Dalit women in the cleaning of grains and other eatables (Shah et al. 2006: 94). It is the prevalence of this form of exclusion which made Ambedkar argue, in 1936, that caste-based occupational division is not just a division of labour but also a division of labourers.[8]

Response to Shame

Questions that arise in retrospect to the experience of stigmatization and shame by Dalit women, and their lack of control on production relations, are: do these women respond to such treatment and if yes, how and what happens next? On examining responses to both stigmatizing working conditions and personalized shame, some commonalities can be found, but there are also some significant differences.

Response to Stigmatized Working Conditions

The two broad ways in which Dalit women respond to the experience of stigma and shame in agricultural production relations is by

---

[8] The division of Dalits and non-Dalit labourers who belong to the same economic class is also used to undermine the potential shared-class identity or proletarian solidarity and fraternity between Dalit and non-Dalit workers (Channa and Mencher 2013).

keeping silent and asking for a change. The proportion of respondents on either side is about 50 per cent. Keeping silent is rooted in the lack of courage, fear of facing the master's anger, and the fear of losing livelihood. Two narratives are noteworthy: 'I don't have that much courage and opportunity [to ask]' (Jaya, HD-Kote)'; and 'If we go [little] late they will get angry and scold. In response ... I will say sorry or ... keep quiet. What can I do, I have to listen and do what they say... if we say anything they get angry' (Narasa, Yadgir). This silence is not a reflection of the experience of shame being taken as a normal incident, but an indication of the internalization of shame. As reported by Narasa from Yadgir, 'we also get angry, but we don't say anything, they are big people.' Further, Manju from Belgaum also said, 'we don't get anything, just a 10-minute break ... we know it is necessary, but we can't demand, we tolerate.'

Unlike Narasa and Manju, not everyone is able to control their anger and they do speak out when limits are crossed. However, unfortunately, this speaking out, instead of betterment, increases the possibilities of further exclusion. A respondent narrated: 'I work from 9 a.m. to 6 p.m., I get Rs 100, I feel it is less. I tell them about this, they say that for the work you do this is what we pay. If you like you may come, otherwise you may leave. Even collectively we all asked ... they say the same.' Further, Narasa from Yadgir was told: 'why do you want to go, don't come again. If you were not well ... or had some emergency, you should have stayed back home only.' Some of the women who reported keeping silent have actually spoken out in the past, but due to their inability to change anything and the fear of further shaming, they now prefer to remain silent and tolerate things as they are.

Though less prevalent, there is also an understanding among some people who are still entrenched in the traditional caste-based division of labour that masters are not obliged to provide anything except wages. As narrated by Naira from Yadgir: 'I never asked for food, water, or tea, because it is a practice, previous people did this, that is why we are also doing it ... Why should we ask, why should they give us?.'

Response to Personalized Shaming

The response to personalized shaming is broadly the same as that of stigmatizing working conditions, however, its nature of operationalization is different. The Dalit women, at times, adopt a humble demeanour and a submissive posture by keeping silent, making no eye contact, and bowing their heads. They even submit to sexual harassment due to the fear of losing their jobs (Shah et al. 2006: 120). Sometimes they speak out, snub the masters by giving bad looks, and report the case to the head of the village, and at other times, they use protective and remedial responses to deflect attention, such as appearing unattractive by dressing shabbily and staying dirty (Shah et al. 2006: 225).

However, when it comes to speaking out in family and community there is a great difference between stigmatizing working conditions and personalized shaming. Such expression in case of personalized shaming is rarely reported, and whatsoever has been reported has rarely led to any positive outcomes; instead like the earlier case, it only increased the possibility of further exclusion. From a well-being point of view, one could argue that stigmatization in working conditions is a lesser evil, because these women are more likely to speak out or give vent to this stigmatization in families and community, compared to personalized shaming. Within personalized shaming, there appears to be a compartmentalization—they are likely to talk about the feeling of being ignored, helpless, embarrassed, however, they will not speak about the incidents of use of abusive language by masters, particularly, physical and sexual abuse. The reason being prioritization of community values, norms, and rules over the individual, which is a very strong element of collective cultures (Walker 2014). While this is a common practice across all castes and communities in South Asia, for a Dalit woman it is highly significant because her community has been historically experiencing an extreme form of shame because of being lower caste, and any further shame would be very disastrous.

The feeling is that if physical and sexual abuse, in particular, is reported at home or in the community, it might lead to multilayered shaming. One, if a case becomes public, the Dalit woman is blamed, without any stigma being attached to the non-Dalit man (Shah et al. 2006: 120). That particular woman is exposed to the scrutiny of the entire village and becomes a focal point of discussion and common teasing, with the landlord getting impunity. Two, there is shame for that Dalit family and community with possibilities of inter-family/community physical violence. As reported by Puttama from HD-Kote:

If I face any kind of physical harassment such as my master takes off my sari (clothes) I will keep this incident to myself. I can't tell this to my husband or father. If my husband or father fight with my master, it is [a] big shame. If something happens to my husband, what will I do? I will keep this incident to myself and not go to work for that master.

The statement of such incidents in front of the interviewer also appeared to be shameful for a large number of respondents. While they reported such incidents taking place in production relations, rarely anyone reported it as having happened with them: for example, 'with me it has not happened but with others it has happened' (Lakshi, Belgaum).

Shame–Lack of Alternate Livelihood Nexus: A Discussion

There are several things that we take away from the aforementioned findings. First, there is prevalence of stigma and shame in many forms, and at many levels, in the production relations of female Dalit agricultural labourers. This shame is an outcome of their previous caste-influenced (bonded labour) and present (daily wage worker) status in production relations, and the perpetuators of this shame are people with authoritarian personalities (masters) who are usually more prone to stigmatize and shame because of their religious, caste, political, and economic control in the mode of production.

Second, the personal or felt stigma (Baumberg et al. 2012) or a sense of personal failure (Walker 2005) or self-stigma is not only a manifestation of institutional shaming (Walker 2014), but also of social stigmatization. The social stigmatization and shame that Dalit women have experienced in the past (during bonded labour) from their masters, has remained unhealed and has therefore taken the form of deep personal shame (through internalization), which affects their current life in several ways. Further, even though most of them and their families are no longer involved in bonded labour, this past identity, continues to haunt them through social stigmatization by the other (ex-masters) in non-workplace settings. This felt stigma and shame in non-workplace settings gets further exacerbated by degrading treatment at the hands of masters and lack of rights at workplace (current production relations).

Third, what we see is that even though the Indian society has grown tremendously, both politically and economically, since the conception of caste-based class hierarchies, the change in the experience of stigma and shame by Dalit women in agricultural labour or in their lives has been marginal. There is a continuity of the remnants of feudalism and colonialism in rural agriculture, where upper-caste landlords still control the economic and political power and the lives and livelihoods of Dalit women as *beti chakri*[9] workers and/or as agricultural labourers; particularly if we count since the late Mughal period, for which we have some first-hand evidence of the experience of shame by untouchable women in agriculture. The current experience of stigma and shame clearly indicates a continuation of colonial and pre-colonial slavery-based production relations. This uncovers the widespread misconception that release from the bonded labour contract is freedom from bonded labour. In reality, it is merely a physical distancing, a move from the state of slavery to semi-slaves, which has given them physical freedom while keeping them imprisoned psychologically, socially, and even economically. The unfortunate fact is that some of them are not even able to recognize this semi-slavery because of a lack of consciousness due to the continued disillusion with karma orthodoxy and/or lack of exposure to a different life and work environment due to a community-wide shared experience.

Finally, consistent with Sen's (2000: 27) theory, there is the existence of both unfavourable inclusion (inclusion in the shameful and stigmatizing production system) and unfavourable exclusion (leaving or forced to leave stigmatizing and shameful production systems and struggling for basic survival). However, unlike Sen who suggested that both of them have similar consequences, it was found that unfavourable inclusion is preferred over unfavourable exclusion because of its economic value for survival; in other words, prioritization of poverty with stigmatizing and shameful livelihoods over destitution. As noted by Shobu (from Belgaum):

---

[9] A form of bonded labour in which a woman goes to the master's house every day for 2–3 hours to clean the cowshed and toilet, and also helps them during festivals and other functions. In return she gets a bag of millets at the end of the year and access to the master's farm for open defecation and grazing cattle.

'Rs 100 is less, but we have to earn our livelihood ... somehow we have to feed ourselves. We are losers [sic] if we don't go, they have nothing to lose.' Further, Manju (from Belgaum) said, 'I will lose money and work ... it has happened with me ... what [will I do] ... whom to share it with. To fill our stomach, I have to go to work anyway.' The entire response system to the experience of stigma and shame, highlighted earlier, is also influenced by this fear of unfavourable exclusion.[10] Earning the displeasure of masters by speaking out (Hjejle 1967) does not stop only at loss of livelihood but also leads to restriction of access to other assets; in other words, further poverty and destitution, as reported during FGDs: 'if they have anger, they would say don't graze cattle in our land'.

What we see is Dalit women's consistent powerlessness to resist, which inherently emerges from their unavoidable dependence on non-Dalit landlords. The only interest of these landlords is to extract more and more wealth, irrespective of what happens to the labourers. As reported by Shobu (from Belgaum), 'we are anyway working fast; even then they are forcing us to do [the work] faster.' These masters are aware of the fact that there is a huge labour supply and they are the only work providers, hence they can hire and fire anyone at will. As reported during an FGD in Advagolavarahalli: 'for them [masters], work is all that needs to be done, irrespective of us or someone else. [If we speak, we will lose our job] they can get extra persons from elsewhere.' This unavoidable economic dependence, which forces labourers to enter into this semi-slavery mode of production and bear the burden of shame and stigma from upper-caste authoritarian, unaccountable, and exploitative landlords, is rooted in their lack of access to decent alternate livelihoods after getting free from bonded labour. This per se reflects a failure of bonded labour abolition policies in independent India to enhance these women's opportunities; and this policy failure resembles quite closely to the anti-slavery policies of colonial India (Slavery Abolition Act, 1843), which according to Hjejle (1967) failed because they were not accompanied by the

---

[10] With the exception of not disclosing personalized abuses and harassments to family and community, which is more influenced by the feeling of protecting family and community values and avoiding larger shame.

availability of alternate livelihoods, and the feudal landlords were instrumental in creating such a situation because it interfered with their economic interests.

Overcoming Dalit Women's Shame in Agriculture: A Collective Approach

This continuing problem of Dalit women in agricultural relations is definitely a shame of India—a state failure, where the state is becoming more and more ambivalent towards untouchables. On the one hand, it has put in place various laws and legislations without which substantial change in the condition of untouchables cannot be achieved. On the other hand, these measures are too limited in scope and too poorly implemented to overcome the pervasive subordination and poverty of these people (Mendelsohn and Vicziany 1998: 268). Particularly on the issues of bonded labourers, the government has become silent (Prasad 2008) and the commitment towards overcoming untouchability after 70 years of independence has resulted in almost nothing (Shah et al. 2006: 64). The demands and sources of stigma and shame of untouchables—ritualistic and economic—still persist (Mendelsohn and Vicziany 1998). An ideal Marxist way to overcome this was by overthrowing imperialism, which could never happen in Indian history. Instead, what has been happening is that untouchables are resisting both (ritualistic and economic) stigma and shame, while facing upper-caste confrontations and backlashes, which sometimes also lead to violence (Mendelsohn and Vicziany 1998). Those who achieved economic mobility, as shown earlier, have been able to overcome economic stigma and shame, but they continue to face ritualistic shame and in newer forms (Shah et al. 2006). Those who are static in production relations, like rural Dalit women, continue to face both.

History is witness, especially from the twelfth-century Mughal era, to the fact that access to decent alternate livelihoods has worked as the first step towards breaking this cycle of stigma and shame for Dalits, particularly the shame of production relations. This study also highlights some outcomes of access to alternate livelihood and/or access to additional sources of income leading to reduced experience of stigma and shame. For example,

Ninga, a 34-year-old woman from Mysore, was studying in Class 10 before marriage and did not know much household or labour work. After marriage, her husband did not allow her to continue her studies and got her involved in domestic work at home and agricultural work at a master's farm. Since she did not know how to perform either of these tasks well, she used to face continuous shame from the masters, including physical harassment at times. Her husband also used to beat her regularly, which ultimately forced her to run away and go back to her parents' house 19 years ago. In 2003, she got a job as a mid-day meal cook at a local public school. This not only empowered her economically with an earning hike from Rs 300 to Rs 2,000 per month, but also reduced other forms of stigma and shame, with all castes treating her with dignity and respect. Even the master, who had harassed her 15 years ago, was now talking to her and addressing her as 'madam' whenever they came in contact, since they were both living in the same community.

Further, the quantitative results in Figures 2.7 and 2.8 show that Dalit women's access to additional sources of income—cultivable land and livestock—have reduced their dependence on masters

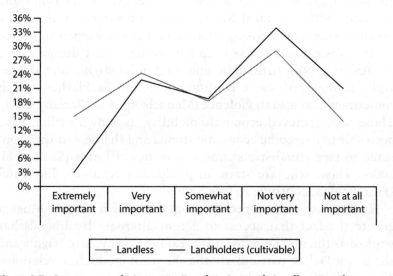

Figure 2.7 Importance of Masters in Family's Survival: Landless Families versus Landlord Families

Source: Primary field study.

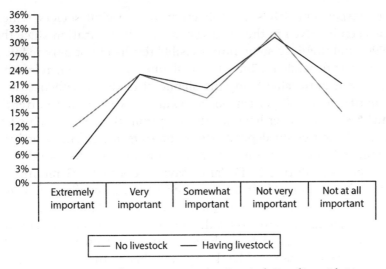

Figure 2.8 Importance of Masters in Family's Survival: Families with Livestock versus Families without Livestock

Source: Primary field study.

for their family's survival. This implies that the availability of an economically viable asset is working as financial security, thereby reducing the importance of exploitative masters in the Dalit women's life, which consequently means reduced vulnerability to stigma and shaming.

However, based on historical experience, it seems more appropriate to approach the case of these women through collective economic action, instead of individualized action, because collectivization has several merits. First, individual livelihoods are more vulnerable to opposition and threat from the upper caste, as reflected by the past experiences so far. Second, collective livelihood is internally more motivating, powerful, and sustainable. Third, the current public policies, especially the credit structures in India, are more inclined towards collective livelihoods. Fourth, if we go through contemporary writing on the Dalits, there is a great deal of agreement that collective movement can lead to overcoming not only economic stigma and shame but also social/ritualistic and political exclusion.

However, facilitating them requires conscious and collaborative effort on the part of state and civil society (Shah et al. 2006: 170).

Our respondent SHGs are collectivized by a civil society which has been involved in the process of such collectivization since the 1990s and there are some initial visible results of not only reduced economic dependence but also of shame in production relations. The most noticeable being the shame of credit dependence, as a majority of the 50 per cent of respondents who are not currently indebted to a master have taken loans from their SHGs. This has reduced their credit dependence on masters and strengthened the members' interest in the collectivization process. As narrated by a respondent during FGD: 'after saving money for 3 months ... I took loan and repaid it back. Seeing all these benefits, I felt that this group should keep going' (SHG, Bailhongal). This has also pressured some masters to reduce the interest rates. As narrated in two FGDs: 'we don't stretch our hands in front of Gowdas [landlords] seeking money' (SHG, Matakaray) and 'hence they have reduced the interest rate' (SHG, Bailhongal).

While these collectives have started giving promising economic dividends and creating a culture of resistance against the existing semi-feudal production relations, they are too small and unsustainable in their current form to act as sustainable and decent alternatives to the existing semi-colonial and semi-feudal system. As observed from the field, the need is to federate them and strengthen their capacity in two areas: internal collective dynamics and collective economic enterprise. This is where state action and support is mandatory, especially when the state's economic empowerment policies have, to a large extent, moved from individual to collective livelihood support. However, such policy support has to be extended without hurting the dignity of the Dalits, that is, without using terms like Dalit capitalism, and implemented without shaming, an example being the National Rural Employment Guarantee Act (NREGA) (Pellissery and Mathew 2014b).

Dalit women's economic collectivization, in the longer run, is also visionary and futuristic for the larger political mobilization and movement against the remnants of ritualistic and social shame which most of the Dalits continue to face even after getting economic mobility. Also, it is crucial to the process of organizing agricultural labourers for bigger changes in the system because they represent a dominant force among agricultural labourers, are more proletarianized (landless for a longer period) and low paid, and have less family or caste ties to rich peasants (Omvedt 1977: 16).

References

Baumberg, B., K. Bell, and D. Gaffney. 2012. *Benefits and Stigma in Britain*. London: Turn2us.
Bhowmik, S.K. 1992. 'Caste and Class in India', *Economic and Political Weekly* 27(24–5): 1246–8.
Breman, J. 1974. *Patronage and Exploitation*. London: University of California Press.
Buchanan, F.H. 1809. *A Journey from Madras through the Countries of Mysore, Canara, and Malabar*. London: Cadell.
Channa, S.M. and J.P. Mencher (eds). 2013. *Life as a Dalit: Views from the Bottom on Caste in India*. New Delhi: SAGE.
Chatterjee, I. 1999. *Gender, Slavery and Law in Colonial India*. New Delhi: Oxford University Press.
Choudhry, S. 2014. 'The Wealth of Poverty-Induced Shame in Urdu Literature', in E. Chase and G. Bantebya-Kyomuhendo (eds). *Poverty and Shame: Global Experiences*, pp. 35–47. Oxford: Oxford University Press.
Dubois, A.J. and H.K. Beauchamp. 1905. *Hindu Manners, Customs, and Ceremonies*. New York: Cosimo Inc.
Dutt, C. 1927a. 'Capitalist Exploitation in Indian Agriculture: Part I', *Labour Monthly* 9(11): 669–76.
———. 1927b. 'Capitalist Exploitation in Indian Agriculture: Part II', *Labour Monthly* 9(12): 669–76.
Goffman, E. 1963. *Stigma: Notes on the Management of Spoiled Identity*. New York: Touchstone [Simon & Schuster].
Guru, G. 2009. *Humiliation: Claims and Context*. New Delhi: Oxford University Press.
———. 2016. 'Shifting Categories in the Discourse on Caste and Class', *Economic and Political Weekly* 51(47): 21–5.
Habib, I. 1995. *Essays in Indian History: Towards a Marxist Perception; With the Economic History of Medieval India: A Survey*. London: Anthem Press.
Hjejle, B. 1967. 'Slavery and Agricultural Bondage in South India in the Nineteenth Century', *Scandinavian Economic History Review* 15(1–2): 71–126.
International Labour Organization (ILO). 2017. Available at http://ilo.org/global/topics/working-conditions/lang--en/index.htm; last accessed on 21 December 2017.
Iyer, L.K. 1988. *The Mysore Tribes and Castes*, five volumes. New Delhi: Mittal.
Kosambi, D.D. 1956. *An Introduction to the Study of Indian History*. Mumbai: Popular Prakashan.

Kotovskii, G.G. 1950. 'Indian Agricultural Laborer: A Soviet View', *The Economic Weekly*. Available at https://www.epw.in/system/files/pdf/1956_8/15/indian_agricultural_labourer_a_soviet_view.pdf; last accessed on 5 April 2019.

Kumar, D. 2013. *Land and Caste in South India*. Cambridge: Cambridge University Press.

Marla, S. 1981. *Bonded Labour in India: National Survey on the Incidence of Bonded Labour: Final Report, January, 1981*. New Delhi: Biblia Impex.

Mendelsohn, O. and M. Vicziany. 1998. *The Untouchables: Subordination, Poverty and the State in Modern India*, Vol. 4. Cambridge: Cambridge University Press.

Mukherjee, R. 1999. 'Caste in Itself, Caste and Class, or Caste in Class', *Economic and Political Weekly* 34(27): 1759–61.

Omvedt, G. 1977. 'Women and Rural Revolt in India', *Social Scientist* 6(1): 3–18.

———. 1978. 'Women and Rural Revolt in India', *The Journal of Peasant Studies* 5(3): 370–403.

Patterson, O. 1982. *Slavery and Social Death*. USA: Harvard University Press.

Pellissery, S. and L. Mathew. 2012. 'Hard Times and the Experience of Shame in India', Poverty, Shame and Social Exclusion Working Paper 2: India, Oxford Institute of Social Policy, the UK.

———. 2014a. 'I am Not Alone', in E. Chase and G. Bantebya-Kyomuhendo (eds), *Poverty and Shame: Global Experiences*, Chapter 11, pp. 138–48. Oxford: Oxford University Press.

———. 2014b. 'Thick Poverty, Thicker Society and Thin State: Policy Spaces for Human Dignity in India', in E.K. Gubrium, S. Pellissery, and I. Lødemel (eds), *The Shame of It: Global Perspectives on Antipoverty Policies*, pp. 37–60. Bristol: Policy Press.

Prasad, K.K. 2008. *Understanding and Eradicating Bonded Labour in India*. Bangalore: Jana Jagrati Prakashana.

Ray, R. 1988. *The Naxalites and Their Ideology*. New York: Oxford University Press.

Rege, S. 2006. *Writing Caste, Writing Gender: Reading Dalit Women's Testimonios*. New Delhi: Zubaan.

Sen, A. 2000. 'Social Exclusion: Concept, Application and Scrutiny', Social Development Papers No. 1, Asian Development Bank, Manila, the Philippines.

Shah, G., H. Mander, S. Thorat, S. Deshpande, and A. Baviskar. 2006. *Untouchability in Rural India*. New Delhi: SAGE.

Walker, R. 2005. *Social Security and Welfare: Concepts and Comparisons*. Milton Keynes, UK: Open University Press.

———. 2014. *The Shame of Poverty*. Oxford: Oxford University Press.

3

Gender Equality and Women's Empowerment

Ambedkar in Contemporary Context

RAJESH RAUSHAN

The status of women in India has undergone several changes over the years. As a visionary and pioneer reformer, B.R. Ambedkar expounded multiple problems faced by women and other depressed classes. He strongly believed that women empowerment can be achieved by welfare of women and, in this regard, his contribution to the social, economic, and political development and progress of women is noteworthy. He claimed that women have immense power, potential, and courage to contribute to economic development, further arguing that economic development is impossible without improving the socio-economic and political status of women and ensuring their equality. Thus, his philosophy was based on liberty, equality, and fraternity (Ambedkar 1987, 1989; Massey 2003; Singh 1997). According to Ambedkar, women were the victims of the oppressive, caste-based, and rigid hierarchical social system. He also believed that gender relations were artificially constructed by sociocultural forces, especially by the Manusmriti and Hindu religion. Ambedkar attacked Manusmriti as a major source which legitimized the denial of freedom and self-respect, as well as the right to education, property, divorce, and so on, to women by attributing a lofty ideal to them (Zelliot 2007).

In fact, women having considerably lower social status and autonomy compared to men seems to be associated with poor outcomes. The ability of women to make decisions which affect circumstances of their own lives is an essential aspect of empowerment (Kabeer 1999). Two broad developmental perspectives, namely, social and economic, may also respond in shaping the development, autonomy, and empowerment of women in any society (Batliwala 1994; Kabeer 1999).

Ambedkar on Gender Equality and Social Justice

The world over, gender equality, gender mainstreaming, and financial freedom are essential aspects of women empowerment, and the activities for empowering women worldwide should follow the vision of Ambedkar. The idea of 'social justice' was the root of Ambedkar's vision of gender equality. Hence, as the architect of the Indian Constitution, Ambedkar provided strong constitutional safeguards to women. He also included women in the process of social reform by involving them in the struggle for the eradication of caste system and upliftment of the underprivileged sections. He realized the vulnerability of women across all spheres and understood that this could not be erased without liberating the women themselves. Therefore, he put due stress on gender equality and the need for education. Ambedkar's perception of women's issues, namely, emphasizing their right to education, equal treatment with men, right to property, and involvement in the political process, resembled the global feminists' demands in later years. The Hindu Code Bill, introduced in Parliament by Ambedkar, especially highlighted the issues regarding women's property rights. Indeed, his greatest contribution towards women empowerment, emancipation, and gender equality was the Hindu Code Bill (Omvedt 2000; Sinha 2007). The Bill was an attempt at demolition of the entire structure and fabric of Hindu society. The very foundation not only of one pillar but of all the pillars on which the Hindu society rests is shaken (Sinha 2007). In reality, the Bill was a threat to patriarchy on which traditional family structure was founded, and that was the major reason behind the opposition to it (Ambedkar 1987; Omvedt 2000).

Globally, in the early 1990s, the International Conference on Population and Development (ICPD), Cairo (1994), and Beijing

Conference on Women (1995) were centred on empowering women and mainstreaming gender equality to fasten the development of a nation and achieve better outcomes. On these lines, India framed the National Policy for Empowerment of Women in 2001 (GoI 2001b). The aim of the National Policy for the Empowerment of Women (2001) was to bring about advancement, development, and empowerment of women in the country. The policy claims, 'The underlying causes of gender inequality are related to social and economic structure and practices.... Consequently, the access of women, particularly those belonging to weaker and marginalized sections ... for education, health, and productive resources, among others, is inadequate. Therefore, they remain largely marginalised, poor and socially excluded' (GoI 2001b). The objectives of this policy include: creating an environment through positive economic and social policies for full development of women to enable them to realize their full potential; equal access to participation and decision-making of women in the social, political, and economic life of the nation; and strengthening legal systems aimed at limitation of all forms of discrimination against women.

So, to examine Ambedkar's view of social justice for gender equality and women empowerment and progress over the period in the aforementioned policy framework, this study has been framed to explore and examine the progress on gender equality and women empowerment, and their interlinkages with other developmental outcomes in the country.

Method and Materials

Data Source

The study is based on secondary data collected by the GoI on the dimensions included to examine gender equality and women empowerment in the country on selected developmental indicators and outcomes. Two different data sources, that are, Census of India and National Family Health Survey (NFHS), have been used. The Census of India data are collected by the Indian government every 10 years to provide population headcount on demographic, sociocultural, and economic characteristics. In this study, Census of India data have been used to calculate child sex ratio (CSR), missing girls, and effective female literacy rate. Data for 1961–2011 have been used for the calculation of sex ratio. For CSR and missing girls at state level, data from 1991 to 2011 have been used (GoI 1991, 2001a, 2011). The effective female literacy rate is estimated only for 2011 Census year (GoI 2011). The second data source, the latest wave of NFHS conducted in 2015–16, NFHS-4, has also been used. Use of NFHS data in this study is appropriate as it is a large-scale, multi-round survey conducted in a representative sample of households throughout the country. The survey provides state and national information on fertility, infant and child mortality, maternal and child health, reproductive health, nutrition, anaemia, utilization and quality of health services, and women's autonomy and empowerment (International Institute for Population Sciences [IIPS] and ICF 2017).

Methodology

A state-level analysis has been carried out to examine the progress of women in terms of gender equality and empowerment on demographic, nutritional, autonomy, and empowerment aspects. In order to understand disparity, exclusion, and unequal treatment of females, descriptive statistics are calculated for trends of sex ratio and its regional variations, followed by trends of missing girls in Indian states. Preference for male children is one of the socio-cultural phenomena responsible for discrimination and exclusion in resource allocation, care giving, and support for the progress of women. Hence, I_m and SR_b are used appropriately to delineate the prevailing situation of preference for male child in India.

Finally, to understand the complex phenomena of gender inequality and empowerment, a multivariate technique, namely, factor analysis method, is employed. The factor analysis method simplifies complex and diverse relationships pertaining to a set of observed variables by uncovering common dimensions or factors that link together the seemingly unrelated variables, and consequently provides insight into the underlying structure of the data (Dillon and Goldstein 1984; Raushan et al. 2017). Factor analysis is undertaken using principal component method of extraction with varimax rotation criterion. The principal factor method extracts factors in such a way that each factor accounts for the maximum possible amount of the variance contained in the set of variables being factored. The number of factors is restricted to Kaiser's criterion of the eigen values (e-values) greater than unity.

Hence, structural relationship on three different components is extracted using various indicators having worth, and these can be found in the Appendix (Table A3.2). The first set of relationship is examined for the effect of sex preference and female literacy on demographic and health outcomes for the female child. The second set of relationship is examined on interlinkages of women's household autonomy, freedom of movement, and economic empowerment. Finally, the third set of relationship is examined on interlinkages of discriminatory practices, sex preference, demographic and health outcomes, women's autonomy, and economic empowerment. All three sets of structural relationships in the study are examined through a structural matrix of factors extracted on the set of variables. The state is the unit of analysis for each of the indicators.

Here, I would like to emphasize that Ambedkar's vision of empowering women can be easily understood through their progress, participation, and achievement. So, the inclusion of various indicators related to individual, household, and community (state) have value in understanding Ambedkar's idea of gender equality and empowerment.

Variables under Study

Indicators have been selected in such a way so as to capture gender inequality, exclusion, discriminatory practices, and vulnerability, which lead to poor status and progress of women in the country. First, this is examined through sex ratio and missing girls. Second, to deepen the issue of gender inequality, health and nutritional outcomes, along with preference for male child and female literacy rate, have been included. As a third step, indicators of women's autonomy and empowerment on decision-making, freedom of movement, and economic empowerment are included. The methods used for estimation of different indicators in the study have been provided in following section.

Sex Ratio (SR)

Sex ratio for the whole population (person sex ratio [PSR]) and 0–6-year-old children (CSR) is calculated for the 1961–2011 Census period as:

$$\text{Sex Ratio }(SR) = \frac{F_t}{M_t} \times 1000$$

where,

F_t = total number of females in the population
M_t = total number of males in the population

In case of PSR, the number of males to females will be for the whole population, and for CSR it will be only for children within 0–6 years of age.

Missing Girls (G_m)

Calculation of missing girls is based on surplus of male children in the 0–6 year age group at the given point of time and is presented in percentage. The percentage of missing girls (G_m) in the study varies between 0 and 100 per cent. Increasing value of 'G_m' denotes the increase in the number of missing girls and vice versa. Zero denotes gender equality. Negative sign shows surplus girls over boys at a given point of time in any population. It is calculated as:

$$\text{Missing Girls } (G_m) = \frac{M_{0-6} - F_{0-6}}{C_{0-6}} \times 1000$$

where,

M_{0-6} = male child aged 0–6 years
F_{0-6} = female child aged 0–6 years
C_{0-6} = children aged 0–6 years

Sex Ratio at Birth (SR_b)

Sex ratio at birth provides evidence of gender bias and discriminatory practices for the female child and preference for the male child. In absence of manipulation, sex ratio at birth is remarkably consistent across human populations. Sex ratio at birth is calculated as:

$$\text{Sex Ratio at Birth } (SR_b) = \frac{M_y}{F_y} \times 1000$$

where,

M_y = total number of male children born during a specified period
F_y = total number of female children born during a specified period

Index of Sex Preference (I_m)

Index of sex preference in the study provides evidence of preference for the male child. It is the surplus of male children out of total children a woman wanted as additional children. Its calculation is based on:

$$\text{Index of Sex Preference } (I_m) = \frac{E}{C} \times 100$$

where,

E = percentage of woman who preferred male children

C = cumulative percentage of woman/couple who specified the sex of additional child

The index of sex preference (I_m) in the study will vary between −100 and +100. Depending on sex preference, the sign of index would be positive or negative. Movement of I_m from zero towards positive represents increasing preference for male child and movement in the opposite direction represents increasing preference for female child. Notably, extreme values will represent either only-female or only-male child preference. In case of gender equality, the value of index will be zero (0).

Mortality Rate (MR_f)

In demographic and health studies, neonatal mortality rate (NMR; observes death within the first 28 days of life), infant mortality rate (IMR; observes death within the first year of life), and under-five mortality rate (U5MR; observes death within the first four years [59 months] of life) are widely considered to capture progress on health of the population. These mortality-related indicators are estimated usually on probability of death per 1,000 out of total live-born children within the specified time period. The mortality indexes in this study have been estimated only for female children born in the last five years. Mortality rate is calculated as:

$$MR_f = \frac{D_f}{C_t} \times 1000$$

where,

D_f = total number of deceased female children of defined age within a specified period

C_t = total children of specified age born within a specified time period

Child Nutrition

To examine the disparity and inequality in resource allocation, malnutrition and anaemia have been calculated. Poor allocation of food results in highly malnourished children. For the purpose, this study has considered stunting (height for age) and underweight (weight for age). The Z-score of a child below minus two standard deviations (-2 SD) from the median of the reference population is considered as malnourished, and above –2SD is considered as healthy. The calculation of Z-score is based on World Health Organization's (WHO) child growth standards of 2006, which is the latest in this regard. In case of anaemia, a haemoglobin level below 11 gram/decilitre is considered as anaemic. For malnutrition, female child of less than 5 years (age up to 59 months) and for haemoglobin, 6–59 month old female child is included.

Effective Female Literacy Rate (ELR_f)

To examine gender equality and its linkages with health outcomes and nutrition achievements, female literacy may be a good indicator and it has been examined on effective female literacy rate (ELR).

$$ELR_f = \frac{\text{Number of literate females aged 7 and above}}{\text{Females aged 7 and above}} \times 100$$

Women's Autonomy and Empowerment

Autonomy and empowerment are examined through decision-making ability, freedom of movement, and economic independence. Household autonomy is measured by a women's decision regarding her own healthcare, and freedom of movement is measured based on whether she is allowed to go to the market, to health facilities, and visit family/relatives alone. Economic autonomy and empowerment are measured based on whether women have an account in their own name, have money to spend as per their wishes, and have the right to decide how to spend their own and their husband's earnings. Other important dimensions include females in households having land on their own name and females as heads of their household. For all the aforementioned indicators, a woman's independence to make a decision is considered as 'Yes', otherwise, 'No'.

Results of the Study

Declining CSR, Sex Preference, and Missing Girls

This section explores gender disparity and sex ratio, and also studies the preference for a male child and the issue of missing girls in the country. Discriminatory practices towards the girl child can be easily observed through the male-skewed CSR: Over the years, CSR has been continuously declining and reached 918 female children for every 1,000 male children in 2011 (Figure 3.1). However, PSR was found to be declining continuously till 1991, with some elevations in between, and thereafter it has been on an increase and reached 940 females per 1,000 males during the same period. In contrast, the CSR has not shown an increase in any single Census period. If we study the data tabulated for 1961–2011, it is evident that the CSR has declined by 49 points in the last 50 years. The pace of decline has been found to be the highest in north India and lowest in south India, mainly Kerala. Not a single state has reported an increase in the CSR. From Figure 3.1, it can easily be observed

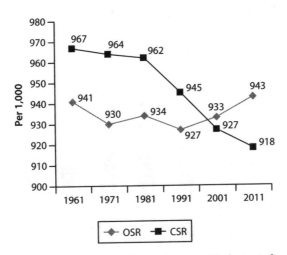

Figure 3.1 Trend in Sex Ratio and Sex Ratio at Birth in India (per 1,000): 1961–2011

Note: OSR: overall sex ratio.
Source: Author calculations based on Census of India data for various years.

that the decline in the CSR was very fast and during 1981–91, the CSR declined by a maximum of 17 points. The state-level scenario of CSR from the last 20 years has been presented in the Appendix (Table A3.1). Studies on sex ratio in India have pointed out a clear regional dichotomy, with pronounced masculinity in the north-western part of the country. The trend has been attributed to the regressive cultural practices in the north-western region and the relatively female-friendly culture in the south-eastern part of the country (Dyson and Moore 1983).

Persisting male-skewed CSR in a country like India is a reflection of male child preference, which may lead to discrimination resulting in less number of female children. The number of young girls, particularly in the 0–6 year age group, is affected by the sex ratio at birth and differential mortality by sex after birth (You et al. 2010). This has been explored though sex preferences for male child and can be easily observed through sex ratio at birth. Sex ratio at birth is an evidence of discriminatory behaviour with regards to female children. The natural or normal sex ratio at birth should be between 943 and 970 females per 1,000 males for most of the societies (Arnold et al. 2002). In India, sex ratio at birth was 918 girls per 1,000 boys in 2005–6, 935 girls per 1,000 boys in 1998–9 and 951 girls per 1,000 boys in 1992–3 (IIPS and Macro International 2007). In Figure 3.2, sex ratio at birth is provided for 2010–15 and it can be observed that except for 2013, the sex ratio

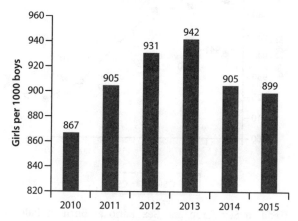

Figure 3.2 Sex Ratio at Birth in India: 2010–15

Source: Author calculations based on Census of India data for various years.

Gender Equality and Women's Empowerment

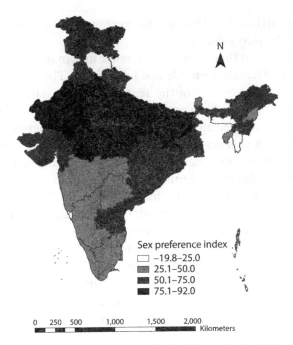

Figure 3.3 Index of Sex Preference for Male Children in India: 2015–16

Notes: (i) This map is based on available data prior to the bifurcation of the state of Jammu & Kashmir into Jammu & Kashmir union territory and Ladakh union territory. The new boundary came into existence on 31 October 2019.
(ii) This map does not represent the authentic international boundaries of India. It is not to scale and is provided for illustrative purposes only.
Source: Author calculation based on NFHS-4 (2015–16) data (IIPS and ICF 2017).

at birth has remained very low, ranging from 867 to 931 female children per 1,000 male children. This shows persisting preference for the male child.

Figure 3.3 reveals the preference for male child among women of reproductive age, that is, 15–49 years, in India in 2015–16. It has been found that around 70 per cent women wanted more male children in their lifetime (Table A3.1). There is an obvious north–south division in the preference for more male children. Surprisingly, the index of male preference in Uttar Pradesh and Bihar has crossed the 90 per cent level. On the other hand, preference for male child has been found to be the lowest in Goa (11 per cent). Only Meghalaya has been found to have more female than male children. There are nine large states where sex preference for male children has been found to be higher than the national average and all those states lie in north India (see Table A3.1).

It is also evident that the high preference for a male child increases the chances of female foeticide and infanticide. The practice of foeticide may indeed be one of the reasons for the male-skewed sex ratio at birth that has been presented earlier (Figure 3.2). However, it is the unequal treatment and discriminatory practices towards female children that results in missing girls. Missing girls reflect the number of girls less than the number of boys at a given point of time. Globally, the issue of missing girls got importance during the 1990s when Sen (1990) raised it for the first time. The 2011 Census has revealed that there are around 7 million missing girls in the country, with this number increasing by 0.81 million in the last 10 years (GoI 2001a, 2011). The data reveals that 2.81 per cent girls were missing during the 1991 Census and 3.77 per cent were missing in 2001, which increased to 4.25 per cent in 2011 (Table A3.1). From the regional picture of the missing girls, it can be understood that during the 1991 Census, 7 states reported missing girls above the national average, which increased to 9 in 2001, and further to 11 states during the 2011 Census.

Resource Allocation and Vulnerability in Outcomes: Interdependence

The major barrier towards balanced gender structure is gender inequality, regulated by sociocultural context and poor resource allocation, which translates into poor health outcomes and achievements among females. Underpinning the issue, Table 3.1 provides evidence of strong interdependence of sex preferences with poor health and nutritional outcomes for female children in India. The underlying relationship is examined through factor analysis which extracts number of factors restricted to eigen value criteria. The details of the indicators included in Table 3.1 are provided in the Appendix (Table A3.2). Within the factor analysis, all the nine selected indicators extracted with high communalities, ranging from around 0.721 to 0.983, except for the preference for female child that carved out with communalities of 0.650. The overall variance explained across the factors is close to 83 per cent. Interestingly, high female mortality at younger age is a dominant factor of poor care, treatment, and resource allocation, leading to poor nutritional outcomes.

Table 3.1 Varimax Rotation Factor Score of Sex Preferences and Female Mortality, Nutrition, and Literacy across States/Union Territories in India

	Rotated Component Matrix			Communality
	F-I	F-II	F-III	
NMR_f	0.921	0.080	0.254	0.918
IMR_f	0.955	0.264	0.031	0.983
$U5MR_f$	0.884	0.419	0.075	0.963
$STNTD_f$	0.349	0.817	0.243	0.849
$UNDWT_f$	0.216	0.611	0.628	0.815
$ANMIA_f$	0.127	0.084	0.871	0.782
$CHLDP_f$	−0.075	−0.007	−0.803	0.650
$CHLDP_m$	0.123	0.753	−0.373	0.721
$LTRCY_f$	−0.288	−0.705	−0.432	0.767
Eigen Value	4.555	1.738	1.154	
Variance Explained (%)	31.452	26.273	25.028	
Total Variance Explained = 82.753%				

Source: Calculated by author using the factor analysis on nine demographic, malnutrition, and development indicators.

Perusal of first factor (F-I) reveals high mortality and poor nutrition among female children in India. The preference for male child increases the risk of poor nutrition among female children, and also has a negative association with female literacy (F-II). Further, preference for female children is found to be negatively linked with underweight and anaemia among female children. These findings strengthen the discrimination and disparity in recourse allocation associated with preference for male children in the country. However, high level of female literacy is associated with less chance of sex preferences on the one hand, and better nutrition among female children on the other, extracted on factors two and three. There is a possibility that allocation of resource is positively linked with status, autonomy, and empowerment of women (Dyson and Moore 1983; Kabeer 1999; Kishor 1992, 1993, 1995; Raushan et al. 2016), and this is examined in the next section.

Women's Autonomy and Economic Empowerment Interlinkages

The previous section tried to delineate discriminatory behaviour towards the female child and preference for male child, reflected

Table 3.2 Varimax Rotation Factor Score of Women's Autonomy and Empowerment in States/Union Territories in India

	Rotated Component Matrix				Communality
	F-I	F-II	F-III	F-IV	
$BNKAC_f$	0.350	0.185	0.489	0.371	0.534
$MNYSL_f$	0.256	−0.018	0.097	0.855	0.806
$SEED_f$	0.069	0.690	−0.322	0.388	0.735
$HEED_f$	0.213	0.802	0.064	−0.283	0.773
$HCDCN_f$	−0.237	0.676	0.156	0.354	0.663
$VFDCN_f$	0.317	0.869	−0.039	−0.059	0.860
$MKTAN_f$	0.948	0.116	−0.032	0.106	0.925
$HFCAN_f$	0.940	0.160	−0.003	0.168	0.937
$FVAN_f$	0.950	0.055	−0.151	0.074	0.934
$LAND_f$	−0.195	−0.065	0.931	0.099	0.918
$HHFH_f$	−0.050	−0.027	0.920	−0.033	0.850
Eigen Value	3.121	2.414	2.117	1.285	
Variance Explained (%)	28.369	21.941	19.249	11.684	
Total Variance Explained = 81.244%					

Source: Calculated by author using the factor analysis on 11 women's autonomy and empowerment indicators.

through high factor loadings on each other in Table 3.1. This section tries to understand the interlinkages of women's autonomy and empowerment indicators (Table 3.2). These are the indictors widely used across the world to depict gender equality, empowerment, and their linkages with other development indicators. It has also been examined in the same way as for Table 3.1. The indicators included in Table 3.2 are found to be highly interlinked and extracted with high communalities above 0.70, except for women having a bank account (0.534) and women's decision on self-healthcare (0.663). Overall variance explained by the 11 selected indicators (details in Table A3.2) is around 81 per cent. Four factors have been extracted based on the selected indicators of autonomy and empowerment. Freedom of movement has been extracted on factor one (F-I), whereas intra-household decision-making ability has been extracted on factor two (F-II). Notably, the ability to take decisions about spending self-earned as well as husband's earnings increases the chance to decide on self-healthcare and visits to family and relatives (F-II). Economic empowerment, reflected mainly by female head of the household, female having a bank account, and female having land in her name, is found positively associated (F-III). Also, having a bank account increases the chance of women having money to spend on themselves as well as making decisions regarding spending the money earned by self (F-IV).

The gender equality framework—examined through a set of women's autonomy and empowerment indicators on various demographic, health, nutrition, and socio-economic development characteristics—reveals that poor health outcomes among females are well connected with high preference for male child and increased number of missing girls. In addition, preference for male child results in high mortality and poor nutrition among female children. Table 3.3 clearly depicts the persisting scenario of development of women being directly linked with developmental outcomes among female children. For example, high malnutrition among female children is positively linked with sex preferences and negatively linked with female literacy, women having bank account, as well as women's decision for self-healthcare (F-I). Notably, women-headed households and women having land reduces the preference for specific sex and increases the sex ratio at birth (F-III). Higher sex ratio at birth shows less discrimination against female children. Further, women's economic independence reduces the risk of discriminatory practices towards female children and increases the decision for better healthcare, and those practices reduce gender inequality among them (F-V).

Keeping in mind Ambedkar's views on women empowerment, this study tries to understand if improvement in gender equality and women empowerment leads to better social and economic development. The study finds a continuous decline in CSR and an increase in missing girls in the country. There is evidence of discriminatory behaviour towards, and less desire for, female children, which increases the risk for female children, as shown by other studies too (Agnihotri 2000; Malhotra et al. 1995; Miller 1981; Raushan et al. 2016). A plethora of studies have shown that these issues hinder the process of gender equality (Bhat 2002a, 2002b; Bhat and Zavier 2001; Dasgupta and Bhat 1997; Guillot 2002; Jha et al. 2006; Kishor 1993, 1995; Patel 2008; Raushan et al. 2016).

As many studies have highlighted these issues, the government has stepped in to stop gender discrimination. It is committed to

Table 3.3 Varimax Rotation Factor Score of Gender Equality, Health, Nutrition, and Empowerment in States/Union Territories in India

	Rotated Component Matrix					Communality
	F-I	F-II	F-III	F-IV	F-V	
NMR_f	0.205	0.838	0.042	0.280	−0.235	0.880
IMR_f	0.248	0.908	−0.093	0.106	−0.115	0.918
$U5MR_f$	0.391	0.850	−0.140	0.089	−0.101	0.913
$STNTD_f$	0.811	0.426	−0.065	−0.047	0.041	0.848
$UNDWT_f$	0.832	0.243	0.025	0.217	0.080	0.805
$ANMIA_f$	0.391	0.108	−0.025	0.720	0.202	0.724
SRB	0.190	−0.289	0.607	−0.158	−0.456	0.721
INDSF	0.572	0.256	−0.547	0.307	−0.186	0.821
CSR	0.101	−0.184	0.260	−0.891	0.104	0.916
$MSNG_f$	−0.106	0.184	−0.263	0.889	−0.103	0.915
$LTRCY_f$	−0.688	−0.358	0.397	−0.039	0.020	0.761
$BNKAC_f$	−0.715	−0.062	0.292	0.137	0.244	0.679
$HFCAN_f$	−0.516	0.056	−0.180	0.038	0.533	0.587
$HCDCN_f$	0.153	−0.344	0.448	0.501	0.358	0.722
$VFDCN_f$	−0.067	−0.397	−0.056	0.035	0.800	0.807
$HEED_f$	0.032	−0.118	−0.017	−0.073	0.886	0.806
$LAND_f$	−0.192	0.009	0.893	−0.102	−0.106	0.856
$HHFH_f$	−0.226	0.035	0.824	−0.244	−0.027	0.792
Eigen Value	6.095	3.034	2.138	1.797	1.407	
Variance Explained (%)	19.507	17.468	15.535	15.098	12.787	
Total Variance Explained = 80.396%						

Source: Calculated by author using the factor analysis on 18 demographic, malnutrition, women's autonomy, empowerment, and development indicators.

gender equality, but the state has to monitor and evaluate the various programmes and schemes related to eliminating gender discrimination and empowering women (Patel 2008; Raushan and Raushan 2012; Raushan et al. 2016). Although the National Policy for the Empowerment of Women (2001), that aims to bring about advancement, development, and empowerment of women in the country, has made a difference, it needs a more focused implementation. This can be done through a bottom-up approach, that is, start from the community level to strengthen to state-level programmes and policies. Community-based sensitization and awareness to stop dangerous and discriminating behaviour can reduce gender inequality and would be a major step in this regard. Ambedkar had clearly stated that social awareness and social responsiveness are the basic ingredients of women empowerment (Malini 1993; Zelliot 2007). However, intra-household, community, and societal resources, and their equal availability and accessibility for both men and women, will strengthen the idea of social justice for the development of the nation, along with the development of women in the country.

References

Agnihotri, S.B. 2000. *Sex Ratio Patterns in the Indian Population: A Fresh Exploration*. New Delhi: Sage.

Ambedkar, B.R. 1987. 'Philosophy of Hinduism', in Vasant Moon (ed.), *Dr. Babasaheb Ambedkar: Writings and Speeches*, Vol. 3, pp. 3–92. Bombay: Education Department, Government of Maharashtra.

———. 1989. 'Annihilation of Caste: With a Reply to Mahatma Gandhi', in Vasant Moon (ed.), *Dr. Babasaheb Ambedkar: Writings and Speeches*, Vol. 1, pp. 25–96. Bombay: Education Department, Government of Maharashtra.

Arnold, F., S. Kishor, and T.K. Roy. 2002. 'Sex Selective Abortions in India', *Population and Development Review* 28(4): 759–85.

Batliwala, S. 1994. 'The Meaning of Women's Empowerment: New Concepts from Action', in G. Sen, A. Germain, and L.C. Chen (eds), *Population Policies Reconsidered: Health, Empowerment and Rights*, pp. 127–38. Boston: Harvard University Press.

Bhat, P.N.M. 2002a. 'On the Trail of "Missing" Indian Females: Search for Clues', *Economic and Political Weekly* 37(51): 5105–18.

———. 2002b. 'On the Trail of "Missing" Indian Females: Illusion and Reality', *Economic and Political Weekly* 37(52): 5244–63.

Bhat, P.N.M. and A.J.F. Zavier. 2001. 'Fertility Decline and Gender Bias in Northern India', Discussion Paper No. 33, Institute of Economic Growth, Delhi, India.

Dasgupta, M. and P.N.M. Bhat. 1997. 'Fertility Decline and Increased Manifestation of Sex Bias in India', *Population Studies* 51(3): 307–15.

Dillon, W.R. and M. Goldstein. 1984. *Multivariate Analysis: Methods and Applications*. New York: John Wiley & Sons.

Dyson, T. and M. Moore. 1983. 'On Kinship Structure, Female Autonomy and Demographic Behaviour in India', *Population and Development Review* 9(1): 35–60.

Government of India (GoI). 1991. *Primary Census Abstract, Census of India: 1991*. New Delhi: Office of Registrar General and Census Commissioner of India.

———. 2001a. *Primary Census Abstract, Census of India: 2001*. New Delhi: Office of Registrar General and Census Commissioner of India.

———. 2001b. *National Policy for Empowerment of Women, 2001*. Ministry of Women and Child Development, Government of India. Available at https://wcd.nic.in/sites/default/files/National%20Policy%20for%20Empowerment%20of%20Women%202001.pdf; last accessed on 20 October 2019.

———. 2011. *Primary Census Abstract, Census of India: 2011*. New Delhi: Office of Registrar General and Census Commissioner of India.

Guillot, M. 2002. 'The Dynamics of the Population Sex Ratio in India, 1971–96', *Population Studies* 56(1): 51–63.

International Institute for Population Sciences (IIPS) and ICF. 2017. *National Family Health Survey (NFHS-4), 2015–16: India*. Mumbai: IIPS.

IIPS and Macro International. 2007. *National Family Health Survey (NFHS-3), 2005–06: India*, Vol. I. Mumbai: IIPS.

Jha, P., R. Kumar, P. Vasa, N. Dhingra, D. Thiruchelvam, and R. Moineddin. 2006. 'Low Male-to-Female Sex Ratio of Children Born in India: National Survey of 1.1 Million Households', *The Lancet* 367(9506): 211–18.

Kabeer, N. 1999. 'Resources, Agency, Achievements: Reflections on the Measurement of Women's Empowerment', *Development and Change* 30(3): 435–64.

Kishor, S. 1992. 'All "Devis" but Not All Wanted: A District-Level Analysis of Female Discrimination in India 1961–1981', Paper presented at the annual meeting of the Population Association of America, Denver, Colorado, USA, 30 April–2 May 1992.

———. 1993. 'May God Give Sons to All: Gender and Child Mortality in India', *American Sociological Review* 58(2): 247–65.

———. 1995. 'Autonomy and Egyptian Women: Findings from the 1988 Egypt Demographic and Health Survey', Occasional Papers No. 2, Macro International Inc, Calverton, Maryland, USA.

Malhotra, A., R. Vanneman, and S. Kishor. 1995. 'Fertility, Dimensions of Patriarchy and Development in India', *Population and Development Review* 21(2): 281–305.

Malini, M. 1993. 'Caste and Patriarchy: Ambedkar's Insight into the Status of Women', in K.S. Chalam (ed.), *Relevance of Ambedkarism in India*, pp.129–38. Jaipur: Rawat.

Massey, J. 2003. *B.R Ambedkar: A Study in Just Society*. New Delhi: Manohar.

Miller, B.D. 1981. *The Endangered Sex: Neglect of Female Children in Rural North India*. Ithaca: Cornell University Press.

Omvedt, G. 2000. 'Towards a Theory of Brahmanic Patriarchy', *Economic and Political Weekly* 35(4): 187–90.

Patel, V. 2008. *Female Foeticide: Implication for India*. New Delhi: Planning Commission, Government of India.

Raushan, R. and M.R. Raushan. 2012. 'Sex Ratio Imbalance: A Study of Recent Changes with Special Reference to Haryana', *Man and Development* 34(3): 49–64.

Raushan, R., M.R. Raushan, and S.B. Kumari. 2017. 'Demographic Outcomes and RCH Services Utilization in Bihar: Where Is the Gap?', in H. Sahoo, F. Ram, B. Paswan, H. Lhungdim, and D. Govil (eds), *Population Issues: Studies from Uttar Pradesh and Bihar*, pp. 134–53. Mumbai and Jaipur: IIPS and Rawat.

Raushan, R., G. Sahu, and M.R. Raushan. 2016. 'Declining Child Sex Ratio and Missing Girls in India', *Man and Development* 38(2): 87–106.

Sen, A. 1990. 'More than 100 Million Women Are Missing', *New York Review of Books* 37(20): 61–6.

Singh, S. 1997. 'Ambedkar's Contribution to Social Justice', in Mohd. Shabbir (ed.), *B.R. Ambedkar: Study in Law and Society*, pp. 86–8. Jaipur: Rawat.

Sinha, C. 2007. 'Images of Motherhood: The Hindu Code Bill Discourse', *Economic and Political Weekly* 42(43): 49–57.

You, D., G. Jones, K. Hill, T. Wardlaw, and M. Chopra. 2010. 'Levels and Trends in Child Mortality, 1990–2009'. *The Lancet* 376(9745): 931–3.

Zelliot, E. 2007. 'Empowerment of Women', in S. Thorat and Aryama (eds), *Ambedkar in Retrospect: Essays on Economics, Politics and Society*, pp. 317–31. New Delhi: Rawat.

Appendices

Table A3.1 Missing Girls over Decades in Indian States: 1991–2011

States/Union Territories	Child Sex Ratio (per 1,000)*			Missing Girls (%)*			Sex Preference Index**
	1991	2001	2011	1991	2001	2011	2015–16
Andaman & Nicobar Islands	973	957	968	1.39	2.21	1.62	15.7
Andhra Pradesh	975	961	939	1.27	1.99	3.14	52.1
Arunachal Pradesh	982	964	972	0.92	1.84	1.44	71.8
Assam	975	965	962	1.26	1.78	1.92	67.6
Bihar	953	942	935	2.41	2.97	3.35	90.4
Chandigarh	899	845	880	5.32	8.4	6.4	31.3
Chhattisgarh	984	975	969	0.82	1.29	1.59	67.6
Dadra & Nagar Haveli	1013	979	926	−0.64	1.04	3.86	77.2
Daman & Diu	958	926	904	2.17	3.85	5.03	77.5
Delhi	915	868	871	4.44	7.06	6.88	61.0
Goa	964	938	942	1.82	3.23	2.98	11.2
Gujarat	928	883	890	3.75	6.21	5.83	64.4
Haryana	879	819	834	6.45	9.95	9.04	84.5
Himachal Pradesh	951	896	909	2.49	5.51	4.76	18.4
Jammu & Kashmir	NA	941	862	NA	3.03	7.42	61.9
Jharkhand	979	965	948	1.05	1.76	2.69	86.0
Karnataka	960	946	948	2.06	2.78	2.65	31.8
Kerala	958	960	964	2.14	2.03	1.83	26.6
Lakshadweep	941	959	911	3.06	2.1	4.67	18.3
Madhya Pradesh	941	932	918	3.02	3.5	4.28	81.5
Maharashtra	946	913	894	2.77	4.55	5.58	38.7
Manipur	974	957	930	1.3	2.18	3.63	67.9
Meghalaya	986	973	970	0.71	1.38	1.54	−19.8
Mizoram	969	964	970	1.57	1.82	1.54	13.6
Nagaland	993	964	943	0.35	1.85	2.92	31.8
Odisha	967	953	941	1.7	2.43	3.03	69.0

Puducherry	963	967	967	1.91	1.68	1.65	33.4
Punjab	875	798	846	6.67	11.22	8.31	73.3
Rajasthan	916	909	888	4.36	4.77	5.9	87.4
Sikkim	965	963	957	1.8	1.9	2.2	26.1
Tamil Nadu	948	942	943	2.66	2.99	2.92	29.8
Telangana	NA	NA	NA	NA	NA	NA	44.0
Tripura	967	966	957	1.67	1.73	2.18	48.7
Uttar Pradesh	927	916	902	3.8	4.41	5.13	91.4
Uttarakhand	949	908	890	2.62	4.84	5.8	74.1
West Bengal	967	960	956	1.7	2.05	2.26	54.1
India	**945**	**927**	**918**	**2.81**	**3.77**	**4.25**	**68.8**

Note: * Census of India data for 1991–2011;
** NFHS-4 data for 2015–16.
Source: Author's calculation based on GoI (1991, 2001a, 2011) and IIPS and ICF (2017).

Table A3.2 List of Variables Included in the Study

Sl. No.	Variables	Description	Data Source
1	NMR_f	Neonatal mortality rate of the girl child	NFHS-4
2	IMR_f	Infant mortality rate of the girl child	NFHS-4
3	$U5MR_f$	Under-five mortality rate of the girl child	NFHS-4
4	$STNTD_f$	Percentage of stunted girls (under 5 years age)	NFHS-4
5	$UNDWT_f$	Percentage of underweight girls (under 5 years age)	NFHS-4
6	$ANMIA_f$	Percentage of anaemic girls (under 5 years age)	NFHS-4
7	SRB	Sex ratio at birth for 2012–16	NFHS-4
8	INDSF	Index of sex preferences	NFHS-4
9	$CHLDP_f$	Percentage of women having a preference for a female child	NFHS-4
10	$CHLDP_m$	Percentage of women having a preference for a male child	NFHS-4
11	CSR	Child sex ratio in 2011	Census
12	$MSNG_f$	Percentage of missing girls in 2011	Census
13	$LTRCY_f$	Female literacy rate in 2011	Census

(*Cont'd*)

Table A3.2 (Cont'd)

Sl. No.	Variables	Description	Data Source
14	$BNKAC_f$	Percentage of women having bank accounts	NFHS-4
15	$HFCAN_f$	Percentage of women allowed to visit health facilities alone	NFHS-4
16	$HCDCN_f$	Percentage of women who can take decisions on self-healthcare	NFHS-4
17	$MKTAN_f$	Percentage of women who can go to the market alone	NFHS-4
19	$FVAN_f$	Percentage of women who can visit their family/relatives alone	NFHS-4
20	$VFDCN_f$	Percentage of women who can decide to visit family/relatives	NFHS-4
21	$HEED_f$	Percentage of women who can make decisions about their husband's earnings	NFHS-4
22	$SEED_f$	Percentage of women who can make decisions on how to spend their own earnings	NFHS-4
23	$MNYSL_f$	Percentage of women who have money to spend on themselves	NFHS-4
24	$LAND_f$	Females who have land in their name	NFHS-4
25	$HHFH_f$	Female is head of household	NFHS-4

Note: NFHS 4 data for 2015–16; *Census of India* data for 2011.
Source: GoI (2011) and IIPS and ICF (2017).

4
Ambedkar as a Feminist Philosopher

SUNAINA ARYA

B.R. Ambedkar as a scholar is a rare image in mainstream Indian mindset which volunteers to restrict him into the domain of a 'social reformer'. Although Ambedkar as a philosopher is not acceptable to the academic circles in India (Rathore 2017), his perspective on everyday issues, such as gender, is becoming a topic of curiosity for people around the world. Our ignorance of Ambedkar's philosophy lies in the prejudices against the wisdom of an outcasted, devalued Dalit, similar to our casual questioning of the feminist possibilities of a man. This chapter explores the theme 'Ambedkar as a feminist philosopher', defying the preconceptions of both philosophy and feminism, towards a 'philosophy by all' and 'feminism by all'.

Ambedkar's philosophy is based on three principles, namely, liberty, equality, and fraternity, which are exposited in his conception of justice (Ambedkar 2003b: 25). His idea of a just society includes justice for everyone—Dalits, women, labourers, rural dwellers, and so on. Given the patriarchal structure of social organizing, women as a significant unit are deprived of fundamental rights. Ambedkar investigates into the roots of their degradation and seeks to establish a system with a dignified life for them. I seek to establish his theoretical analysis and advocated principles to enhance women's conditions as a feminist philosophy. Ensuring each has access to basic human rights, Ambedkar's objective is not meant to favour women but to uplift and empower them as equal citizens of the country.

As explicated further in various sections of this chapter, Ambedkar lays the groundwork for gender justice in India. The following section includes his feminist critique of grand narratives which support patriarchal norms, namely, the Ramayana, the Mahabharata, and the Manusmriti. He investigates the ways in which women-degrading practices are preached and manifested by the idealized characters of Hindu tradition, thereby exposing their irrationality and ethical failure (Arya 2017). In his quest for gender justice, Ambedkar forwards evidences from other ancient literature, namely, Patanjali's *Mahabhashya*, Kautilya's *Arthashastra*, and several Buddhist texts, as testimonials to gender equality in ancient Indian culture. The next section deals with Ambedkar's alternatives to the prevailing social order based on patriarchal norms. It exposits his views on the kind of treatment a woman should be given in family and society, which is evident in his founding of gender-just laws in the form of Hindu Code Bill. It also highlights the kind of difference these laws bring about in the lives of Indian women for their progress. The section that follows scrutinizes debates in Indian feminist discourse in light of Ambedkar's feminist philosophy. The positions of contemporary Indian feminist thinkers, such as, Gopal Guru, Nivedita Menon, Sharmila Rege, Uma Chakravarti, and V. Geetha, are discussed and debated with regard to those issues. It also includes a discussion of major standpoints of feminist discourse as dealt by Indian thinkers, namely, Marxist feminist, liberal feminist, and Dalit feminist standpoints. In conclusion, I seek to gestate the relevance of Ambedkar's feminist philosophy in the present context.

Ambedkar's Feminist Critique of Patriarchal Grand Narratives

Among grounds of conceiving Ambedkar as a feminist philosopher is his theoretical contribution to women's emancipation. What renders the failure of struggles towards gender justice is the religious preaching for gender hierarchies. Through a philosophical engagement with these epics, Ambedkar seeks to dismantle the inhuman and illogical justification for patriarchal norms. First, he challenges the socially idealized relation of a woman and a man within the institution of marriage.

Critique of Rama from the Ramayana

While reading the phase from the Ramayana where Sita is freed from Ravana's abduction and Rama expresses disregard to her, Ambedkar contemplates:

> It would be difficult to believe [that] any man with ordinary human kindness could address to his wife in such dire distress as Rama did to Sita ...: 'I have got you as a prize in a war after conquering my enemy, your captor. I have recovered my honour and punished my enemy. People have witnessed my military prowess and I am glad that my labours have been rewarded. I came here to kill Ravana and wash-off this dishonour. I did not take this trouble for your sake.' Could there be anything more cruel than this conduct of Rama towards Sita? He does not stop here. He proceeded to tell her: 'I suspect your conduct. You must have been spoiled by Ravana. Your very sight is revolting to me. Oh daughter of Janaka! I allow you to go anywhere you like. I have nothing to do with you. I conquered you back and I am content, for that was my object. I cannot think that Ravana would have failed to enjoy a woman as beautiful as you are.'[1] ... To give him no excuse ... She enters the fire and comes out unscathed.[2] It is then that Rama agrees to take her back to Ayodhya. (Ambedkar 2003c: 327-8)

We see that Ambedkar's reading of the Ramayana highlights that Sita had a commodified value for her husband, Rama, because he called her a 'prize'. What is tragic about the epic is that the reason for her suffering such mischief from Rama was because she was kidnapped by Ravana. After staying away from her for more than 10 months, Rama sends Hanuman not to bring her back, but 'to inform her that he is hale and hearty' after killing Ravana (Ambedkar 2003c: 327). He does not hesitate to say that he killed Ravana not as revenge for kidnapping his wife, but to show-off his masculine power being a Kshatriya.[3]

---

[1] Valmiki, *Ramayana*, Yudha Kanda Sarga 115, slokas 1-23, cited in Ambedkar (2003c: 327).

[2] This test of purity performed by Sita is known as *agnipareeksha*.

[3] Kshatriya is the second caste in the Hindu *varna* system (that is, the social categorization of professional duties according to the Vedic process of personal evolution and community cooperation) after Brahmin, whose prescribed profession is to fight, as decided by their birth, according to Hindu religion.

When she conveyed her longing to see Rama, she was told that he bore no relationship with her. Again, why? It must have been because she must have been 'enjoyed' by Ravana. Though it was not Sita's fault that she was kidnapped by Ravana, Rama was not really concerned about her situation. The notion of being enjoyed showed that Sita was reduced to a sexual object, which could only be possessed by one man in her lifetime. In case of misfortune of sexual violence by Ravana, her love and regard for Rama immediately turned nil. She was taken to her husband's home only after she proved her purity through surviving the fire (agnipareeksha). This shows that Rama had no love, affection, or esteem for his own wife, whose beauty he acknowledges. It would not be an exaggeration to say that Rama valued only her body, and that was his sole possession, not Sita as a person. However, as a devoted wife, Sita did not hesitate to go through agnipareeksha to prove her chastity. Rama taking Sita along after the agnipareeksha proves that what mattered to him as a husband was the singular possession of a sexual servant.

When Sita conceived Rama's children after he resumed kingship in Ayodhya, people in the kingdom started gossiping about her chastity. In response, he did not hesitate to abandon her, without even thinking about her agnipareeksha. In Ambedkar's words, he took 'the shortest cut' and 'the swiftest means' to disembarrass himself. Ambedkar brings to notice other considerable means of getting rid of that defamation. For one, Rama could have informed the people about Sita performing agnipareeksha or he could have volunteered to declare that she conceived after returning to Ayodhya. However, he did not do so; instead, he chose to take the ultimate step at the very beginning. This unfortunate situation shows why even today public gossiping has so much value in our society—because Rama–Sita are still hailed as an ideal couple by orthodox patriarchal culture. This culture of 'shame' for defying irrationality supports that a husband owns *his* wife even while not bearing affection or concern for her. What is regarded as improvement in 'modern' marriages is the responsibility of her livelihood, but protecting the wife's purity is still a major concern for husbands today, as it was for Rama.

Sita's pregnancy did not distract Rama from his patriarchal anxiety of cleansing the shame, and even the thought of his own child could not replace that feeling. Ambedkar emphasizes that Rama abandoned 'a woman, in somewhat advanced state of pregnancy in a jungle, without friends, without provision, without even notice in a most treacherous manner' (Ambedkar 2003c: 328). Ambedkar's concern comes on basic humanitarian grounds that Rama should have considered the physical and psychological troubles Sita would go through with a pregnant body; pregnancy is a stage in a woman's life when she needs support, care, and wellness the most. Another aspect which Ambedkar calls attention to is that Rama, being a king, should have followed some procedure of legislation before issuing her a notice to leave the palace. He could have issued a prior notice, or sent her along with some basic support, that is, a caretaker or a friend. What we find in the end is that Sita ceased to be a queen even after proving her innocence by sitting through the fire flames, whereas Rama continued to remain a king after punishing her for no crime of hers.

From the entire Ramayana, as reflected in Ambedkar's writings, we can draw the following characteristics of the 'ideal man', Rama, as regarded in the sacred Hindu text: he regards his wife as a prize or reward for his masculinity; his 'honour' or public image is his greatest asset; he sees a woman as an object of pleasure for a man; he tests her celibacy through agnipareeksha for himself, but abandons his pregnant wife in order to avoid gossip shaming, that is, he hesitates to tell the truth to people; and he does not feel love, affection, or care for his own unborn children. Such incidents from Valmiki's Ramayana show that the queen of a godly man has been, time and again, demeaned by her king-husband.

Ambedkar argues that such dehumanizing view of a woman does not comply with the basic aspects of being a human. He evaluates Rama's actions through the lens of social philosophy and finds that these are not only unjust to a woman but also highly unethical. Rama never did count the subjectivity and individuality of Sita in the entire epic. Therefore, Ambedkar dismisses the validity of the Ramayana as a guiding principle of an ideal form of living as it preaches slavery of women in the institution of marriage, which is against his idea of social justice. Ambedkar concludes that Rama–Sita relation in a marriage is anti-justice and preaches inequality, and what we need to strive for is an egalitarian society with dignity for all women and men. What comes next in Ambedkar's theoretical contribution to feminism is studying another narrative which is preached as a source of morality, through fundamental principles of ethics.

Critique of Krishna from the Mahabharata

Ambedkar reads the Mahabharata and finds that Krishna, the 'incarnation of the Supreme Being', had eight chief wives, namely, Rukmini, Satyabhama, Jambavati, Kalindi, Mitrabinda, Satya, Bhadra, and Lakshmana, 1.8 lakh children, and 16,100 wives, whom he married on the same day (Ambedkar 2003c: 333–43). Most of his wives were acquired through fights, theft, or dishonesty. He carried off Rukmini a day before her proposed marriage with his cousin, Sishupala. Satyabhama was given to him by her father as he was afraid of Krishna. He got Jambavati as a peace offering on defeating her father in a war. Kalindi went through a series of austerities in order to get Krishna as her husband and was thus rewarded by him. Mitrabinda was a cousin of Krishna who was carried off by him from her *swayamvara*[4] grounds. Satya was won by Krishna for killing a number of naughty bulls belonging to her father. Lakshmana was carried off by him from her swayamvara grounds. Krishna even advised Arjuna to carry his half-sister (Balarama's sister), Subhadra, off 'like a brave Kshatriya' without depending on the chances of swayamvara.

Observing the disregardful and disrespectful treatment of women, Ambedkar comments that Krishna did not take the pain of arguing and acted on his own whims. We can derive from the Mahabharata that the incarnation of God Vishnu, Krishna, and the respective fathers of the women demeaned, objectified, and commodified them. They were rewarded to Krishna for victory in fights; or they were offered to him as a penalty or compensation for defeat and in fear. He not only carried them off from their swayamvaras but also advised other men to carry off women, including his half-sister. Krishna did not care for the consent of a woman. His regardless attitude towards socio-political standards explicates that social ethics were far from his way of living. Ambedkar criticizes the Mahabharata from a feminist perspective because it preaches dehumanization of women. Hence, Ambedkar dismisses its validity as a source of morality on the grounds that it does not

---

[4] Swayamvara is a Hindi word which is constituted by the combination of *swayam*, that is, self, and *vara*, that is, groom. It is a ceremony where the bride chooses her groom among the various men who compete in order to win her heart.

comply with the basic principles of ethics. The next text is what makes him furious for the madness involved in its principles. The Ramayana and the Mahabharata were narratives which persuaded people for patriarchy as norm, but the Manusmriti was written as the 'law book' propounding misogyny as a rule. This is regarded as *dharmashastra,* or main source of religious regulations to refer to find what is permitted and what is punishable in our everyday practices.

Critique of the Manusmriti

Ambedkar writes:

> Manu can hardly be said to be more tender to women than he was to the Shudra.... For Manu does not prevent a man from giving up his wife.... But what he does is to prevent the wife from becoming free. ... The meaning is that a wife, sold or repudiated by her husband, can never become the legitimate wife of another who may have bought or received her after she was repudiated. If this is not monstrous nothing can be. But Manu was not worried by consideration of justice or injustice by his law. (Ambedkar 2003b: 429–30)

Ambedkar compares the laws of Manu for women with that for the Shudras. Manu not only demeans and commodifies women but also assures their slavery. The women, irrespective of their caste and age, are precluded from being free in any condition or at any stage of life. Indeed, he 'declared a new rule that killing a woman was only an *Upapataka,* i.e. it was a minor offence'.[5] In other words, slaying a woman is not considered a serious crime, rather it is an easily excused act, according to Manu's laws. Therefore, Ambedkar concludes that Manu did not have the slightest degree of regard for justice.

After analysing Manu's laws from the perspective of social standards, Ambedkar finds no logic behind his degradation of women. He quotes from the Manusmriti (IX.18): 'women have no knowledge of religion because they have no right to know the Vedas.... As women cannot utter the Veda Mantras they are as unclean as untruth is' (Ambedkar 2003f: 119). Ambedkar regards this view of women as 'an insult and an injury to the women of India'

---

[5] According to Manusmriti (XI.67), cited in Ambedkar (2003b: 432).

(Ambedkar 2003f: 119): injury because, without a justification, women were denied their fundamental right to acquire knowledge, which further forbids them to take *sannyas*[6] for attaining the *Brahma*;[7] and insult because after that denial they were declared unclean like untruth. Ambedkar shows that Manu's argument is circular because a woman is prohibited 'to realise her spiritual potentiality' and then she is 'declared to be barren of spiritual potentiality' (Ambedkar 2003f: 119). The later judgement made by Manu regarding women requires the truth of the first one for its validity, that is, unless a woman is given an opportunity to realize her potential, it is irrelevant to make a judgement about whether or not she has that potential. Thus, Ambedkar shows that the laws made by Manu were neither logically correct nor ethically sound to follow.

Ambedkar's argument against Manu's patriarchal laws is very similar to Simon de Beauvoir's take on patriarchal restrictions on women in Western society. She writes: 'A woman is shut up in a kitchen or a boudoir and one is surprised her horizon is limited; her wings are cut and then she is blamed for not knowing how to fly. Let a future be open to her and she will no longer be obliged to settle in the present' (Beauvoir 2010: 660).

Like Ambedkar, Beauvoir refutes the general notion that women are incapable of competing with men in any field of life, thereby exposing the fallacy in such beliefs. She claims that women's perspectives towards things are limited only because they have been forced to limit themselves to domestic affairs throughout their lives. She argues that if a woman is able to avail freedom and resources, she too will compete equally with men and contribute greatly to the development of society. Thus, Ambedkar's feminist thought is similar to that of Beauvoir.

In his quest for a minimal logic in Manu's commands, Ambedkar finally regards it as 'madness'[8] (Ambedkar 2003c: 215) because it

---

[6] It is a form of asceticism where a person renunciates from the desires of material world, including marriage, and thus he/she is known as a 'sannyasi'.

[7] It is that stage of spiritual life wherein a sannyasi is said to have attained the power of godly bliss, after acquiring complete freedom from worldly life.

[8] Ambedkar calls Manu's Brahmanic explanation for the origin of mixed castes as 'madness', according to which everything a person is allowed/

has no other explanation than the Brahmanical superiority complex. By 'Brahmanical superiority complex',[9] I mean the psyche of people who regard themselves as superior to their fellow human beings only because they accidentally (that is, by birth) belong to a dominant gender, that is, men, in a patriarchal structure of society. It is termed as a complex because there are no logical grounds for such a (mis)belief. This complex renders a person incapable of exercising their rational and logical abilities because of such prejudices, and they perceive reality differently not only about others but also about themselves.

Ambedkar compares the prevailing position of women with that in pre-Manu time and in the Buddhist regime where women were allowed to take sannyas or *parivraja* (monkhood). Based on his reading of Buddhist literature, that is, *Anguttara Nikaya* (cited in Ambedkar 2003d: 83), *Samyutta Nikaya* (cited in Ambedkar 2003a: 62), and other texts, Ambedkar writes that Buddha 'held the view that those families are saved from a downfall which places a woman in authority over their affairs, [he] ... had no hesitation in describing woman as one of the seven Treasures and a thing of supreme value' (Ambedkar 2003f: 118). Ambedkar argues that women were treated not only equal to men, rather greater than them. They had great respect, power, and possession in the Buddhist tradition.

Ambedkar also refutes the existing notion that women are not capable of pursuing intellectual endeavours and cites examples from some of the ancient texts which describe women's active participation in the public domain. On the basis of his analysis of Patanjali's *Mahabhashya*, Ambedkar (2003b: 432) writes, 'The stories of women entering into public discussions with men on most abstruse subjects of religion, philosophy, and metaphysics are by no means few.' He argues that women's intellectual potential is in no way less than that of men as they have been engaging with very difficult topics from well-developed disciplines, such

---

disallowed to do is defined by one's birth and not by any logical reason. Similarly, if one is born as a female or a male, s/he is disallowed/allowed to perform certain acts accordingly.

[9] By using 'Brahmanical superiority complex', I am trying to emphasize and articulate how an individual behaves under the influence of the caste psyche, which I am bringing in the context of gender.

as metaphysics, philosophy, and religion. Therefore, Ambedkar suggests that nurturing the potential of both men and women is equally important to develop the society.

Based on his reading of Kautilya's *Arthashastra*, Ambedkar compares the status of women in the times of Kautilya and Manu. In Kautilya's time, women had the right to knowledge, right to property, right to divorce, right to claim maintenance, right to remarry, and so on. Also, there were practices of monogamy, widow remarriage, inter-caste contacts; and laws relating to fine, penalties, and punishment for men who indulged in extra-marital sexual contacts. Men were charged an abundant fine and punished if they remarried due to their desire for a male child, without waiting for the determined time period by law, that is, 8–12 years under the given conditions. Women could seek justice from the court for defamation and assault by their husbands. Ambedkar concludes that they were 'free and equal partners' of their husbands at that time (Ambedkar 2003b: 433–7). The better status of women in pre-Manu times shows that women were degraded and demeaned by Manu. Ambedkar, therefore, refutes all the patriarchal and unjust laws made by Manu because they bear no logical grounds for justification.

Ambedkar's engagement with the ancient texts that support patriarchal norms and his problematization of the gender issues provide strong evidence for his feminist insight. The kind of critiques he offers to the gendered hierarchical system come entirely from a feminist perspective. He considers the subjectivity, autonomy, and dignity of women as equal to that of men, which is positively denied in the Ramayana, the Mahabharata, and the Manusmriti. The poverty of social values and ethics in prevailing laws maintaining the social order in Hinduism poses great danger to human life in Indian society. Therefore, Ambedkar conceives of a better society which maintains equal respect for every human life.

Ambedkar's Alternatives to the Prevailing Social Order Based on Patriarchal Norms

Ambedkar's material contribution to women's emancipation can be seen in his drafting of the Hindu Code Bill, after a careful study of the highly patriarchal social system, which he actively defends in the courtroom. Also, he makes great efforts to encourage women's active participation in the social, economic, and political domain. Highlighting the role of women as agents of social change and development, he writes, 'I measure the progress of a community by the degree of progress which women have achieved' (Ambedkar 2003g: 282). He analyses the Indian social structure and argues that the society can never be uplifted unless the most downtrodden are uplifted. Therefore, he emphasizes on women's upliftment and gender aspects.

Ambedkar holds strong confidence in the potential and strength of women's organizations in altering the existing social order. He says, from his experience (Ambedkar 2003g: 282), that women have played a very significant role in improving the conditions of the weaker sections and classes. Ambedkar believes that if women are truly taken into confidence, they may change the present picture of a society which is highly stratified and unjust. He advocates that unity is meaningless without the accompaniment of women, education is fruitless without educated women, and agitation is incomplete without the strength of women (Ambedkar 2003g: 273–6). Hence, he strongly recommends equal status for women in order to uplift the socio-economic and cultural condition of the society at large.

In independent India, in order to provide equality to women, Ambedkar dwells upon the political as well as the social realm and comments upon the legitimate treatment that women should get. He suggests, 'let each girl who marries stand up to her husband, claim to be her husband's friend and equal, and refuse to be his slave' (Ambedkar 2003f: 283). He strongly advocates for the complete abolishment of the slavery of women under patriarchal systems of society by establishing strong equality for women in the very fundamental social institution, that is, the institution of marriage. Therefore, he proposes such laws which guarantee the upliftment of their socio-economic and political conditions. The Hindu Code Bill thus covered unprecedented issues, such as the abolition of birthright to property, property by survivorship, half-share for daughters, conversion of women's limited estate into an absolute estate, abolition of caste in matters of marriage and adoption, and the principle of monogamy and divorce (Ambedkar 2003h: 4–11).

Ambedkar also strongly advocates for women's education, along with men's, in his speeches. Addressing the All-India Depressed Classes Women's Conference in Nagpur, he says, 'Give education to your children. Instil ambition in them ...', further suggesting that they should have a proper hold of resources before getting married or getting their children married (Ambedkar 2003f: 283). This shows that he wants each and every citizen of the nation, regardless of their gender, to avail education, which can help them in living a dignified life. He suggests instilling ambition in children so that they tend to believe in hard work and efforts, not in fate. He believes that education is the primary requirement for a rational life and advocates for education to all in order to uplift the society on a larger scale.

While introducing the Maternity Bill, he emphasizes that it is in the interest of the nation that the mother get a certain amount of rest in the prenatal period. Subsequently, the concept of the Bill is based entirely on that principle (Ambedkar 2003e: 274–7). It explicates the greatness of his vision that he considers the well-being of each future citizen of the country even prior to their birth.

While resigning from the post of law minister in protest against the opposition to Hindu Code Bill, Ambedkar asserts, 'The Hindu Code was a right step towards a Civil Code. The laws should be easily understandable and be applied to all society irrespective of regional barriers' (Ambedkar 2003g: 396). The proposal of feminist laws, such as the Marriage Act, Maternity Act, Divorce and Maintenance Act, and Adoption Act, shows his genuine commitment to avail equality for each and every woman in India, irrespective of caste, class, region, religion, and any other social identity (Ambedkar 2003h: 4–11).

One pertinent question to enquire into Ambedkar's feminist endeavours is: what difference has B.R. Ambedkar brought about in the lives of women in India? Comparing the status of women in pre-Ambedkar time and post-Hindu Code Bill, we find that Ambedkar has championed freedom from slavery for women in India. Some of the examples are as follows: before the implementation of Ambedkar's feminist ideas in India, women were regarded *as property*, and later with the Hindu Succession Act (HSA), they have become women *with property*. Earlier, women were treated as *slaves* to their husbands and now they have the power to stand at par with their husbands as their *friends*. Earlier women had no right to education and now, they are getting educated and leading millions of people due to the implementation of the fundamental right to education. Now, they bear rights not only to be educated but also to educate others. Earlier, women were easily demeaned and repudiated by their husbands under polygamy, but now, with Divorce and Maintenance Act, if they face inhuman behaviour from their husbands, they can choose to leave them. Earlier women's health issues were grossly ignored even during pregnancy, which was the case with Sita, but with the Maternity Act, their health is given proper consideration even at the workplace.

Ambedkar's Feminist Philosophy in Light of Contemporary Debates in Feminism in India

As a strong advocate of equality and social justice, Ambedkar championed the cause of progress and independence of all women in India. Sharmila Rege is the first thinker who finds the foundations of feminist discourse of India in Ambedkar's writings and practices. She not only collects and highlights the feminist philosophy from Ambedkar's writings and speeches but also links his perspective with contemporary debates in feminism in Indian academia. In the present context, in support of Ambedkar's standpoint, Rege (2013: 193) holds: 'Ambedkar's forceful counsel to the Constituent Assembly to frame a Common Civil Code through the Hindu Code Bill needs to be seen as an effort to recognise the politically equal Indian woman citizen as an individual, and not merely as the bearer of the "honour" of the family, kinship, and community.' Rege argues that the Hindu Code Bill facilitates/ strengthens a woman to be recognized as an equal and 'free'[10] individual citizen as men, rather than less than a member of a family or something to be gained and protected, namely, honour. She claims that Ambedkar's deep concern for gender equality is vibrantly visible from his active defence of the Hindu Code Bill in courtrooms. She also mentions that he fought not only for women's citizenship in the nation but also for their equal status in domestic and social life. She attempts to highlight Ambedkar's endeavours for the empowerment of all women citizens of India in all spheres of life.

---

[10] Free, in the sense, means to possess certain rights and freedom of choice and authority for decision-making.

Nivedita Menon, a Marxist feminist, criticizes some crucial acts of the Hindu Code Bill on the grounds of advantages made available to women over men through matrilineal practices at some places in India. She writes, 'The Hindu Succession Act (HSA) nullified the better position of daughters under matrilineal laws, making sons equal inheritors' (Menon 2012: 27). She argues that the HSA (1937) equalized the women's socio-economic status under matrilineal practices with that of the men's; so, women ceased to enjoy higher position than men.

I argue that making son(s) equal inheritors of their mother's property should not be seen as disempowering daughters. In order to sincerely seek gender justice, we must avoid such paths or steps which do injustice to men in the end. The feminist enterprise must not cause the victimization of men. Extremist positions, like that of Menon, can cause the entire struggle for gender justice to be futile. For, in keeping sons out of heirship, we leave a space for the possibility that men will require struggling for gender justice after a period of time. Such a method would make feminist struggle circular and lead us nowhere. In the same line of debate, Rege (2013: 208) holds that the Bill seeks to maintain an equality of position between the son and the daughter. In other words, Ambedkar attempts to equalize the economic status of men and women by HSA, which is a necessary step to end gender injustice.

Contemporary debates on feminist issues in Indian academia give a significant place to sex work, pornography, and bar dancing. In the same context, Menon argues that works such as sex work should be seen with respect as they are chosen professions. She writes: 'There is no more or less agency exercised in "choosing" to work as a domestic servant in multiple households for a pittance and with minimum dignity, or to be exploited by the contractors in arduous construction work, than there is in "choosing" to do sex work—whether as the sole occupation or alongside other work' (Menon 2012: 182). Thus, according to Menon, an equal degree of agency is exercised by women in choosing sex work and choosing other domestic or construction labour work. She also mentions the findings of the first pan-India survey of sex workers: about 71 per cent of female sex workers *choose* to prefer sex work over other occupations (Menon 2012: 180). The reasons for this, as found in the survey are: low pay; insufficient salary; no profit in business;

no regular work; no seasonal work; not getting money even after work; and inability to run their home with the income earned from other occupations (Menon 2012: 180–2). In order to strengthen her argument to dignify sex work, Menon gives the example of the institution of marriage. She says that we must find ways to improve the status of women in sex work, instead of abolishing that 'profession' (Menon 2012: 180), just like we make laws to empower women under marriage, instead of abolishing it (Menon 2012: 184).

There are several flaws in Menon's position on sex work. First, in order to regard one's action as a 'choice', her freedom and availability of sufficient options is necessary. The women involved in 'sex-work' opt one of the two demeaning options. To simplify this case, let A denote the domestic help, vendor, construction labourer, and such jobs, and B denote, sex work. Now, a woman has to choose between these two groups: (*i*) condition: neither A nor B avails dignity to the woman; (*ii*) action: the woman chooses B; and (*iii*) reason: B provides higher wage than A.

We clearly see that the unavailability of dignity is common to both A and B, which qualifies them to fit into one category, in terms of jobs with and without dignity. Although the woman who makes the choice of sex work is an equal agent as the ones choosing other jobs, her agency has no meaning if she does not have sufficient opportunity to exercise her freedom. In this context, if women can avail another dignified job with the same wage, they would prefer to choose that one over sex work. Therefore, I argue that sex work as a profession is *not preferred* by women, rather it is the result of the unavailability of sufficient job options and hence, it is *not chosen*.

Second, the category of being a 'sex worker' alienates women from female non-sex workers because they treat them as the 'other' (Rege 2013: 147).[11] In this context, Menon's comparison of women's unjust status in sex work and that in the institution of marriage does not hold. Such a dominant practice of discrimination, in the form of *othering*, must not be ignored in our endeavours to establish a gender-just society; for, the purpose of feminist discourse can never be met unless each and every woman is assured equal treatment and status in society.

---

[11] For details, see Nair (1993).

Third, a strong critique of the Marxist feminist standpoint on sex work comes from reports by National Federation of Dalit Women (NFDW) and National Campaign on Dalit Human Rights (NCDHR), which prove structural violence in terms of caste-ordained linkages between sexuality and labour (Rege 2013: 20–1). Menon completely ignores the factual aspect of the issue which calls attention to the foundations of such dehumanization of women. For example, she includes custodial deaths, lesbian suicides, honour killings, and so on, in one form of violence based on gender (Menon 2012: 8). Here, she misses the point that the victims of honour killing would not have suffered had they been among the upper-class residents of urban areas because illegitimate institutions like *khap panchayat*,[12] which play the fundamental role in their killing, do not exist in metropolitan cities. Menon (2012: 164) also claims that an 'upper'-caste, urban Hindu woman's experience of discrimination is no less than that of an Other Backward Class (OBC) or Muslim woman. This claim can be strongly criticized by incorporating the idea of intersectionality into the context. A rural subordinate caste, OBC, or Muslim woman is more prone to violence as compared to an urban, 'upper'-caste Hindu woman because the former is victimized at the intersections of caste, class, region, and gender, while the later suffers violence based only on gender. Therefore, I argue that had she been able to see the concerned issue from an intersectional perspective, she could have altered her claim. Her feminist enterprise turns out to be an academically non-serious standpoint, or a shallow understanding, of the feminist discourse in the context of India because of its limited engagement with revealed facts.

Ambedkar's feminist philosophy provides a clear standpoint on the concerned issue. He advocates that women should give up the 'disgraceful' life of prostitution (Ambedkar 2003g: 150–1). Some critics accuse Ambedkar of showing disdain towards some women by calling them a 'shame to the community' (Ambedkar 2003g: 150) on the grounds that such a view attempts to curb women's freedom to deploy their sexuality in the manner they desire. However, those critics have grossly ignored his advice in the same speech: 'do not

---

[12] Khap panchayat is a non-state institution generally constituted by the old men of a village who take major decisions about any controversy as per their age-old traditional customs, rituals, and belief system.

live under conditions *which inevitably drag you into prostitution'* (Ambedkar 2003g: 151).[13] This statement brings out the caste-ordained linkages between sexuality and labour. Here, he is referring to the traditional practices of *devadasis, muralis,* and *jogtinis*. According to these practices, young women from 'untouchable'[14] communities were first sent into religious consecration, which included abandoning their houses and staying in temples. Then, they were taught to be sexually available to the priests of those temples. As the women already had sanctioned their lives, they were disallowed to abandon that way of life, which consequentially pushed their lives into prostitution. Such practices can also be called 'religious prostitution' because religion becomes the cause for those women's entry into prostitution.

In such a historical context, one can derive that 'sex work', as referred by Marxist feminists, is not a profession but rather a brutal form of exploitation; and the subordinate caste women continued to live such lives of exploitation or in Rege (2013: 146) words, 'less than ideal lives in a more than imperfect milieu'. For the said reason, Ambedkar advocates abandoning such conditions which play a fundamental role in degraded lives of women from subordinate castes. In words of Rege (2013: 149), Ambedkar's appeal to introspect into their humiliation is 'an epistemological act' and to express their perspective to their oppressor is 'a political act'. He encourages them to be self-sufficient in terms of their dignified identity and to be assertive of their identity in terms of their political strength.

Based on Ambedkar's analyses of the issue and survey reports, Rege (2013: 146) concludes that subordinate caste women's 'entry into a life of sex work is dictated by their birth into specific untouchable communities that are expected to provide sexual favours to caste Hindu men, and not by choice'.[15] She provides a strong critique to mainstream feminism that Indian women's life is degraded not by *choice* but by *birth*. The revealed linkages between caste and gender show that their disgraceful life is predetermined

---

[13] Emphasis added by Rege (2013: 146).

[14] Indian citizens who are constitutionally categorized as Scheduled Castes were called 'untouchables'. Also, see Ambedkar (2003d).

[15] In support of her argument, Rege mentions the work of poet Namdeo Dhasal, who has competently described the life of Kamatipura's women.

in a caste-stratified society. Therefore, she argues that 'caste determines the division of labour, sexual division of labour and division of sexual labour' (cited in Rege 1998: WS44).

In her article, 'Intersections of Gender and Caste', Rege et al. (2013: 36) argues: 'in analysing the caste and gender matrix in Indian society, merely pluralising the term patriarchy is not enough. The task is to map the ways in which the category "woman" is being differently reconstituted within regionally diverse patriarchal relations cross-hatched by graded caste inequalities.'

The intersection of caste and gender produces a kind of experience not reducible to patriarchy alone, nor to caste-oppression alone. A concrete example that may be useful for understanding this is the case of Bhanwari Devi (1992), a Dalit *saathin*.[16] Devi, along with members of the District Women's Development Agency, was campaigning against a one-year-old girl's marriage and was consequently gang-raped by five 'upper' caste men who were related to one other (three brothers, their uncle, and their brother-in-law) in the presence of her husband who was flogged by the assailants (Mody 2013: 190). This brutal rape was intended to punish Devi for 'interfering' in their household, where child marriage was customary, and this is indicative of the fact that a caste-stratified society finds the assertions of a Dalit woman repugnant. Had she been from an 'upper' caste family, it is less likely that she would have been regarded as sexually available by those men. Had she been a male, she might have suffered some other kind of violence but not rape. Had she not been from a lower class, options beyond working as a saathin would have been available to her. A single-axis framework for such a case thus renders a dysfunctional analysis. A merely additive evaluation of a Dalit woman's marginalization is distorting, but adequately capturing their 'difference' can play a positive role for legislative as well as social justice. That is, in their experience, the difference is not of degree but of kind.

Gopal Guru (1995), in his article, 'Dalit Women Talk Differently', puts forward several arguments to show how Dalit women are more oppressed and victimized, which results in the difference in their way of talking and living; consequentially, they become more prone to patriarchal and structural violence. The reason for

---

[16] A grassroots worker employed for a women's development project for the Government of Rajasthan.

the need of their talking differently, he argues, is that they suffer 'on the basis of external factors (non-dalit forces homogenising the issue of dalit women) and internal factors (the patriarchal domination within dalits)' (Guru 1995: 2548). The phenomenon of talking differently is regarded as an act of dissent against their exclusion from both politics and culture. He argues that since the reality is perceived from a specific social location, non-Dalit feminist theories fail to capture the reality of Dalit women. Consequentially, Dalit women's representation by non-Dalit women is 'unauthentic' (Guru 1995: 2549). Therefore, a new branch of feminism known as Dalit feminism is introduced.

In her seminal article, 'Dalit Women Talk Differently: A Critique of "Difference" and towards a Dalit Feminist Standpoint Position', Rege (1998) revisits the historical evolution of feminist discourse from Western feminism, to black feminism, to the introduction of Saidian[17] framework in feminism. She shows how white feminists fail to capture the issues of black women and how racism turns out to be 'the sole responsibility of black feminists'. The black feminists criticize the established discourse on the grounds of the difference of their experience of combined discrimination based on race and gender. Similarly, she unfolds how the problems regarding caste become 'the sole responsibility of the dalit women's organisations' in India and argues for adding more difference to the (established) difference (Rege 1998). Therefore, she suggests for an ideological position for the unrecognized plurality of women. Rege writes: 'It is imperative for feminist politics that "difference" be historically located in the real struggles of marginalised women' (Rege 1998: WS39). Based on this *difference*, she further advocates for a Dalit feminist standpoint. Rege suggests that the ignorance of the category of caste in feminist discourse also causes limited perception of violence against Muslim and Christian women, that is, only in terms of *talaq* or divorce, which is contradictory to the survey reports. The survey reports reveal a dominant linkage between caste-determined professions and violence against women involved in them. Hence, Rege reasserts that caste as a category plays a major role in 'the collective and public threat of rape, sexual

---

[17] Saidian refers to Edward Said (1935–2003), a Palestinian-American literary theorist and public intellectual who helped found the critical theory field of postcolonialism.

assault and physical violence at the workplace and in public' (Rege 1998: WS43); and therefore, the Dalit women suffer most.

Uma Chakravarti formulates a significant order of privilege and deprivation on the basis of her analysis of intersection of caste and gender in Indian society: the 'upper'[18]-caste men are most privileged; upper-caste women are more privileged; 'lower'-caste men are more deprived; whereas lower-caste women are most deprived (Chakravarti 2013[2003]). Lower-caste women are most prone to violence as they face oppression at three levels (Chakravarti 2013[2003]: 142–3): (*i*) caste-based oppression at the hands of upper castes; (*ii*) class-based oppression, as labourers mainly at the hands of upper and middle castes, who form the bulk of landowners; and (*iii*) gender-based oppression, as women who experience patriarchal oppression at the hands of all men, including men from their own caste.

In this way, subordinated caste women suffer caste-based discrimination in the vertical structure of society, and gender-based discrimination in the horizontal structure of society. Based on Ambedkar's analysis, Chakravarti (1993) conceptualizes 'Brahmanical patriarchy' or 'graded patriarchy' arguing that the question is incomplete in the absence of understanding its inherent relation with caste. We all know that cases of 'honour killing' do not belong in the domain of arranged marriages.[19] Rather, those who violate the norms of endogamy, which is a standard of socially accepted marriages, are the ones who become victims of honour killing. The couple is murdered for choosing a life partner who does not belong to their caste and has not been chosen by their parents, which is considered as bringing disgrace to their family's and community's 'honour'. Clearly, caste is regarded as honour, and anything anti-caste is considered a threat to brahmanical repute.

Rege mentions the 29 September 2006 Khairlanji case. She says that due to lack of adequate focus on the caste–gender links, the violence against Dalit women is either marked as *caste atrocity* or

---

[18] 'Upper' and 'lower' denotes the preached hierarchy of castes according to a caste-stratified system, that is, Brahmanism. I support equality of all human beings and believe that no person is upper or lower in logical terms.

[19] 'Honour killing' is the term used for such murders where people believe that they are protecting their 'honour' by killing the couple in love. However, I believe honour killings are dishonourable.

sexual atrocity (Rege 2013: 20). From a Dalit feminist standpoint, she writes:

> In the absence of such critiques of brahmanical, class-based hetropatriarchies, the political edge of sexual politics is lost. No politics committed to caste based society can overlook sexual politics. It is therefore important to revision it rather than give it up or pose the upper caste women alone as the only needy constituents of such a politics. (Rege 2000: 493)

Rege further argues that mainstream feminism does not capture the uniqueness of marginalization at the intersection point of different types of discrimination, that is, a woman faces a kind of discrimination at the intersections of her multiple identities which she may not face if she singularly belonged to any one social, cultural, economic, political, or regional category. This perspective converges with that of Ambedkar's understanding of the issue.

Ambedkar underlines the inadequacy in understanding the caste system as the 'idea of pollution' (Ambedkar 2003a: 7) and argues that its fundamental characteristic is *endogamy*, that is, the absence of intermarriage, which is its *essence* (Ambedkar 2003a: 9). In order to maintain the numerical balance between the sexes of the society, inhumane rituals like *sati pratha*,[20] enforced widowhood,[21] and child marriage were advocated by the Brahmins (Ambedkar 2003a: 14). As controlling the sexuality of women is one vital way to sustain the caste system, Ambedkar regards patriarchy as the twin of Brahmanism. Thus, the intrinsic connection between caste and gender is revealed by Ambedkar's scholarly analysis.

Chakravarti (2013[2003]: 86) and V. Geetha (2009: 108) formulate a concept of 'Dalit patriarchy' to define the patriarchal practices carried out by the members of the Dalit community. They suggest that the Dalit men, as part of their exploitation by uppercaste men, also face taunts regarding their masculinity in terms of not being able to protect their women, which results in their

---

[20] Sati pratha was the custom of a Hindu widow burning herself to death or being burned to death on the funeral pyre of her husband.

[21] Enforced widowhood describes the practice according to which a widowed woman has to alienate herself from all kinds of colours, festivals, delicious food, wedding ceremonies, deity worship functions, and so on, and she is not allowed to marry any other man.

aggressive behaviour towards their families. I argue that this concept does not hold well for two reasons. First, we do not find anything unique in the patriarchal practices followed by Dalit men: whether or not they are mocked by symbolic 'emasculation', they behave in the same manner as the non-Dalit men, very similar to even those who taunt them (Arya 2020). Therefore, the attempt to coin a different term for the same practice known as 'patriarchy' turns out to be futile. Second, as per Geetha's conception, even middle-caste (namely, OBC) men are prone to such 'emasculation', so shall we call their patriarchal practices as OBC patriarchy? Similarly, Muslim men may also face such taunts, so will their patriarchal behaviour be termed as Muslim patriarchy? Further, men from each and every caste face such discrimination by the immediate 'upper caste' and all 'upper-caste' men, so will there be plural patriarchies called Mahar patriarchy, Kunbi patriarchy, Kayastha patriarchy, or Rajput patriarchy? This will lead such a concept into the fallacy of infinite regress.

Additionally, from their writings, it is not clear whether this concept is motivated by the concept of Brahmanical patriarchy, as exposed by Ambedkar. If this is the case, these feminists fail to understand the meaning of Brahmanical patriarchy, which does not refer to the patriarchal practices followed by Brahmin men; instead, it represents the multilateral nature of patriarchy against women. Thus, the concept 'Brahmanical patriarchy' explains a specific kind of patriarchy by explicating a set of discriminatory levels, which is unique in India.

Also, if 'Dalit patriarchy' has been conceived by thinking about the new development in feminist discourse known as 'Dalit feminism', then it misses the point of the later concept. Dalit feminism in India has evolved on similar grounds of intersection as black feminism in the Western world. Black feminism recognizes the multiple deprivations faced by black women based on race and gender. Similarly, Dalit feminism recognizes the multiple deprivations faced by Dalit women based on caste and gender. They are considered as 'easy prey' by upper-caste men (Geetha 2009: 108). The concept of 'Dalit patriarchy' falls in the same fallacious category as black patriarchy would. Also, Ambedkar's feminist perspective would refute the concept as it does not stand on a logical basis. He might ask: If women are patriarchal, will we call it 'women patriarchy' or 'feminist patriarchy'?

Through the given discussion, we find that Ambedkar's perspective on issues concerning gender justice holds strong relevance in the present context and seeks to provide relevance in future also for its logical coherence, egalitarian approach, and rich ethical values. He has consistently raised the issues of inequality and degradation of women throughout his reading of those religious texts which preach inequality based on caste and gender. He strongly criticizes the commodified notion of women as a prize, property, sex object, and so on, as described in the laws made by Manu and the practices preached in the Ramayana and the Mahabharata. He also dwells upon the inbuilt linkages between caste and gender and proposes alternatives to the patriarchal norms. His critique of the ancient texts supporting patriarchal norms is logically sound. He not only evaluates the existing norms from the standards of social and political philosophy but also regards them as the founding principles to incorporate new laws for gender justice.

Ambedkar's alternatives to the patriarchal practices come in the form of HSA, Maternity Bill, the equal wage for equal labour and other feminist laws, as propounded in the Indian Constitution. He actively defends these laws, showing how they are eminently profound and practically sound, in order to pass them in the Constituent Assembly. Through these laws, he has altered the objectified value of women to a dignified member of the family and a free and equal citizen of the nation. Thus, he has attempted to ensure freedom from slavery and ignorance for Indian women through his formulation of the Hindu Code Bill, which can be seen as an instance for his pragmatic philosophy.

The contemporary relevance of Ambedkar's feminist philosophy has been discussed using the critical and hermeneutical method. His concern for the upliftment of women is clearly visible in his formulation of laws for women, irrespective of their region, religion, language, caste, and class. His feminist philosophy, just like his contributions to other disciplines, is based on three basic principles of social philosophy, namely, liberty, equality, and fraternity, and is explicitly visible across the board in his writings, speeches, and practices. The criticisms on his perspective have been counter-criticized through analytical and hypothetical methods. Thus, Ambedkar's basic principle of feminist philosophy—gender justice for all—holds strong relevance beyond the boundaries of space and limits of time (Arya and Rathore 2020). Inspired by his groundwork on feminist epistemology, let us extend our efforts to a better society with justice, equality, and freedom for everyone.

References

Ambedkar, B.R. 2003a. *Dr. Babasaheb Ambedkar: Writings and Speeches*, Vol. 1 (compiled and edited by Vasant Moon). New Delhi: Dr Ambedkar Foundation, Government of India.

———. 2003b. *Dr. Babasaheb Ambedkar: Writings and Speeches*, Vol. 3 (compiled and edited by Vasant Moon). New Delhi: Dr Ambedkar Foundation, Government of India.

———. 2003c. *Dr. Babasaheb Ambedkar: Writings and Speeches*, Vol. 4 (compiled and edited by Vasant Moon). New Delhi: Dr Ambedkar Foundation, Government of India.

———. 2003d. 'Untouchables or the Children of India's Ghetto', in *Dr. Babasaheb Ambedkar: Writings and Speeches*, Vol. 5 (compiled and edited by Vasant Moon), pp. 3–112. New Delhi: Dr Ambedkar Foundation, Government of India.

———. 2003e. *Dr. Babasaheb Ambedkar: Writings and Speeches*, Vol. 10 (compiled and edited by Vasant Moon). New Delhi: Dr Ambedkar Foundation, Government of India.

———. 2003f. *Dr. Babasaheb Ambedkar: Writings and Speeches*, Vol. 17, Part 2 (compiled and edited by Vasant Moon). New Delhi: Dr Ambedkar Foundation, Government of India.

———. 2003g. *Dr. Babasaheb Ambedkar: Writings and Speeches*, Vol. 17, Part 3 (compiled and edited by Vasant Moon). New Delhi: Dr Ambedkar Foundation, Government of India.

———. 2003h. *Dr. Babasaheb Ambedkar: Writings and Speeches*, Vol. 14, Part 1 (compiled and edited by Vasant Moon).

Arya, Sunaina. 2017. 'An Enquiry into Ambedkar as a Feminist Philosopher', MPhil dissertation, Centre for Philosophy, Jawaharlal Nehru University, New Delhi, India.

———. 2020. 'Dalit or Brahmanical Patriarchy? Rethinking Indian Feminism', *CASTE: A Global Journal on Social Exclusion* 1(1): 217–28.

Arya, Sunaina and Aakash Singh Rathore (eds). 2020. *Dalit Feminist Theory: A Reader*. Oxon, London, and Delhi: Routledge.

Beauvoir, Simon de. 2010. *The Second Sex* (translated by Constance Borde and Shiela Malovany-Chevallier). New York: Alfred A. Knopf.

Chakravarti, Uma. 1993. 'Conceptualising Brahmanical Patriarchy in Early India: Gender, Caste, Class and State', *Economic and Political Weekly* 28(14): 579–85.

———. 2013[2003]. *Gendering Caste: Through a Feminist Lens*. Kolkata: Stree.
Geetha, V. 2009. *Patriarchy*. Kolkata: Stree.
Guru, Gopal. 1995. 'Dalit Women Talk Differently', *Economic and Political Weekly* 30(41–2): 2548–50.
Menon, Nivedita. 2012. *Seeing Like a Feminist*. New Delhi: Penguin India.
Mody, Zia. 2013. *10 Judgements that Changed India*. Delhi: Penguin India.
Nair, Janaki. 1993. 'From Devadasi Reform Act to SITA: Reforming Sex Work in Mysore State, 1892–1937', *National Law School Journal* 1: 82–94.
Rathore, Aakash Singh. 2017. 'Indian Academia's Shunning of Ambedkar the Philosopher Reeks of Social Exclusion: Why Is He Untouchable by the Standards of Philosophy Departments?' *Huffington Post*, 4 April.
Rege, Sharmila. 1998. 'Dalit Women Talk Differently: A Critique of "Difference" and towards a Dalit Feminist Standpoint Position', *Economic and Political Weekly* 33(4): WS39–WS46.
———. 2000. 'Real Feminism and Dalit Women', *Economic and Political Weekly* 35(6): 492–5.
———. 2013. *Against the Madness of Manu: B.R. Ambedkar's Writings on Brahmanical Patriarchy*. New Delhi: Navayana.
Rege, Sharmila, J. Devika, K. Kannabiran, M.E. John, P. Swaminathan, and S. Sen. 2013. 'Intersections of Gender and Caste', *Economic and Political Weekly* 48(18): 35–6.

5

Ambedkar on Women's Empowerment and the Status of Dalit Women in Karnataka

MALA MUKHERJEE

Babasaheb Bhimrao Ambedkar is remembered as the prime architect of the Indian Constitution and the chief crusader against untouchability and caste system. Born in a Mahar family at Mhow in Madhya Pradesh on 14 April 1891, Ambedkar faced both caste oppression as well as social rigidity. This encouraged him to challenge the social order from a rational point of view. He left India for higher studies and completed his doctoral thesis from Columbia University in the United States (US), and then pursued a law degree from England. He came back to India as an advocate and decided to fight for the plight of the oppressed castes. He penned down the agony of the lower castes in his journals, *Mooknayak* (1920) and *Bahishkrit Bharat* (1927). His famous book, *Annihilation of Caste*, openly urged for eradication of the caste system which was maintained through 'caste endogamy' (Ambedkar 1990). Ambedkar was one of the few social reformers who realized that annihilation of caste was not possible without women empowerment, as women were the means to maintain caste purity through 'endogamy' or 'arranged marriages'. Thus, women in India were not only facing patriarchy but also experiencing 'caste–patriarchy' nexus, which could be obliterated through 'inter-caste marriage'.

He believed that development of women leadership in social reform movements would help to bring in positive changes and simultaneously, he also encouraged married women to take part in their husband's activities and abandon the life of household slaves (Gunjal 2012). During the 1927 Mahad Satyagraha (in present-day Raigad district in Maharashtra), women marched in the procession along with men (Dhanvijay 2012).

His main achievement towards women empowerment was the codification of the Hindu Code Bill (1956), which ensured Hindu women's equal rights in marriage, adoption, inheritance, and guardianship of minors. At the same time, the Bill abolished polygamy, legalized inter-caste marriage, and ensured women's right to claim divorce. The Hindu Code Bill faced strong opposition in the Parliament and this compelled Ambedkar to resign from his post of law minister; however, later on, it was adopted in four phases.

Gender-sensitive labour laws based on the norms of equal work and equal wage, maternity leave, and banning of women workers in underground mines were his other contributions towards women empowerment. During the drafting of the Constitution, he ensured universal adult suffrage or equal voting rights for men and women, along with gender and caste equality before law. The Directive Principles of the State Policy ensured affirmative action for women to access their basic rights as well as citizenship.

Long before the term 'women empowerment' was coined, Ambedkar believed that a community's progress could be measured only by the degree of progress achieved by women (Ambedkar 1990). In his book, *The Rise and Fall of Hindu Women*, he portrayed how women of ancient India, who once enjoyed equal rights as their male counterparts, had fallen into the trap of male chauvinism, supported by some scriptures, and lost their right to access education and employment (*Mahabodhi* 1950). They gradually lost their right to choose life partners and were compelled to accept 'arranged marriage' or 'caste endogamy' as their destiny.

Gail Omvedt (1994), an eminent sociologist, remarked that 'Dalit women are Dalit among Dalit'. Ambedkar, too, described the Hindu caste system as having a pyramidal hierarchy in which the Brahmins and Kshatriyas were at the top and the Shudras were at the bottom. Within each of these castes, men were at the top and women were at the bottom (Paswan and Jaideva 2002: 72).

The United Nations' (UN) concept of 'women empowerment' is not different from that of the Ambedkarite philosophy. The UN has defined women empowerment through five components: (*i*) women's sense of self-worth; (*ii*) women's right to have and determine choices; (*iii*) women's right to have access to opportunities and resources; (*iv*) women's right to have control of their own lives, both within and beyond home; and (*v*) women's ability to influence the direction of social change to create more just social and economic order. These five components can be achieved by promoting gender equality, gender mainstreaming, networking, leadership, and financial freedom. However, quoting Ambedkar, we can say that it is important to 'organise, educate & agitate' to achieve these five components, rather than pleading for equality (Ambedkar 1979).

The aim of this chapter, thus, is to analyse the status of Dalit women in Karnataka in light of Ambedkar's philosophy. To achieve this, the following objectives have been adopted:

1. To establish a linkage between gender, caste intersectionality, and women empowerment in light of Ambedkar's view.
2. To analyse women empowerment across social groups through educational attainment and access to employment.
3. To assess vulnerability of women from different socio-economic spheres by addressing social group-wise gap in accessing resources and services, with special focus on Karnataka.

Data Sources and Methodology

This chapter is based on secondary data sources collected from various literature, official documents, and reports to highlight women-specific issues among the Dalit community. The phases and evolution of Dalit women's movement in Karnataka are described in the following section to link it with contemporary women issues. Based on this history, contemporary data are analysed to find out the present status of Scheduled Caste (SC) women in terms of access to education and employment, and to find out the inbuilt causes behind gender gap in all these parameters.

Statistical techniques have been employed to analyse the Census data. For pictorial representation, ArcGIS software has been used to make thematic maps showing regional variation in the status of SC women within the state.

Linkage between Dalit and Women's Movements in Karnataka

The socio-religious movement that began among the Dalit population in Karnataka took three different paths. The first one remained within the Hindu social order and tried to reform the society. The second one encouraged embracing another religion to escape from caste-divided Hindu social order. This second stream was influenced by Ambedkar's philosophy and embraced Buddhism to escape untouchability. The third stream declared a separate 'identity' for the Dalit population, as the indigenous people of the land. The Adi Dharmi movements in the form of Adi Dravida and Adi Karnataka sprang up in the state. Though Ambedkar launched his anti-caste movement in Maharashtra, his work and Jyotirao Phule's philosophy influenced the Dalit leaders of Mysore, Madras, and Hyderabad states. Devaraya Ingale, who was two years older than Ambedkar, started the anti-caste movement in the Belgaum region of Karnataka. He tried to denounce surnames indicating caste status of a particular individual. He also criticized the *devadasi* system[1] and asked Dalits to denounce the practice of eating the flesh of dead animals.

B. Shyamsundar (1930) started the anti-caste movement in the Nizam's state of Hyderabad and established separate educational institutions (Madrasa-e-Pastakam) and hostels for Dalit children (Yadav 1998). However, Ambedkarite movement in Karnataka gained momentum in the 1960s due to the establishment of Ambedkar's statue at the main road in Bidar city. B. Shyamsundar's Dalit movement took off with a new zeal. In 1968, he established Bhim Sena at a big rally in Gulbarga. Gradually, Bhim Sena became popular in other states and it started fighting for Dalit rights against upper-caste landlords (Yadav 1998). This movement

---

[1] Devadasi is a term that means 'servant of god'. This is a system in which a girl is dedicated to god. It involves a traditional ceremony and is performed before the girl hits puberty.

advocated for separate universities, constituencies, and political parties for the Dalits. Though this movement was mainly focused on Dalit rights rather than women's rights, it fought against two inhuman practices prevalent against the women belonging to the Dalit community. The first one was the devadasi system, which was prevalent among the Yellamma cult. This system forced poor women to marry the goddess and enter into temple prostitution. Another evil practice was *bettale seve* or nude worship of Goddess Renukamba in Chandragutti temple of Shimoga district. Devotees took bath in the Varada River and ran up to the temple, covering a distance of 5 kilometres, without clothing, to fulfil their vows. The 'Chandragutti Incident' of 1986 was in response to the protest demonstration organized by Dalit activists to stop women from performing this ritual. It forced the government to ban such inhuman practices in the name of religion (Epp 1992).

Basavalingappa, a Karnataka cabinet minister, resigned from his post and formed the Dalit Sangharsha Samiti (DSS) to continue the battle of oppressed castes for an equitable society. In 1978, the first state meeting of DSS was held in Bhadravati town and it incorporated various wings for students, activists, workers, and women, but did not support any existing political parties' agenda. However, 1990s onwards, the DSS started supporting candidates to gain political power, without supporting their party agenda (Subramaniam 2006; Yadav 1998).

The journal *Dalit Voice* fostered Basavalingappa's extreme anticaste ideology through its writings and tried to strengthen the Dalit movement of Karnataka. Though the movement initiated by DSS remained localized, it provided a platform to the Dalit people to protest against caste-based discrimination. Initially, Dalit movements raised women issues but later adopted a protectionist approach, in which women were treated as 'vulnerable' and required 'protection' to save community honour.

Ruth Manorama, a crusader for Dalit women's rights, took initiative to organize the socially marginalized women, especially the slum dwellers in Bengaluru city, and began to speak about 'triple oppression' of Dalit women under 'poverty, patriarchy, and untouchability'. Her efforts created a separate platform for Dalit women and encouraged the government to launch the Mahila Samakhya Karnataka (MSK) programme. The MSK aimed to enhance the literacy rate and schooling among Dalit girls along with skill development and participation in various activities, including gram panchayats (Subramaniam 2006). The MSK was not target driven but based on outcomes. Manorama argued that gender inequality must be studied from the caste–class axis of stratification because these mediate every aspect of Indian women's lives and movement. The mainstream Dalit movement could not bring about women leadership and they started analysing women issues as an integral part of the 'community's honour', but women's complex agencies were denied. Therefore, the National Federation of Dalit Women was formed to understand the issues of Dalit women separately.

Dalit Population in Karnataka

The SC population in Karnataka accounts for 17.1 per cent of the total state population and is slightly higher than the national average (16.6 per cent). In 2011, the percentage of SC population was slightly higher than 16 per cent and now, it is above 17 per cent. In rural areas, 20 per cent of the total population is SC and in urban areas, it is 12.6 per cent. Thus, the SC population is mainly found in rural Karnataka.

District-wise variation in population distribution records that Kolar has the highest percentage of SC population (above 30 per cent), followed by Chamarajanagar and Gulbarga which record more than 25 per cent. Udupi, Dakshina Kannada, and Uttara Kannada record the lowest proportion of SC population. In 2001, Chitradurga also recorded very high proportion of SC population, but in 2011, it showed a decline. Coastal Karnataka records very low proportion of SC population and Belgaum and Gulbarga divisions record the highest proportion (Figure 5.1 [A, B]).

Decadal growth of SC population is the highest in Gulbarga, Bidar, Kolar, Koppal, and Gadag, and lowest in coastal Karnataka and the southern part of the state. In Bengaluru (rural and urban), the proportion of SC population is low.

The districts with high percentage of SC population have always remained in the limelight with regard to Dalit movement. Thus, Kolar, Bidar, and Shimoga have always remained the main nerve centres of Dalit movement. On the other hand, Dalit movement has not been so strong in the districts having less number of SC

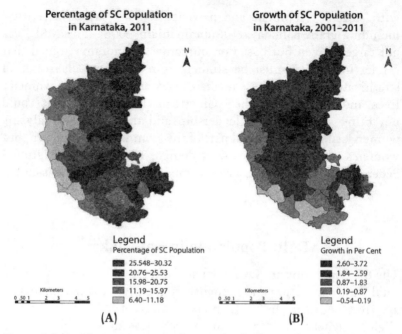

Figure 5.1 (A, B) Percentage and Growth of SC Population in Karnataka (2001–11)

Source: Generated by the author using Census (2011a and 2011b) data.

population. The recent news of the purification of Udupi temple surroundings (2016) after the meeting of Dalit people raises the question of humanism over politics and rituals (*Indian Express* 2016).

Composition of SC Population in Karnataka

The SC population of Karnataka incorporates more than 100 sub-castes and they are not homogenous in nature. Generally, these sub-castes are further divided into *Edgai*, the left-hand caste, and *Balgai*, the right-hand caste. The right-hand SC subgroups are mainly agricultural labourers and the left-hand sub-castes work as sweepers, cobblers, cleaners, and so on. These two sub-castes practise endogamy and do not interdine with each other. The left-hand ones are considered as the untouchables, but the right-hand ones are 'clean Shudra' or 'touchable' (Ghosh 2016; Natraj and Natraj

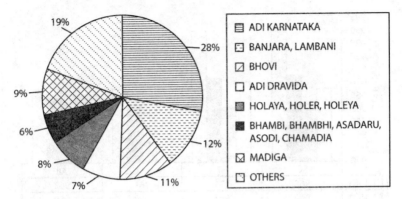

Figure 5.2 Composition of SC Population in Karnataka (2011)
Source: Computed from Census (2011b).

1984). Adi Karnataka is the numerically dominating sub-caste among the SC population, comprising 28 per cent of the total SC population, followed by Banjara (12 per cent), Bhovi (11 per cent), Madiga (9 per cent), Holaya (8 per cent), and Bhambi (6 per cent) (see Figure 5.2).

Women in SC Population

The status of SC population cannot be measured effectively unless and until data on their women population is analysed. Sex ratio is the first important indicator that reveals the male–female composition of a particular population subgroup. The data reveal that the overall sex ratio of SC population is better than that of their non-SC/Scheduled Tribe (ST) counterparts. The overall sex ratio of Karnataka was 968 females per 1,000 males in 2011, with SC and ST population recording 990 females per 1,000 males, which is higher than the state-level average. Sex ratio is also showing an increasing trend over time (Figure 5.3).

District-level analysis reveals that the sex ratio is favourable for women in southern Karnataka (Chikmagalur, Hassan, Udupi, and Kodagu districts). Child sex ratio is also favourable for girls in Chikmagalur, Hassan, and Kodagu districts. The SC adult and child sex ratios are not favourable for women in the districts having high proportion of SC population (Figure 5.4 [A, B]).

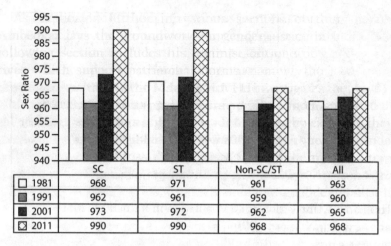

Figure 5.3 Social Group-wise Sex Ratio
Source: Census (2011b).

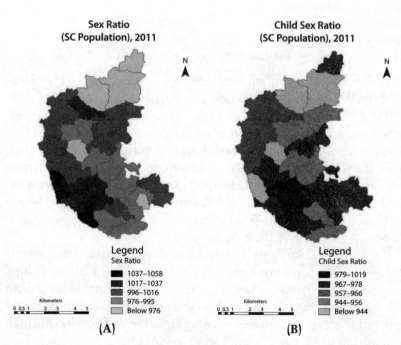

Figure 5.4 (A, B) Adult and Child Sex Ratio of SC Population in Karnataka
Source: Generated by the author using Census (2011a, 2011b, 2011c) data.

Status of Dalit Women in Karnataka

Access to Education

The first and foremost principle of women empowerment is 'educate, organize, and agitate'. Education is the first component which indicates empowerment. However, in India, the female literacy rate is still lower than the male literacy rate, and it is further lower in case of socially excluded communities like the SCs/STs. According to Census (2011a), literacy rate is higher in the southern coast of Karnataka and Bengaluru as compared to the northern districts. Thus, districts recording higher percentage of SC population record low male and female literacy. Udupi records the highest literacy rate (71 per cent), followed by Uttara Kannada; and Yadgir records the lowest literacy rate (35 per cent). Bagalkot, Raichur, Koppal, Bellary, and Gulbarga also record literacy rates lower than 50 per cent. This pattern is observed for both male and female literacy rates. However, the gap in male and female literacy rates is acutely high in Bijapur (more than 20 per cent), Raichur, Yadgir, and Bagalkot.

The gap between male and female literacy rates among the SC community is well supported by other data sources. For example, the highest percentage of children out of school in the age group of 7–14 years is that of SC and ST girls (see Figure 5.5).

Another indicator is the rate of enrolment of SC female candidates in higher education institutes. After the age of 20, it shows a rapid decline and is only 14.5 per cent in the age group of 25–9 years, while the percentage of male candidates shows an increase from 72.7 per cent to 85.5 per cent (Table A5.1). Therefore, it is evident that SC women do not have adequate access to higher education (Figure 5.6 [A–D]).

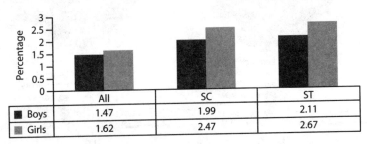

Figure 5.5 Percentage of Children Out of School in the Age Group of 7–14 Years

Source: Census (2011b: 221).

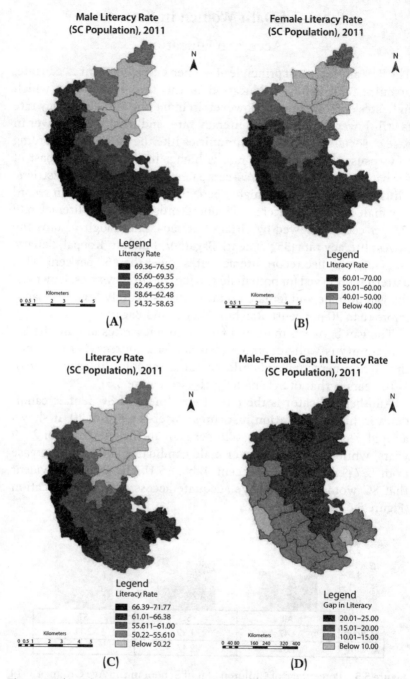

Figure 5.6 (A–D) Literacy Rates and Gender Gap

Source: Generated by the author using Census (2011a, 2011b, 2011c) data.

Access to Employment

Access to employment is another crucial indicator which shows an individual's or community's access to resources. Work participation rate (WPR) is a basic measurement which shows the number of people who are actively employed or looking for jobs. In India, male WPR is much higher than the female WPR, however, this picture largely varies across regions and communities. The SC/ST population generally record higher WPR for women. In Karnataka, SC women in some districts record higher WPR and the gap between male and female WPR is also low. However, an inverse relationship exists between WPR and literacy rates. Districts with higher gap in literacy rates record low gap in WPR. Also, urbanized districts like Bengaluru (urban) and Udupi record lower WPR for SC women (Figure 5.7 [A, B]).

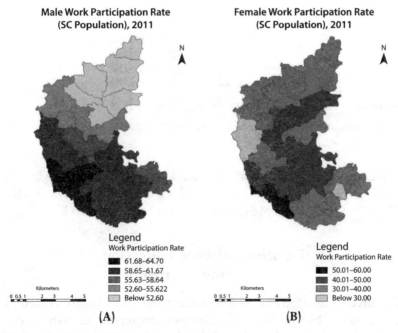

Figure 5.7 (A, B) Male and Female WPR

Source: Generated by the author using Census (2011a, 2011b, 2011c) data.

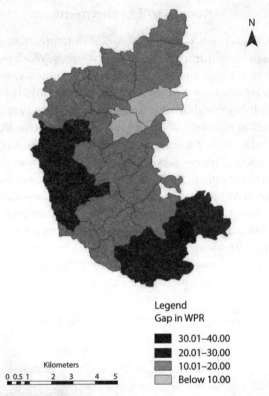

Figure 5.8 Gender Gap in WPR (SC Population), 2011
Source: Generated by the author using Census (2011a, 2011b, 2011c) data.

District-wise data reveal that gender gap in WPR is higher in southern Karnataka and the coastal part, but low in the north, where the percentage of SC population is high (Figure 5.8).

Relation between Education and Employment

The inverse relation between education and employment is further strengthened by the Census data on workers according to their educational level. It has been found that SC female workers are mainly illiterate and work as agricultural labourers. There are very few SC women with graduate and above degree, or technical degree, who are employed as main workers. There are 6.4 per cent SC male workers with graduate or higher degree but only 2.6 per cent female workers are found in this category. More than 85 per cent SC female main workers work as agricultural labourers, while 60.3 per cent males are found in this category. In the 'Other' works, while 68 per cent SC male workers are literate, only 37.7 per cent women workers are literate.

The inverse relationship between women work participation and literacy rate supports the fact that despite high WPR among SC women, most of them are found either in the agricultural sector or in other low-paid jobs (Figures 5.9 and 5.10).

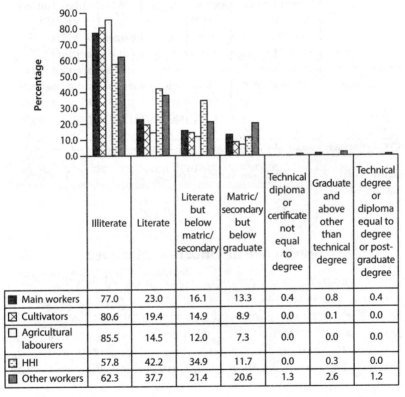

	Illiterate	Literate	Literate but below matric/secondary	Matric/secondary but below graduate	Technical diploma or certificate not equal to degree	Graduate and above other than technical degree	Technical degree or diploma equal to degree or post-graduate degree
Main workers	77.0	23.0	16.1	13.3	0.4	0.8	0.4
Cultivators	80.6	19.4	14.9	8.9	0.0	0.1	0.0
Agricultural labourers	85.5	14.5	12.0	7.3	0.0	0.0	0.0
HHI	57.8	42.2	34.9	11.7	0.0	0.3	0.0
Other workers	62.3	37.7	21.4	20.6	1.3	2.6	1.2

Figure 5.9 Educational Background of SC Female Main Workers in Karnataka (2011)

Source: Calculated from Census (2011a, 2011b, 2011c).

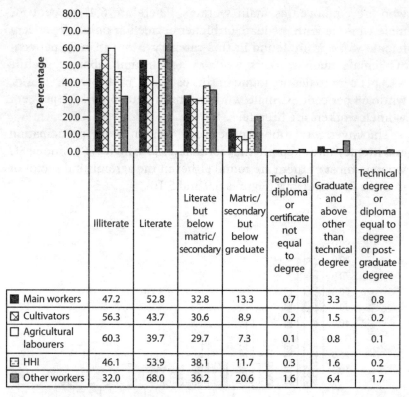

Figure 5.10 Educational Background of SC Male Main Workers in Karnataka (2011)

Source: Calculated from Census (2011a, 2011b, 2011c).

Prevalence of Underage Marriage

The data analysis in the previous section revealed that SC women have less access to education as compared to their male counterparts, due which early marriage is common among the girls. The Census data reveals that there are ever-married[2] girls whose age is under 15 years and their percentage varies largely across the districts. Data from Bagalkot, Bengaluru (urban), Bijapur, Hassan,

---

[2] The term 'ever-married' is used in Census to refer those who have been married only once in their lifetime, including widows, women who are separated, and women whose husbands are alive. This term is used to set these women apart from currently married women or women living with their husbands. The unmarried population is referred to as 'never married'.

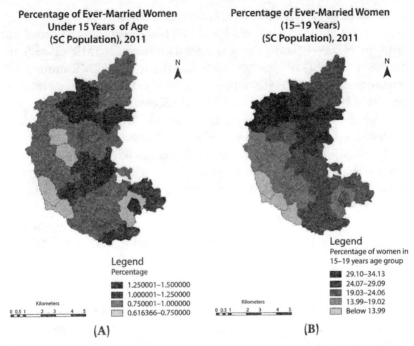

Figure 5.11 (A, B) Percentage of Ever-Married Women in the SC Population
Source: Generated by the author by using Census (2011a) data, F-Series.

Mandya, Mysore, and some other districts shows that more than 1 per cent girls under the age of 15 years are already married.

This percentage increases for the age group of 15–19 years. The legal age for marriage in India is 18 years, so this age group records a sudden increase in the percentage of girls reported as 'ever-married'. The districts of northern Karnataka record (Bagalkot and Belgaum) the highest number of 'ever-married' girls in the 15–19 age group (Figure 5.11 [A, B]).

Health Deprivation

Low literacy rate and prevalence of underage marriage among the SC girls often leads to adverse health outcomes. The SC/ST population records higher infant and child mortality as well as low body mass index (BMI) among women of reproductive age group.

Social group-wise segregation shows that ST and SC population record higher infant mortality rate (IMR), child mortality rate (CMR), and under-five mortality rate (U5MR) as compared to other backward class (OBC) and others. The IMR of SC was 69.9 in NFHS-2 and declined to 57.2 in NFHS-3, but OBCs recorded 53 IMR in NFHS-3, and others recorded the lowest IMR of 43.5 in NFHS-3. The SC population recorded the lowest CMR among all social groups in NFHS-3, which is 8.7 only, while earlier NFHS-2 recorded 37.4. Therefore, it is a big achievement. The U5MR for SC was 104.6 in NFHS-2 and declined to 65.4 in NFHS-3, but U5MR is lower among the OBCs (63.8) and others (60.4) (Table A5.2).

The BMI of women of reproductive age group (15–49 years) shows that Karnataka recorded 38.8 per cent of them as underweight in NFHS-2 and this percentage reduced to 35.5 per cent in NFHS-3. Social group-wise segregation shows that ST records 48.7 per cent and SC records 40.6 per cent underweight women, but the percentage is much lower among the OBCs (33.7 per cent) and others (29.3 per cent) (Table A5.3).

Linkage between Historical Process of Denial and Contemporary Practices of Discrimination

Secondary data analysis reveals the male–female gap in access to education and formal employment, which makes women more vulnerable to underage marriage and leads to negative health outcomes for both mothers and children. This gap can be explained through the historical process of denial that the Dalit population has faced since time immemorial, including discrimination, along with the burden of patriarchy, faced by their womenfolk. Higher education for girls is still a luxury for many poor households. Moreover, if the household is dependent on traditional caste-based occupation, then early marriage of girls and early engagement of boys in workforce provides them economic benefit.

To check this process of historical denial, various policies and programmes have been implemented across the country, and Karnataka is no exception. Universal access to education, introduction of various scholarships for women, especially those belonging to backward communities, and affirmative actions in various sectors of the economy have provided opportunities to everyone for social mobility. In the health sector, especially in maternal and child health, the government has implemented free healthcare facilities for mothers and children. Despite these sincere efforts, why do gaps still exist in all spheres?

To answer this question, one must move beyond secondary data. Field studies conducted by the Indian Institute of Dalit Studies (IIDS) reveal that Dalit women not only face patriarchy within their households but also face untouchability while accessing various services. In the healthcare centres, SC women do not get proper attention from the service providers and remain less informed about the necessary information; this leads to high infant and child mortality among the SC communities (Acharya and Sabharwal 2014). In the schools, separate seating arrangement and utensils for SC children are noticed; this discourages them from continuing their education. In case of girls, dropping out from school often results in early marriages and child-bearing, and also encourages them to work as agricultural labourers to assist their fathers or husbands.

Therefore, the linkage between the historical process of untouchability and contemporary practices of discrimination explains why SC women are lagging behind in terms of education, employment, and health. The gaps explain that inbuilt processes of discriminations are still operating and this is pushing the socially marginalized communities further away from the mainstream, thereby making women belonging to these communities even more vulnerable.

References

Acharya, Sanghmitra and Nidhi S. Sabharwal. 2014. 'Enabling Environment for Social Inclusion in Universal Access to Reproductive and Child Health: Situational Analysis of Selected Villages of Uttar Pradesh, Madhya Pradesh and Karnataka'. A UNICEF-IIDS report, Indian Institute of Dalit Studies (IIDS), New Delhi.

Ambedkar, B.R. 1979. *Dr. Babasaheb Ambedkar: Writings and Speeches*, Vol. 1. Bombay: The Education Department, Government of Maharashtra.

———. 1990. *Annihilation of Caste: An Undelivered Speech*. New Delhi: Arnold Publishers.

Census. 2011a. *F-1: Number of Women and Ever Married Women by Present Age, Parity and Total Children Ever Born by Sex*, Office of the Registrar General & Census Commissioner, India, Ministry of Home Affairs, Government of India.

———. 2011b. SC PCA Series, Office of the Registrar General & Census Commissioner, India, Ministry of Home Affairs, Government of India.

―――. 2011c. 'C-8: Educational Level by Age and Sex for Population 7 and Above'. In *C Series: Social and Cultural Tables*. New Delhi: Ministry of Home Affairs, Government of India.

Dhanvijay, Vaishali. 2012. 'Dr. Babasaheb Ambedkar's Efforts for Women Empowerment and Present Status of Women in Society'. *Electronic International Interdisciplinary Research Journal* (EIIRJ) I(II), ISSN 2277–8721. Available at http://www.irjims.com; last accessed on 3 March 2016.

Epp, Linda J. 1992. 'Dalit Struggle, Nude Worship, and the "Chandragutti Incident"'. *Sociological Bulletin* 41(1–2): 145–68.

Ghosh, S. 2016. 'What Are Scheduled Caste Left and Scheduled Caste Right in Karnataka?' *Oneindia*. Available at http://www.oneindia.com/feature/what-are-scheduled-caste-left-scheduled-caste-right-in-karnataka-2110902.html; last accessed on 1 August 2017.

Gunjal V.R. 2012. 'Dr. Babasaheb Ambedkar and Women Empowerment'. *Social Work* XI(1): 84–5.

Indian Express, The. 2016. '"Purification" Ceremony Conducted in Udupi After Dalit Meeting: Report'. 29 October. Available at http://indianexpress.com/article/india/india-news-india/purification-ceremony-conducted-in-udupi-after-dalit-meeting-report-3105041/; last accessed on 1 August 2017.

International Institute for Population Sciences (IIPS) and ORC Macro. 2000. *National Family Health Survey (NFHS-2), 1997–98: India*. Mumbai: IIPS.

―――. 2006. *National Family Health Survey (NFHS-3), 2004–05: India*. Mumbai: IIPS.

Mahabodhi (Calcutta), The. 1950. 'The Rise and Falls of the Hindu Women', 59.5–6: 139–51. New Delhi: Arya Sudha, Women Gender Equality and the State, Deep and Deep Publications.

Natraj, L. and V.K. Natraj. 1984. 'Backward Classes, Minorities and the Karnataka Elections', in George Mathew (ed.), *Shift in Indian Politics: 1983 Elections in Andhra Pradesh and Karnataka*, pp. 35–60. New Delhi: Concept.

Omvedt, Gail. 1994. *Dalits and the Democratic Revolution: Dr. Ambedkar and the Dalit Movement in Colonial India*. New Delhi: Sage Publications.

Paswan, Sanjay and Paramanshi Jaideva (eds). 2002. 'The Last among Dalits', in *Encyclopaedia of Dalits in India: Women*, Vol. 9, p. 71–80. Delhi: Kalpaz.

Subramaniam, Mangala. 2006. *The Power of Women's Organizing: Gender, Caste, and Class in India*. Lanham, MD: Lexington Books.

Yadav, Manohar. 1998. 'Career of Dalit Movement in Karnataka'. *Journal of Social and Economic Development* 1(1): 107–27.

Appendix

Table A5.1 Percentage of Male and Female SC Students Attending College and Higher Education Institutes, 2011

Age Group (years)	Male (%)	Female (%)	Gap (%)
Total	72.7	27.3	45.5
20–4	75.4	24.6	50.9
25–9	85.5	14.5	71.0

Source: Census (2011c).

Table A5.2 Infant and Childhood Mortality Indicators for Social Groups

Year	IMR					CMR					U5MR				
	SC	ST	OBC	Others	All	SC	ST	OBC	Others	All	SC	ST	OBC	Others	All
1998–9 (NFHS-2)	69.9	85.0	60.6	56.4	62.3	37.4	38.9	18.7	14.2	22.9	104.6	120.6	78.2	69.8	83.3
2005–6 (NFHS-3)	57.2	45.8	53.0	43.5	53	8.7	33.6	11.4	17.7	13.9	65.4	77.9	63.8	60.4	66.2

Note: IMR: infant mortality rate; CMR: child mortality rate; U5MR: under-five mortality rate; SC: scheduled caste; ST: scheduled tribe; OBC: other backward class.

Source: National Family Health Survey (NFHS)-2 and NFHS-3 (International Institute for Population Sciences [IIPS] and ORC Macro 2000, 2006).

Table A5.3 Percentage of Underweight Women (BMI < 18.5) between Ages 15 and 49

Years	SC	ST	OBC	Others	All
1998–9	44.2	49.0	40.1	32.8	38.8
2005–6	40.6	48.7	33.7	29.3	35.5

Source: NFHS-2 and NFHS-3 (IIPS and ORC Macro 2000, 2006).

6

Constructing a New Female Subjectivity

Ambedkar's Perspective

KOMAL RAJAK AND N. SUKUMAR

This chapter interrogates the emergence of a new female subjectivity in colonial India based on the philosophical contributions of Ambedkar. It attempts to delineate the practices, nature, process, outcomes, and ideals of such an endeavour. Very often, there prevails a reductionist understanding of Ambedkar based on his writings and discourses on caste. However, he also developed a unique feminist epistemology. The predominantly Brahmanical scholarship is guilty of academic erasures when it comes to radical intertwining of caste hierarchy and gender oppression. In his scholarly writings and public addresses, Ambedkar never failed to exhort women to shed their cultural veil of purity and participate in the public sphere. In his efforts to liberate women from the stranglehold of tradition, Ambedkar inverted the Altekarian paradigm. The triumvirate of Phule, Ambedkar, and Periyar strove to dismantle the structural roots of female oppression in Indian society. Starting from the 1920s, Ambedkar raised various issues concerning women in his journals, *Mooknayak* and *Bahishkrit Bharat*.

Pure and Impure Bodies

In Indian society, caste occupies an omnipresence which is unparalleled. This idea is further buttressed through scriptural injunctions and sanctified by cultural codes. Needless to say, women are the vital element in maintaining and perpetuating the system. In the Brahmanized universe, the purity of caste is contingent on the purity of women and so they have to be kept under constant surveillance. They are the producers of producers. For apprehending the patriarchal structure and gendered inequality, extrapolating the substructure—that is, caste system—is required, which provides fuel to the functioning and preservation of patriarchy in the Indian context.

A popular proverb states that women have no caste and just like water poured into a vessel, her identity gets shaped by the family or community she belongs to. For instance, though a caste Hindu woman might be oppressed in the domestic sphere, she enjoys more privileges than the men belonging to the lower social strata. The patriarchy, based on caste identity, subjugates both women and men from the lower castes. They are denied any right over their selves and are treated worse than slaves. The Brahmanical scriptures use derogatory terms for those who transgress caste norms. Even extreme violence is sanctioned against such people in order to restore faith in the 'system'. The lower-caste women bear the triple burden of gender, caste, and class. Their male counterparts are constantly ridiculed for failing to 'protect' their women from the predatory caste Hindu males. No wonder, Ambedkar was scathing in his critique of such an obnoxious social order:

> Caste has killed public spirit, destroyed the sense of public charity and made public opinion impossible. A Hindu's 'Public' is his caste. His responsibility and loyalty is restricted merely to his caste. Virtue and morality have become caste-ridden and caste-bound respectively. There is no sympathy for the deserving, no appreciation of the meritorious, and no charity to the needy ... there is charity but commences with caste and ends with caste. There is sympathy but not for men of other castes. (Ambedkar 2008: 29–30)

When it comes to the question of women, many scholars have described the intersectionality of caste and gender. As argued by Shailaja Paik:

Gender within a caste society is defined and structured in such a manner that the 'manhood' of the caste is determined both by the degree of male control over women and the degree of passivity of the women of that particular caste. By the same argument, demonstrating control by humiliating women of another caste is a[n] irrefutable way of reducing the 'manhood' of those castes. (Quoted in Kannabiran and Kannabiran 2003: 254)

In this, caste Hindu women too have taken the stance of men of their community, which was reflected in the Khairlanji massacre in 2006 (Teltumbde 2010) and the Chilakurti case in 1991 (Kannabiran and Kannabiran 2003: 254). In the anti-Mandal agitation, many girls carried placards that they do not crave for unemployed husbands (Chakravarti 2003a: 1). This replicates the notion of purity attached to the *dvija*[1] castes and how 'their' girls are not ready to accept qualified lower-caste men as their prospective partners. They prefer to align with their community, instead of gender, in order to perpetuate the idea of the purity of Brahmin caste, and this notion of purity functions through endogamy, therefore turning women into virtual gateways of the caste order (Ambedkar 2013[1916]: 11–12).

Sharmila Rege similarly argues that in the Brahmanical social order, caste-based division along with sexual division of labour are intermeshed in a very complicated way and the elevation in caste status is preceded by the withdrawal of women of that particular caste from productive processes in the public domain. Due to their marginal economic status, lower-caste women are forced to work, which renders them visible and available to men belonging to the superior castes. The entrenched Brahmanism locates the 'lower-caste' women's participation in the public sphere as the failure of 'their' men in controlling the women and thereby rendering them impure (Rege 2003: 94).

Caste and gender are deeply entwined in the Indian subcontinent, which makes women's suppression distinctive in its own way. This entanglement stifles the women hierarchically, in which lower-caste women are besmirched more than caste Hindu women.

---

[1] It means 'twice-born', which, as a concept, is premised on the belief that a person is first born physically and later, born for a second time, spiritually, usually when he undergoes the rite of *Janeu samskara* that is believed to initiate him into his caste.

As Gopal Guru (1995) holds, lower-caste women are subjugated through a twofold patriarchal structure, constituted by Brahmanical patriarchy which intensely stigmatizes lower-caste women because of their 'lowered' caste status on the one hand, and patriarchal control of lower-caste men over the sexual and economic labour of 'their' women on the other hand.[2]

The dominant feminist discourse that developed during the 1970s does not consider women's inferior stipulation with its caste angle, and undertakes caste as the solitary concern of lower-caste women only. Thus, it bypasses the need for all women to critically interrogate the complex histories of caste and gender oppression (Rege 2003: 4). This dominant feminism takes woman as a collective identity that is suppressed just because of its 'womanhood'. Since 'woman' is not a homogenous category, especially in the Indian milieu, the issues of women's sexuality, which is a primary site of contest for superiority of Brahmins, are intrinsically linked with caste.[3] Therefore, women's enslavement cannot be even addressed without posing challenges to its base structure, namely, Brahmanism,[4] and the feminism that does not defy Brahmanism or caste structure is simply a 'Brahmanized feminism' which is considered as lifestyle feminism by Rege (2003: 90–3), while Uma Chakravarti (2003b: 164) has termed it as dominant class ideology of gender relations.

Thus, there prevails an epistemological vacuum, wherein the dominant feminists display a warped understanding towards thinkers and activists who hail from the lower rungs of society, despite their struggles to enable women in accomplishing an equal footing in society. Anupama Rao (2003), in the introduction of her anthological work, *Gender and Caste*, argues that Indian feminism is exclusionary as it excludes some groups of women, especially women belonging to the lower castes, from its focus area because it works in a casteist structure of society. Lower-caste women do experience patriarchal control both by Brahmins, whether it is men or women, who perceive them as inferior sexual objects, and by the men of lower caste, who see them as sexual property.

---

[2] Rao (2003: 1) also argued on this parameter.

[3] B.R. Ambedkar (2013), Sharmila Rege (2003), Uma Chakravarti (2003b), and Mary E. John (2008) elaborated this in their respective works.

[4] It works through the ideology of caste superiority and inferiority.

Rao's argument is similar to Ambedkar's ideas on the centrality of gendered relationships, within and between the castes, where caste supremacy has been replicated. In these gendered relationships, lower-caste women have been made to suffer sexual violence from upper-caste men and have also been made available to high-caste men for fulfilling their carnal desires through *religiously sanctioned* customs, such as *devadasis*[5] and so on.

Women's Subjugation: Ambedkarian Premise

Ambedkar philosophizes the question of gender and caste and offers interesting insights to elucidate the functioning of caste patriarchy. For him, Indian patriarchy is Brahmanical as it is conceived intentionally by Brahmins in order to perpetuate their caste superiority. Caste system and its notions of purity and pollution—according to which some castes are considered pure in their very origin, while others are considered inferior—depend upon the 'blood purity' of caste group, which can be upheld merely through endogamy.

In his very first scholarly analysis of the prevailing social hierarchies, *Caste in India: Their Mechanism, Genesis and Development* (Ambedkar 2013[1916]), Ambedkar presents women's concerns wherein he propounds the organic connections between the origin and sustenance of the caste system and, by way of its functioning, the subjugation of women. Here, endogamy emerges as an instrument through which this liaison works, as he argues that without endogamy, caste hierarchy cannot persist and castes will get muddled up otherwise. For Ambedkar, caste system is the quintessence of Hinduism which survives merely through an embargo on inter-caste marriages as it is based upon the notion of purity—caste purity hinges upon blood purity since the purity of caste can remain intact, as it is claimed, only if both parents are of same caste. Since women are considered as the gateway of caste system because of their procreational capacity, the burden of maintaining caste purity falls upon them and hence, it is essential to maintain strict surveillance over them (Ambedkar 2014, Vol. 3: 144). Thus, caste and consequently, the Hindu cultural ethos provide the underlining structure of women's subjugation.

---

[5] This custom is like an 'extramarital but socially accepted' affair for 'high-caste' men.

Ambedkar asserts that:

> To retain 'caste-system', one has to ensure that (s)he will not [seek] marriage outside the circumscribed circles. In order to implement it, ensuring the equality between both the sexes of same age, within a caste group, is essential. But it is not possible always as it is not necessary that a couple will depart this life together. Since after death of one partner, another becomes a surplus man or woman and their remarriage, within caste,[6] would spoil the parity between the further marriageable units, so, remarriages were not allowed at once. But, then, (s)he may violate the rules of endogamy by marrying outside the caste.
>
> In order to prevent such violations of the cultural code, suttee or widow burning on her husband's pyre is a way to dispose of surplus woman and if that is proved to be too difficult, enforced widowhood[7] is more feasible to tackle the problem. Again, enforced celibacy is not considered suitable for men as they are considered to be superior beings. So, the Brahmanical forces do try to find out a suitable partner for him within his caste circle. As it is difficult to get a woman of his age-group, his marriage would be arranged with a girl of not-yet-marriageable group. (Ambedkar 2014, Vol. 3: 296–8)

Thus, in this way, sati (suttee), enforced widowhood, and girl child marriage solve the problem of surplus men and women for sustaining the parity between marriageable units within the caste circle and to prolong the endogamous character of caste society (Ambedkar 2014, Vol. 3: 301).

Theoretically, this is the model system of caste, but human nature, in contrast, is something that cannot be bound in shibboleths. Every rule is violable but there is a mechanism to address such problems. Since caste is an enclosed unit, if one member of the caste marries a person from outside her/his caste, s/he would be excommunicated from the original caste group, whereas other castes too will not accept them, so they form a new caste (Rege 2013: 153–67). Thus, excommunication results in the shaping of a new caste. As this newly constructed caste does not possess 'purity of blood', it will be of inferior status in comparison to 'pure' castes. The notion of caste purity also has a binary aspect. For instance, if a Brahmin man has a carnal interaction with a

---

[6] Inter-caste marriage cannot be allowed so as to retain case purity.
[7] State of enforced celibacy.

woman from another caste, his caste purity will not be blemished but the offspring from such a union would be a *chandala*.[8] Thus, a high-caste man is permitted to have sexual liaisons with low-caste women without his purity being tarnished as he is the ritual superior. On the contrary, a high-caste woman cannot engage in sexual encounters with low-caste men since it will discolour, allegedly, her caste purity. Thus, the purity of caste depends on the successful control of women.[9] However, there also exists an economic criterion attached to the notion of purity. Caste is also the division of labourers, as pointed out by Ambedkar. Women in lower-caste families have to go outside to work for their very subsistence. They are considered as 'fallen' because they may be sexually exploited by the owner of the land or factory where they work. By implication, their menfolk are ridiculed as they are unable to 'protect' their women.

Manu, as cited by Ambedkar, underlined the rule that:

> For the first marriage of a twice born class man, a woman of the same class is recommended but if they want to have 'another woman' or to marry again, women in the direct descending order of the classes is preferred. Next to implication, a *Shudra* woman must be the wife of a *Shudra* man merely; she and a *Vaishya* woman can be the woman of a *Vaishya* man; these two and a *Kshatriya* woman, of a *Kshatriya* man; these three and a Brahman woman of a Brahman man. (Ambedkar 2014, Vol. 3: 26–7, 339)

However, this does not mean that Manu took a stand for inter-caste marriage. He highly opposed it, but merely as a preferred practice. A man was allowed to have multiple wives or concubines even from castes lower than his, yet his first wife was supposed to be from his own caste. This reference underscores that while a caste Hindu man is allowed to indulge in 'extramarital but "socially-legitimate" affairs' and exploit the lower social order women as mistresses or through the devadasi custom, in contrast, an untouchable man is not allowed to even marry a caste Hindu woman (Ambedkar 2014, Vol. 3: 27). Thus, *Pratiloma* marriages[10] and relations are

---

[8] Chandala refers to an 'untouchable' caste in the Hindu social order.
[9] At present, it seems to reflect the honour or dishonour of the family or caste.
[10] When a lower-caste man marries a high-caste woman.

prohibited, whereas *Anuloma* marriages[11] are permitted. Thus, this is nothing but merely a matter of carnal intercourse, which is a humiliation[12] of the lower *varna*s and a matter of privilege for the dominant castes to fulfil their carnal desires. It is based upon the principle of slavery which, in the Indian context, works with its caste character.

This reflects the intersectionality between caste and gender. Both men and women belonging to the lower caste are subjugated by their social superiors. Caste Hindu women are also suppressed by the men of their caste. For the shudra-untouchable women, it is a multi-layered oppression from the men of their community, as well as men and women from the caste Hindu communities. In all this, the women are never seen as equal partners to men and are viewed merely as powerless objects, primarily for satisfying men's lust.

Constitutional Rights and the Hindu Code Bill

The history of women's rights can be traced to the British period with the enactment of the Hindu Women's Rights to Property Act, 1937, by the Indian central legislature, which granted Hindu widows, for the first time, the right to claim a share in their husband's property and to stipulate for the partition of his undivided family estate (Banningan 1952: 174). Although this was only a limited interest, as on her death, it would be inherited by her husband's heirs (Sinha 2007: 51), in 1940, this right of women was not validated in a matter of agricultural property by a federal court. So, the (British) government decided to examine the case and, for this, a committee under the chairmanship of B.N. Rau was appointed. This committee recommended the inevitable: to revisit the entire Hindu law which existed in bits and pieces. The Rau Committee sketched out two bills—the Hindu Marriage Bill and the Intestate Succession Bill—which were introduced in the central legislature in 1943, but were eventually discarded because of opposition from the conservative element. These bills were revived in 1944 and restructured

---

[11] It is a marriage between a man of high caste and a woman of low caste. This marriage is considered as a 'natural marriage'.

[12] Humiliation because lower-caste women are generally taken merely for concubinage kind of relations.

into a draft code (Ray 1952: 273–4), known as the Hindu Code Bill, dealing specifically with succession, maintenance, marriage and divorce, minority and guardianship, and adoption (Som 1994: 170). It was introduced in the Parliament on 1 August 1946, but not acted upon. Subsequently, after Independence, it was reintroduced by the Government of India in the Constituent Assembly on 11 April 1947 (Banningan 1952: 174). This time, it was emendated by Ambedkar, law minister of the first cabinet of Independent India. Ambedkar's major concern for women's status was reflected in the Hindu Code Bill. He explained that the 'bill was to codify and modify the Hindu law relating to seven different matters of rights to property of deceased Hindu[s] who died intestate or without making a will, the order of succession of the property of an intestate deceased among the different heirs and above specified issues' (Ambedkar 2014, Vol. 14, Part I: 5). In other words, the Bill was to, according to Austin (1996: 140–1), 'invalidate the Hindu personal law' as women were subjugated through these personal laws.

The Bill challenged the entrenched gender bias of Hinduism. For Hindus, there were two laws—*Mitakshra* and *Dayabhaga*—regarding inheritance, marriage, adoption, and so on. In Mitakshra rule of law, property of a man was not an individual property, it also belonged to coparcenaries or shared ownership of male lineage, that is, father, son, grandson, and great-grandson, by their very birth only, while in Dayabhaga set of laws, 'the ownership of property has its individual character which means anyone who inherits property from their progenitors has absolute right over that property. This latter strand of the laws was adopted in the Hindu Code Bill by Ambedkar and it was sought to make it a common law' (Ambedkar 2014, Vol. 14, Part I: 6). However, in Dayabhaga,[13] there was discrimination among female heirs on the basis of their status of being married or not, having children or not. This discrimination was proposed to end through this Bill (Ambedkar 2014, Vol. 14, Part I: 6), wherein Ambedkar placed the widow, daughter, and the widow of a predeceased son on an equal standing. In order to restore equity of gender, 'daughter's share, as equal to the son, was prescribed in her father's as well as her husband's property and she was made as equal heir as to the son, widow, the widow of the predeceased son,

---

[13] Only in Dayabhaga law, a woman was prescribed some sort of property rights, while in Mitakshra law, she was ostracized absolutely.

the son of predeceased son of the predeceased son, and the widow of a predeceased son of the predeceased son [sic]' (Ambedkar 2014, Vol. 14, Part I: 280). Moreover, Ambedkar brought absolute equality between son and daughter by making a provision of son's share in mother's property as he held that 'son also would get a share as equal to girl's share in mother's property, even in *Stridhana* too' (Ambedkar 2014, Vol. 14, Part I: 264). Thus, all heirs were brought on equal and balanced ground.

Through the Bill, it was proposed that women would get absolute right regarding all property, not merely her 'stridhana'.[14] In Dayabhaga law, a woman was entitled only to 'life estate' over the property, which meant that she could enjoy the property during her lifetime but could not sell it under any condition and after her death, this property would go to someone from her husband's family. Ambedkar made a revolutionary change in this matter too, that is, this partial estate was altered into an absolute estate (Ambedkar 2014, Vol. 14, Part I: 7–8). Furthermore, it was also propounded that whatever property was acquired by the woman after the enactment of the Bill would be her absolute property (Ambedkar 2014, Vol. 14, Part I: 150). Another sacrosanct arrangement regarding women's property was that an adopted son would not dispossess the women from the property she got from her deceased husband prior to adopting this son. Hence, after sanctioning the Bill, 'the adopted son would not be in [a] position to divest the mother utterly from her property and by this way [the] widow's position was strengthened' (Sinha 2007: 52). Ambedkar also reckoned in the Bill that the dowry which was given to the daughter by her parents at the time of her marriage, in terms of stridhana, and over which she barely she had the absolute right must be treated as trust property by her in-laws (Ambedkar 2014, Vol. 14, Part I: 8).

Regarding marriage, two new clauses—restitution of the conjugal rights and the judicial separation—were added by the select committee.[15] These two points were not in the original bill prepared by the Rau Committee (Ambedkar 2014, Vol. 14, Part I: 259).

---

[14] Stridhana is something that a woman can claim as her own property within her marital household. It may include her jewellery, gifts presented to her, and the dowry given to her by her family. Generally, gifts given by the bride's family are considered as stridhana.

[15] The committee was headed by Ambedkar.

Prior to the Bill, only sacramental marriage was in practice under the Dayabhaga rule, wherein there was no space for an atheist or antitheist person, whereas Hindu Code Bill commenced two types of marriages: civil and non-civil, that is, a sacramental one (Banningan 1952: 175). The civil marriage granted the highest personal freedom as divorce was made easier. The divorcement of the civil marriage was introduced for the first time from the women's outlook[16] in the proposed Bill, 'on the grounds of impotency, adultery, leprosy, either of the married couple being lunatic or idiotic, and where the marriage was completed by force and without the consent of [a] guardian' (Sinha 2007: 52). Although sacramental marriage was made indissoluble in the Bill, it too could be declared invalid on the grounds, besides the aforementioned, of: 'conversion, not resuming intercourse for two years after an order for judicial separation; and failing to comply for two years with a decree for restitution of conjugal rights' (Banningan 1952: 175). The commencement of civil marriage and its easier stamp out was very much the liberal outlook of Ambedkar's philosophy. Further, to restore women's dignity as a human being in the society, Ambedkar (2014, Vol. 14, Part I: 267) 'prohibited the polygamy and prescribed the monogamy' at the same time. Through this Bill, he took a step further to annihilate the caste system by 'obliterat[ing] the caste precincts regarding marriage[17] and adoption of child' (Ambedkar 2014, Vol. 14, Part I: 10–11).

It is quite evident from the given illustration of the principal features of the Hindu Code Bill that Ambedkar reframed it within the liberal values of liberty, equality, fraternity, and dignity. The seamless entanglement of the overture of women's absolute share in property, purge of caste restrictions in matters of marriage and adoption, elimination of polygamy, and the overture of monogamy would restore these values of social democracy. The Hindu Code Bill challenged the base of patriarchy and awarded women equal position as that of men. Hence, the Bill was against the structure of domination and suppression of women and, by way of this, challenged the very philosophy of Hinduism. Chitra Sinha (2012), in her work, advocates the provisos of the Bill and opines that the Bill was meant to create a unified legislative framework which would

---

[16] Since a man could have abandoned her previously as well.
[17] By proposing the legalization of inter-caste marriage.

provide justice to women in an egalitarian fashion and undermine the practices of Brahmanical patriarchy, which is why the Brahmanical lobby impeded it.

Ultimately, the Bill could not be conceded and was withdrawn because of staunch antagonism from the Hindu orthodox lobby, particularly the Hindu Mahasabha and Bharatiya Jana Sangh. 'The Hindu Mahasabha opposed the Bill in order to prevent any legislative interference in the religious matters of Hindus and it has been stated that it is against the "Indian culture" as it provides the options of divorce, and monogamy that may prevent a man to have [a] son i.e. sacrosanct for salvation and etc' (Banningan 1952: 176). Such religious, conservative, and patriarchal social elements of the society had condemned the Bill's provisions for 'women's property rights, monogamy and divorce'[18] vehemently because 'the bill was considered by them as an ultra-modern invasion into Hindu religious activities' (Sinha 2012: 79).

The antagonism was expressed even by the then president, Rajendra Prasad, who said: 'the bill intervened in Hindus' personal law and would satisfy a few purported progressive people' (Banningan 1952: 175); the then deputy speaker, Ananthasayanam Aiyyangar, also opposed Ambedkar from carrying on further. Indeed, Ambedkar's status of 'being a non-congressman' made it more difficult for him to manoeuvre (Som 1994: 172). It is evident from the treatment the Hindu Code Bill received in the legislature that since Ambedkar was a lower-caste person, mind had been made up already to not let the Bill be passed (Ambedkar 2014, Vol. 14, Part II: 1323–5).

For Ambedkar, the Hindu Code Bill was the culmination of a lifetime of struggles to create an equitable society. However, inevitably, his caste became an impediment, which is evident from the statement of the then Shankaracharya of Sankeswara Pitha, Jereshastri, in the *Nav Bharat* daily:

> Milk or Ganges water may be holy, but if it comes through a nallah or a gutter, it cannot be considered sacred. Similarly, the '*Dharmashastra*' howsoever it may be authentic, it cannot be considered authentic because it has come from a '*Mahar*' like Dr. Ambedkar who is a scholar, whose study of scriptures, as said, is great, but he is an '*antyaja*'. How can the Ganga of Scriptures coming

---

[18] These three elements comprised the most disputable part of the Bill.

from the *nallah* of Ambedkar be holy? It must be discardable like milk coming from the gutter.[19]

Some members openly declared that as long as Ambedkar was piloting the Bill, they would not allow it to pass (Som 1994: 186–7). It is further apparent from the fact that in 1955–6, when Ambedkar was not in the cabinet, this Bill was enacted smoothly, though in a diluted version (Sinha 2012: 143–4) and in four separate acts: Hindu Marriage Act, 1955; Hindu Succession Act, 1956; Hindu Adoption and Maintenance Act, 1956; and Hindu Minority and Guardianship Act, 1956.

Ambedkar's ideas influenced the enactment of many subsequent pro-women acts, such as: the Child Marriage Restraint Act, 1929; Immoral Traffic (Prevention) Act, 1956; Dowry Prohibition Act, 1961; the Maternity Benefit Act, 1961; the Equal Remuneration Act, 1976; the Family Courts Act, 1984; Sati (Prevention) Act, 1987; the National Commission for Women Act, 1990; Protection of Human Right Act, 1993; and Protection of Women from Domestic Violence Act, 2005, to cite a few.

Ambedkar's Hermeneutics

In India, for women's liberation, one has to challenge the philosophy of Hinduism, comprised by the Manusmriti, the Bhagavad Gita, Shankaracharya's *Vedanta*, the Mahabharata, the Ramayana, and the Puranas (Ambedkar 2014, Vol. 3: 239), wherein women are considered as sexual objects. It is evident from these Brahmanical scriptures that women were given to other men just for cohabitation, in order to appease them. One could even marry his own sister or daughter, or they could be given on rent to others (Ambedkar 2014, Vol. 14, Part I: 171–2). In these scriptures, women and their body parts are considered merely as sexual objects that satiate someone, which may result in rape. Ambedkar, thus, argued that the very essence of Hinduism is to subjugate women.

In order to theorize women's subjugation, Ambedkar critically revisited the scriptures, and in his book, *The Rise and Fall of*

---

[19] Available at http://sarvajan.ambedkar.org/?p=4277; last accessed on 4 May 2018.

Hindu Women (Ambedkar 1999), argued that during the pre-Manu period, especially during the Buddhist regime, women occupied a very high position in the intellectual and social life of the state[20] and that the caste system was the main reason for the subsequent degradation of women in India. He argued that Gautama Buddha established a new and rational sect, Buddhism, wherein man and woman, equally, were regulated by the five precepts known as *Panchsila*. The Buddha denounced the varna system and equalized male and female. For the Aryan Hindus,[21] women were placed equal to Shudras and both were denied the basic human right of acquiring knowledge and renunciation, which is the 'only way to get salvation' in Hinduism. The Buddha broke this Aryan rule and paved the way for women's free movement. Now, a woman too could obtain education and become a nun (Ambedkar 2014, Vol. 3: 221). However, over a period of time, the triumph of Brahmanism over Buddhism degraded the Shudras and women yet again, as it induced the system of graded inequality of caste system (Ambedkar 2014, Vol. 3: 275). Ambedkar proclaimed that even in pre-Buddhist Brahmanism, intermarriages between different varnas were in practice and there was no prohibition on widow remarriages, which continued in Buddhism with greater freedom to women; this time marriage did not turn women into their husband's slaves and women could have access to property (Ambedkar 2014, Vol. 3: 309–10).

As Buddhism envisaged an equal status for both Shudras and women, the Brahmanical order would face unprecedented challenges. To counter the challenges posed by Buddhism and its stress on rational enquiry and not blind belief, the supreme Brahmanical lawgiver, Manu, emphasized seductive domesticity that would pay dividends to women. Thus, with the decline of Buddhism, social laws of Hinduism regarding women were converted into state laws so that they become legally enforceable. Thus, patriarchy was buttressed by the scripturally sanctioned state. The liberties for women granted by Buddha were overturned and she was reduced to

---

[20] Whereas Manu deprived women of the right to participate in such activities. In the Manusmriti, he prescribed women's derogatory position and they were denied freedom and right to education.

[21] They prevailed prior to the Buddha's time and were revived by Manu.

a chattel. She was also denied ultimate salvation (Ambedkar 2014, Vol. 17, Part II: 119–21).

For Ambedkar, battling the Hindu scriptures which sanctioned atrocities against the lower-caste men and women was a lifetime's work. For survival, women from the lower castes were forced to work in many occupations which were deeply dehumanizing. How to restore their agential status was the major dilemma. Ambedkar realized that it was extremely urgent to alleviate the stigma attached to such humiliating occupations which denied these women their personhood. He declared that poverty had always been the lot of the untouchables but they should never compromise on their self-respect. He always exhorted women of the lower caste to aspire for a dignified life.

★ ★ ★

For long, feminists in India have resorted to academic erasures while endeavouring to understand the heterogeneous nature of women's issues. Ambedkar has been reduced to simply a lower-caste ideologue and his entire critique of caste-based patriarchy has been sidelined by many scholars. The contemporary political discourse deems it essential to appropriate Ambedkar and reduce him simply to a vote-catching mantra. However, it is extremely difficult for the ruling elite to embrace his agenda for social transformation as that would lead to a complete overhaul of the socio-cultural pyramid. Similarly, many Indian feminists challenge patriarchy but are unwilling to interrogate caste as that would undermine their entrenched privileges. They are unwilling to consider Ambedkar as sufficiently 'mainstream'. There exists a deliberate blindness of insight vis-à-vis mainstream feminists and Dalit feminists. Although Ambedkar could not succeed in getting the entire Hindu Code Bill passed, his endeavours have helped women of all social strata to attain custody of their children, receive alimony (maintenance allowance from husband on getting legally separated), made it possible for widows to adopt children, ensured their rights over parental property, and given them many more rights.

Ambedkar's lifelong struggles against manifold inequities made him sensitive to the multiple fault lines existing in the Indian society. His concern was to ensure justice to the least represented sections of society. If one were to take cudgels against Brahmanical patriarchy, one needs to be equally vigilant against Dalit patriarchy as Dalit women bear the burden of caste, class, and gender. It is essential to introspect and interrogate the interstices of Ambedkarite feminism vis-à-vis other feminisms to create a just society, especially when battling right-wing fundamentalist forces in contemporary India.

References

Ambedkar, B.R. 1999. *The Rise and Fall of Hindu Women*. New Delhi: Blumoon Books.
———. 2008. *Annihilation of Caste*. Delhi: Gautam Book Centre.
———. 2013[1916]. *Castes in India: Their Mechanism, Genesis and Development*. New Delhi: Critical Quest.
———. 2014. *Dr. Babasaheb Ambedkar's Writings and Speeches*, Vols 3, 14(I and II), 17(II). New Delhi: Dr. Ambedkar Foundation, Ministry of Social Justice, Government of India.
Austin, G. 1996. *Indian Constitution: Cornerstone of the Nation*. Oxford: Claredon Press.
Banningan, John A. 1952. 'The Hindu Code Bill'. *Far Eastern Survey* 21(17): 173–6. Available at http://www.jstor.org/stable/3024109; accessed on 2 January 2014.
Chakravarti, Uma. 2003a. *Gendering Caste: Through a Feminist Lens*. Kolkata: Stree.
———. 2003b. 'Reconceptualizing Gender: Phule, Brahmanism and Brahmanical Patriarchy', in A. Rao (ed.), *Gender and Caste: Issues in Contemporary Indian Feminism*, pp. 164–79. New Delhi: Kali for Women and Women Unlimited.
Guru, Gopal. 1995. 'Dalit Women Talk Differently'. *Economic and Political Weekly* 30(41–2): 2548–50. Available at http://www.jstor.org/stable/4403327; accessed on 25 August 2014.
John, Mary E. 2008. *Women's Studies: A Reader*. New Delhi: Penguin Books.
Kannabiran, Vasanth and Kalpana Kannabiran. 2003. 'Caste and Gender: Understanding Dynamics of Power and Violence', in Anupama Rao (ed.) *Gender and Caste: Issues in Contemporary Indian Feminism*, pp. 249–60. New Delhi: Kali for Women and Women Unlimited.
Rao, Anupama (ed.). 2003. *Gender and Caste: Issues in Contemporary Indian Feminism*. New Delhi: Kali for Women and Women Unlimited.

Ray, Renuka. 1952. 'The Background of the Hindu Code Bill'. *Pacific Affairs* 25(3): 268–77. Available at http://www.jstor.org/stable/2752804; accessed on 2 January 2014.

Rege, Sharmila. 2003. 'A Dalit Feminist Standpoint', in Anupama Rao (ed.), *Gender and Caste: Issues in Contemporary Indian Feminism*, pp. 90–101. New Delhi: Kali for Women and Women Unlimited.

———. 2013. *Against the Madness of Manu: B.R. Ambedkar's Writings against the Brahmanical Patriarchy*. New Delhi: Navayana.

Sinha, Chitra. 2007. 'Images of Motherhood: The Hindu Code Bill Discourse'. *Economic and Political Weekly* 42(43): 49–57. Available at http://www.jstor.org/stable/40276597; 2 January 2014.

———. 2012. *Debating Patriarchy: The Hindu Code Bill Controversy in India (1941–1956)*. New Delhi: Oxford University Press.

Som, Reba. 1994. 'Jawaharlal Nehru and the Hindu Code Bill: A Victory of Symbol Over Substance?' *Modern Asian Studies* 28(1): 165–94. Available at http://www.jstor.org/stable/312925; 23 December 2013.

Teltumbde, Anand. 2010. *The Persistence of Caste: The Khairlanji Murders and India's Hidden Apartheid*. Delhi: Navayana.

TWO

Racial Justice

7

Organic Resistance

The Relevance of Ambedkar, Du Bois, and Garvey to Diaspora, Caste, Race, and Women's Liberation

MOSES SEENARINE

This chapter explores the similarities between Ambedkar's struggle against caste-based subjection of Dalits in India and Du Bois's and Garvey's resistance to racial oppression of African-Americans in the United States (US). It also examines caste and class issues within the South Asian diaspora and how Ambedkar's ideas may help this community to face its many challenges.

The chapter begins with my personal journey and experience of attending the same college as Ambedkar, followed by a discussion on Hinduism and migration. Next, it looks at caste and migration in the indentured South Asian diaspora, and how they differ from the more recent migrants to the West who now form a powerful interest group that is driving conservatism and casteism in India.

The chapter then examines whether overseas Hindus are integrating into their host societies and how Ambedkar's ideas may help them improve race relations with other groups. The similarities in the approaches used by Ambedkar, Du Bois, and Garvey to resist cultural oppression in India and the US are explored next. The chapter concludes with a discussion on women's role in the movements led by the three men.

Ambedkar: My Mentor at Columbia

Overseas South Asians constitute the world's largest diaspora. I am part of this dispersion, born in Guyana, South America, six generations removed from South Asia. I am part of an Indo-Caribbean and US–South Asian population that numbers in millions. Though the diaspora includes thousands of Dalits, only a few will openly admit to being Dalit. There is a deep stigma that comes with being poor and lower caste in the diaspora, as in India.

I did not feel like an interloper growing up in South America since my ethnic group forms the majority in that country. I felt fairly normal until I encountered Indian merchants from South Asia in their stores, who acted superior to Guyanese Indians. I knew caste had something to do with it, but for the most part, I tried to ignore caste, hoping that it would go away.

My surname, Seenarine, is derived from an eighteenth-century south Indian Dalit group that advocated conversion and migration to free themselves from caste oppression in South Asia. I should have been pleased about my family's long history of Dalit resistance, but instead I considered my Dalit surname name as a mark of disgrace. I preferred my mother's Ahir family name, Satrohan, with its slightly higher-caste status.

My working-class family migrated to New York when I was 15, and I tried to distance myself from South Asians and Hinduism through Westernization. Being brown-skinned, I was treated like an African, and I identified as being part of the African diaspora. I studied the history of European colonialism and immersed myself in socialist philosophy. However, caste hung around my neck like a yoke. For example, I quickly became defensive whenever I encountered Hindus in the US. Far from camaraderie, I dreaded the ubiquitous question, 'Where are you from?', since it invariably revealed my ascribed low-caste identity.

I became the first on both sides of my family to graduate from college, an achievement I am proud of. I was educated, but still suffered from low self-esteem due to feelings and oppression related to caste and location in the diaspora. At the age of 30, I attended graduate school at Columbia University, determined to find out more about my Dalit heritage.

Columbia is a mostly European American institution and an emotionally sterile space. The South Asians I encountered on campus were upper caste and middle class. Upon learning about my diaspora origins, they acted like I was a clueless Dalit. I felt as much, and so began to research the history of caste and untouchability in South Asia.

You can imagine my surprise when I first learned about the name Ambedkar, the foremost authority on caste, and discovered that he had also attended Columbia 75 years ago. This encounter with Bhimrao Ramji Ambedkar (1891–1956) changed my life forever. I became reborn as an Ambedkarite immediately as I stood in the library staring at his books. Ambedkar's mere existence, and his enormous political and social accomplishments, meant that I would never again feel disgraced simply for being a Dalit.

By serving as an example, Ambedkar demonstrated that Dalits are capable of greatness, and eons of religious oppression was finally eased from my shoulders. I emerged from a cave of social and intellectual darkness into a blinding light that only Ambedkar made possible. After a lifetime of embarrassment and self-doubt, with his book in my hands, I was finally able to stand up and breathe freely.

Through Ambedkar, I discovered that Dalits were not low or impure in any way. According to his historical and social research, Dalits were the indigenous people of South Asia who converted to Buddhism. They were subsequently out-casted as punishment in an epic conflict between Hinduism and Buddhism that saw the latter practically wiped out in South Asia. For example, referring to Dalits as 'Broken Men', Ambedkar (1979: 375) wrote, 'the Broken Men were Buddhists. As such they did not revere the Brahmins, did not employ them as their priests and regarded them as impure. The Brahmins on the other hand disliked the Broken Men because they were Buddhists and preached against them contempt and hatred with the result that the Broken Men came to be regarded as Untouchables.'

Dalits were not always forced to become 'polluted' scavengers and do the work that caste Hindus refused. For example, Ambedkar (1979: 373) argues, 'triumphant Brahmanism was in need of many things. It of course needed to make Chaturvarna the law of the land the validity of which was denied by the Buddhists. It needed to make animal sacrifice, which was abolished by the Buddhists, legal.' Two thousand years ago, Dalits were ordinary villagers who were influenced by Ashoka to follow a plant-based diet and live ethically. For instance, one major edict reads: 'This rescript on morality has been caused to be written by Devanampriya Priyadarsin. Here no living being must be killed and sacrificed. And also no festival meeting must be held. For king Devanampriya Priyadarsin sees much evil in festival meetings [sic]' (Hultzsch 1925). Also, before Buddhism, Dalits were the originators of Harappan civilization; earlier still, they lived peacefully in egalitarian clans for millennia (Ilaiah 2018). Casteism changed all this, and it was Hindus and their religion that was at fault.

Being at Columbia became a magical experience for me as I imagined myself walking in the footsteps of Ambedkar. We have frequented the same halls and may have held the same books in the libraries. The university had many of Ambedkar's books and I was astounded by the breadth and depth of his writings on caste and other topics.

I emerged from the ignorance of caste shame into normality and was influenced by Ambedkar to further his work on social justice. I became proud of my Dalit roots and of Dalits' affiliation to Africans, Native Americans, and other oppressed cultures and minorities across the world. As I researched West Indian history, I noted that early egalitarian Dalit cultures in the diaspora were gradually replaced by a homogenized, un-egalitarian Hinduism (Seenarine 1999a), just as they were centuries ago in South Asia. To document this trend, Ambedkar relied on the accounts of Chinese travellers to develop a timeline of the Hindu practices of impurity and untouchability in South Asia. He observed that 'Fa-Hian's description refers to the Chandalas only while the description given by Yuan Chwang applies to communities other than the Chandalas. This is a point of great importance. No such argument can be levelled against the acceptance of a description since it applies to communities other than the Chandalas. It is, therefore, just possible that when Yuan Chwang came to India, untouchability had emerged. On the basis of what has been said above we can conclude that while Untouchability did not exist in 200 A.D., it had emerged by 600 A.D.' (Ambedkar 1979: 378–9; also see Ilaiah 1996).

I was excited to learn more about Ambedkar's impact in India and spent a year conducting fieldwork among Dalit women in northern Karnataka (Seenarine 2004). I learned that they too were enormously inspired by Ambedkar and wanted to work on social justice. I was able to share my deep gratitude and appreciation for Ambedkar, and I was encouraged by the vast number of Dalits in India who were becoming Ambedkarites. Back at Columbia, I completed a dissertation titled, 'Voices from the Subaltern: Education and Empowerment among Dalit (Untouchable) Women in India' (Seenarine 2004). In the thesis, I argued that knowledge of Ambedkar and his life were critical to the self-esteem and educational ambition of Dalit women and girls in rural India.

Along with Ambedkar's emotional and psychological value, his scholarly influence is equally profound for me. Ambedkar was brilliant, honest, humble, and remained dedicated to removing the burden of caste from Dalits to his very end. He was an organic intellectual[1] who acted with integrity, and was, therefore, beyond corruption. His deep conscientization, or critical consciousness, is a huge source of guidance for me.

Hindu Taboo: Crossing *Kala Pani*

The Wikipedia entry on 'Caste System in India' dismisses and excludes all of Ambedkar's insights on caste.[2] The page describes this social and political stratification as primarily caused by developments during the post-Mughal period and under the British colonial regime. The impression the Wikipedia page creates is that casteism is the fault of the British, and that Hindus are largely innocent of bias, harassment, and atrocities that occurred during colonialism and centuries earlier.

This commonly referenced page on caste ignores evidence of casteism before the seventeenth century, including anti-caste movements dating back thousands of years. Caste reform movements[3] include Buddhism, Ajivika, and the Charvaka school of materialism in the sixth century BCE; the Bhakti movement in the seventh century with Dalit poets like Chokhamela, Soyarabai,

---

[1] An organic intellectual is a member of a social class, as opposed to a member of the traditional intelligentsia that regards itself as a group apart from the rest of society. Organic intellectuals can be social agents having a form of allegiance to a hegemonic class or to a subaltern class aspiring for state power.

[2] Available at https://en.wikipedia.org/wiki/Caste_system_in_India; last accessed on 1 June 2017.

[3] A movement is a program or series of acts working towards a desired end, like a reform movement. Both Buddhism and Sikkhism were religious movements seeking to reform existing practices.

and Ravidas; the Lingayat movement in the twelfth century; and Sikhism in the fifteenth century. These movements, and many others, flourished long before any European colonists arrived. Some scholars even argue that colonialism allowed Dalits to finally break the caste mould by enlisting in the British military and administration (Constable 2001).

Historically, both *varna*[4] and *jati*[5] were fluid for some groups, yet impoverished Dalits and Adivasis were continuously outcasted. From the very emergence of varna, powerful groups used religiously sanctioned ostracism and hierarchy to exploit the poor among their own group. Those with privilege asserted a sense of superiority and the impoverished were deemed 'lower' over time, but still maintained varna status.

'Upper' varnas could only exist if there were 'lower' ones, and this distinction fostered division and competition. The whole varna system was and still is maintained by social and political boundaries that exclude 'outsiders'. Thus, even though they exist within the local environment, Dalits and Adivasis are perpetual 'outsiders' who serve to reinforce the 'insider' status of all Hindus. This misbegotten religion is based on discrimination; and the fear of 'excommunication' keeps each varna in its place. Eons of Dalit resistance and decades of activism by caste reformers has had little influence on Hindus, who remain casteist and exclusionary. Consequently, there has been little change in the 'polluted' and dehumanized condition of Dalits.

India now has over 1.3 billion people and well over 50 per cent of them are caste Hindus. Dalits and tribals represent 25 per cent of the population. Casteism and untouchability negatively affect the lives of over 300 million Dalits and Adivasis in India, and millions more in the diaspora. Hindu supremacy marginalizes a further 170 million Muslims, and millions more Christians and Sikhs (*Indian Express* 2013; *The Hindu* 2015; UNDESA 2018). With the popularity of right-wing Hindu leaders and government, a region that has not

---

[4] A Sanskrit word which means type, order, colour, or class. The term refers to social classes in Brahmanical books, such as the Manusmriti.

[5] Jati is a group of communities and religions in India. Each jati typically has an association with a traditional job function. The term is derived from the Sanskrit word *jata*, 'born' or 'brought into existence', and indicates a form of existence determined by birth.

known social tolerance for 2,000 years is rapidly becoming even more militantly narrow-minded by targeting Muslims and Dalit activists (Bezzi 2020; Parth 2020).

One glaring inconsistency in this immoral religion is the ancient Brahmanical taboo of *samudrayana* or prohibition against overseas travel. Samudrayana is forbidden to an observant Hindu because it involves interaction with non-Hindus, which is almost an 'uncleansable' defilement. To have contact with foreigners, with the *dasyu*, and their food is a fundamental violation of Hindu *shuddhi* or purity of being.

'Making voyages by sea' causes *pataniya* or loss of caste. It is arduous to reclaim varna, so in ancient times few dared to ignore the taboo. Even today, the Tirupati Temple does not allow any priest who has crossed the seas to enter the temple's sanctum sanctorum; and in recent times, foreign travel has been cited as a reason for denying Brahmin priests temple entry and leadership positions (Kerur 2007; *The Hindu* 2007).

'Mobility', that is, leaving the community and being exposed to external influence can translate into loss of caste for members of even the highest caste, that is, the Brahmins. For example, mobile priests in the service of foreign rulers like the Mughals or European companies were deliberately ostracized by their 'fixed' priestly peers. In some cases, their entire family was denied share in ancestral property and income. Sati or the burning alive of Hindu widows was encouraged primarily by the fixed priestly class, in part to assert independence from mobile clans.

Some mobile clans banded together into popular associations, or *sabha*s, to oppose these un-Brahmanic practices, thereby colliding head-on with the orthodoxy of the 'fixed' Hindu society. This dynamic between diaspora and local competition for power is being repeated in the twenty-first century by non-resident Indians (NRIs), and it involves all castes. One possible difference, however, is that the orthodoxy may now reside in the diaspora.

Coolies to NRIs: Arc of the Diaspora

The overseas Indian population is over 30 million, representing the largest diaspora in the world (MEA 2018). From sojourners to settlers, Hindus form a potent force abroad and at home. Religious restrictions against travelling beyond the sea means that the NRIs technically cannot be considered Hindus; thus, in the strictest sense, Hinduism cannot exist outside of South Asia. The samudrayana taboo is selectively applied however, and overseas Hindus simply ignore this and other restrictions, such as those against eating meat, certain vegetables, and so on.

There are many contradictory narratives that exist within diaspora communities, and caste is one of them. For example, in the West, middle-class Hindus were considered more 'foreign' than working-class Dalit Christians. The status of being part of the upper caste got lost in translation and Brahmin superiority was not automatically transferred to the West. In fact, on the contrary, many found that they were now considered as 'blacks' and treated as Dalits by majority of the European American population.

Up until 1965, Asians were largely excluded by law from emigrating to the US; nonetheless, a few managed to travel to the country from the 1700s onwards. With the end of enslavement in the 1800s, there was a larger presence of South Asians in the Americas, especially indentured coolies in the Caribbean.

Starting in 1838, hundreds of so-called 'Hill Coolies' or Adivasis from Bihar were taken to British Guiana and elsewhere to replace formerly enslaved Africans on colonial plantations. Coolies worked as indentured labourers for 10 or more years under similar conditions as enslavement. By 1917, when the indentured system was finally abolished, some 429,286 South Asians had been transported overseas, of whom 238,909 went to British Guiana and 143,939 to Trinidad (Tinker 1993).

Indentured labourers were primarily Dalits as they were the most receptive to 'pull' factors to emigrate, and they also cared the least about samudrayana (Seenarine 1999b). Dalits were more easily 'pushed' to leave via entrapment and capture as well. The descendants of formerly indentured Dalits and other South Asians now comprise 65 per cent of the population in Mauritius, and over 35 per cent in Fiji, Guyana, and Trinidad. In addition, they comprise over 30 per cent of residents in Suriname and Réunion (Non Resident Indians Online 2020; Rooney 2019; United Nations 2019).

Presently, the taboo against migration is fairly obsolete and the economic pull factors are stronger than ever. Millions of Indians serve as temporary workers in other parts of Asia, the Middle East, Africa, Europe, and the Americas. For example, Indians comprise over 30 per cent of the population in the United Arab Emirates (UAE) at any given time.

Compared to nineteenth-century indentureship in the Caribbean, the first wave of South Asian immigrants who landed in the US 70 years later, in 1907, were not that better off. The migrants were predominantly Punjabi Sikh farmers who worked as agricultural workers. Their 'foreign' presence was strongly opposed by European Americans and immigration restrictions specific to South Asians began to be introduced two years later. Consequently, only 6,400 migrated (Takaki 1998). The 1910 US Census (US Department of Commerce 1913) was the first to count South Asians and it recorded 2,545 'Hindus'. The Cold War caused a huge demand for skilled workers and restrictions began to be loosened in the 1950s for South Asian students and professionals. With the Immigration and Nationality Act of 1965, a wave of educated South Asian immigrants began arriving on American shores.

By 2000, Indian-Americans nearly doubled in population to become the third-largest group of Asian-Americans, after Chinese and Filipinos.[6] This group has increasing visibility in high-tech communities, such as in the Silicon Valley and the Seattle area. Indian-Americans have some of the highest rates of academic achievement among ethnic groups in the US. Most Hindu immigrants to the West speak English and are highly educated, which gets translated into class privilege at home and abroad.

NRIs: The Indian 1 Per Cent

The NRIs are 1 per cent of the subcontinent, with enormous influence in society and politics. Overseas Indians send US$ 70 billion (Rs 4.2 lakh crores) in remittances every year to India. This amount is just 25 per cent less than the Indian government's total plan expenditure of US$ 94 billion on social development. Thus, a small community of NRIs transfers money equal to 75 per cent of expenditure of the Indian central government (Anand 2018; India Brand Equity Foundation 2018). They also invest in homes, businesses, and organizations, and contribute to the country's

---

[6] According to the US Census, there were 3,852,293 Asian Indians in 2018, or 1.2% of the total population. (US Census Bureau 2019). Indian people trace their heritage to South Asia, making them one of the fastest-growing immigrant groups in the country.

technology exports. The enormous wealth of NRIs drives national and regional parties to lobby for their support.

National parties, such as the Aam Aadmi Party (AAP) and Bharatiya Janata Party (BJP), have established overseas groups in more than 30 major cities in North America to encourage NRIs to contribute. For example, Indians living abroad donate 30 per cent of the AAP party fund (Thakur and Nagarajan 2014). Regional parties, such as the Shiromani Akali Dal (SAD), Telugu Desam Party (TDP), and Dravida Munnetra Kazhagam (DMK), are also close to their respective diaspora, and NRIs especially play a major part in politics in Punjab. Since the 1990s, the NRI influence has led to a shift to the right in Indian politics, away from democratic socialism (Hundal 2017; Sharma 2019).

Social media reach has increased the diaspora's utility for Indian political parties. The Overseas Friends of BJP use Google Hangouts to connect with members across the world and live-stream conferences to discuss political ideas in India. Also, Indian-American supporters of the AAP volunteer for the party's phone bank to call potential supporters and voters (Campbell 2014).

The NRIs are defining Indian policy as well. For example, the Telugu Association of North America as well as US-based Telugu professionals were active in contributing to Naidu's ideas for reshaping Hyderabad (TANA 2020; *Times of India* 2017). There is high visibility of the diaspora in Gujarat policy too, which may be behind Hardik Patel's and Other Backward Classes' (OBCs) demand for increased reservations in Gujarat and other states.

One acknowledgement of the standing of the NRIs is the central government's establishment of a Ministry for Overseas Indian Affairs, with a mandate to assess, examine, and address issues and concerns of Indian citizens abroad, and to cement partnerships which would benefit both. In 2003, Pravasi Bharatiya Divas (Non-Resident Indian Day) was celebrated in India on 9 January to mark the contribution of the overseas Indian community in the development of India. In 2014, the annual event was attended by 1,500 delegates from 51 countries and President Pranab Mukherjee gave awards to distinguished NRIs. At these gatherings, representatives from indentured and working-class communities in Fiji, Mauritius, the Caribbean, and the Gulf, complain that their issues are ignored as the events mostly cater to the interests of wealthy, Western NRIs (Duttagupta 2014).

Another sign of conservatism among the NRIs is their financing of orthodox Hindu organizations and cultural associations overseas and in India. There are elaborate Hindu temples in many cities in the US, Canada, the United Kingdom (UK), and Continental Europe; and these institutions are contributing to Sanskritization and retention of casteism in the diaspora. The NRIs' funding of conservative Hinduism has led to right-wing Hindu political and social domination in the form of the BJP, Modi wave, anti-beef movement, increased violence against women, Dalits and minorities, and so on. The effect of NRIs' foreign interference is normalization of Hindu supremacy and further entrenchment of casteism in the subcontinent. The BJP's appointment of the sectarian Yogi Adityanath as chief minister of Uttar Pradesh in 2017 is another ominous sign.

These 1 per cent NRIs are out of touch with the situation on the ground in India. This elite group operates with completely different priorities and interests than the average Indian voter. Indian citizens primarily focus on local issues, such as housing, land, crop prices, and safety. In contrast, the economy, trade, and business regulations are the focus of Indians abroad. The extreme poverty and corruption experienced daily in India does not affect the diaspora in any way. Living in the secular West, the problems of casteism are swept under the rug in the NRIs' prevailing narrative of India as the world's largest 'democracy'. Buried also is the fact that India has the largest population of poor on Earth.

In the past decade, Hindu artists and entertainers have become a more visible presence in the Western media. Sanitized Hindu cultural practices, such as food, yoga, meditation, classical music, Bollywood, and more, have gained large followings in the West, leading to increased tourism at home. The NRIs are beginning to have an impact in Western politics too, as elected leaders and grassroots organizers. The US India Political Action Committee, for example, is influential in the US elections and American foreign policy.

After the events of 11 September 2001, Hindus in the West, in particular the Sikhs, have become victims of religious and racial profiling and violence. In response, a few political organizations have rallied to bring awareness to the issue and defend the rights of immigrants. In general, however, South Asians identify more with dominant Europeans than with other minority communities, and have chosen to 'give-in' to an unjust economic system rather than trying to reform it.

Plural Society or Melting Pot?

Diasporic South Asians are typically one among several minority groups in their home countries and have been the subjects of religious and racial prejudices. For decades, anthropologists have debated whether Indians in the diaspora are retaining Hindu customs or adapting to local cultures. Some point to the ongoing process of assimilation and 'creolization' occurring among overseas Indians in terms of language, dress, food habits, social customs, and so on. There are numerous advantages to blending in with the local culture, and second- and third-generation NRIs tend to socialize and intermarry with non-Indians more.

However, diaspora youth and adults face immense social pressures within their family and community to maintain caste, religious, national, and ethnic identities via dress, friendship, dating, marriage, and so on. In addition, they are larger structural forces that foster retention of Hinduism and casteism in the diaspora, and help to maintain Hinduism as a distinct culture in a plural society. There are variations in observance of Indian traditions, but the Hindu diaspora have resisted 'creolization' and merging into the melting pot of their home societies.

The low frequency of intermarriage with other religious and ethnic groups reflects cultural persistence and a separatist framework. Additionally, the retention of Hindu customs and casteism may have a strong influence on the NRIs race relations with the majority and other minority communities, and could be contributing to raising tensions among Indians and non-Indians.

The religion has been transformed in the diaspora into a homogenized form of Hinduism that outwardly claims the non-existence of caste. Although anthropologists argued, from the 1960s onwards, that the caste system cannot survive outside of South Asia, elements of caste do survive, such as: a tendency towards informal relations of superiority–inferiority; a sense of 'difference' among subgroups; family traditions of caste identity; and a preference for marriage within caste. Carolyn Brown (1981) has shown that in Fiji, as caste populations increase, so does the frequency of endogamy.

After fieldwork in Trinidad, Morton Klass (1960) argued that caste membership is the main determinant of status among rural Hindus on the Caribbean island. The American anthropologist noted that other important status indicators, such as income, wealth, occupation, and education, tend to cluster with claims of higher-caste membership. And, in rural Indo-Trinidad villages, claims of higher caste origins are made by leaders and wealthy residents alike.

In terms of politics, Klass (1960) examined the caste affiliations of Hindu members, from various parties, in the Trinidad Legislative Council. He observed that almost all of the legislators claimed membership in the two highest castes, Brahman and Kshatriya. The same is true for Mauritius, Guyana, Suriname, and other former indentured communities (Par n.d.). In Mauritius, there are the fourfold Maraze, Baboojee, Vaish, and Dusadh castes, as well as Chamars.

Even after six generations, many NRIs profess 'awareness' of their caste. Caste endures in the diaspora and along with it, casteism, the oppression of Dalits, and the marginalization of Dalit cultures. There is a close connection between class and caste privileges, and 'Brahmins' and *maulavi*s (Islamic clerics) are held in high regard. Correspondingly, non-Brahmin priests are rare, and women priestesses rarer still. The Hindu diaspora are still embroiled in caste and Ambedkar's call for its annihilation is as relevant to overseas Indians as it is to Indians in the motherland.

Ambedkar's Relevance to Indian Diaspora

While the NRIs have been able to become highly successful in Western secular states, their sponsorship of religious nationalism is having the opposite effect in the subcontinent. Reinforcement of cultural and social boundaries is one of the main obstacles in the path to economic progress, and one sign is that entrepreneurs and corporations in India are small in comparison to those in China and other Asian countries.

Reinforcing the secular state and rolling back the move towards the right, culturally and politically, offers the NRIs an unprecedented economic opportunity in India, but their caste bias takes precedence over progress. In fact, the NRIs oversized influence may doom India into remaining a sink of ignorance and den of religious intolerance for decades to come. There are key social and political issues affecting diaspora communities that are ignored in the process as well.

Almost all overseas Indians face some form of race conflict in their countries of residence. Some examples of this are: the 1907 Bellingham riots against Indians in Washington in the US; the 1964 riots in Guyana; the 1972 expulsion of Indians from Uganda; the 1987 riot against Indians in Fiji; and the 2009 violence against Indians in Australia. These polarizing events point to the widespread and persistent nature of racial conflict facing the diaspora.

Three shootings in America during 2017 further reinforce the vulnerability of overseas Indians to bigotry in the West. The first one, in Kansas, involved a white army veteran who opened fire on two Indian tech workers in a bar, while shouting, 'Go back to your country'. The second shooting involved a Sikh man in a Seattle suburb who was injured in his driveway after a gunman opened fire while yelling the same thing. In the third case, a South Carolina business owner was gunned down outside his house for no apparent reason (Dwyer 2017; Ismail 2017; PTI 2017).

Hindu supremacy and Indian national pride may be useful psychologically for the NRIs, but they do little else. The diaspora in the West need to recognize that they cannot pass for 'white' and may always be viewed as 'untouchables'. For example, Romas have lived for over 1,000 years in Europe and are still considered 'outsiders'. The NRIs are trapped within caste and regional boundaries and this limits vision of a way forward.

Ambedkar's ideas of 'liberty, equality, and fraternity' can help the NRIs to build a bridge between different caste, religious, regional, and language groups, and with other non-Indian communities. In an undelivered talk, published as 'Annihilation of Caste' in 1936, Ambedkar writes; 'fraternity ... is only another name for democracy. Democracy is not merely a form of government. It is primarily a mode of associated living, of conjoint communicated experience. It is essentially an attitude of respect and reverence towards fellowmen' (Ambedkar 1979[1936]: 24).

The NRIs do practice fraternity, but only in relation to their varna and jati. They need to extend a helping hand beyond their narrow circle to others in their plural societies, as well as to people living in South Asia. Seeped in education and class privilege, diaspora Indians lack compassion towards others who are less fortunate. Ambedkar (1979[1936]: 24) addresses privilege when he asks, 'shall we treat them as unequal because they are unequal? This is a question which the opponents of equality must answer.'

He argues further, 'if it is good for the social body to get the most out of its members, it can get most out of them only by making them equal as far as possible at the very start of the race. That is one reason why we cannot escape equality' (Ambedkar 1979[1936]: 24). Secular organizations in the West can help privileged NRIs to contribute to their professions and help disadvantaged communities overseas and in South Asia. If the diaspora becomes more involved in social and economic justice, this will greatly reduce the racial tensions they face.

The diaspora will significantly be impacted by climate change. A vast number of overseas Indians reside on islands and in countries below the sea level. Will India allow millions of climate migrants to return from overseas communities? Diaspora organizations should include climate change in their agenda and help communities where they live, and in affected countries, to become more climate resilient.

India is already experiencing a warming climate. The former union environment minister, Jairam Ramesh, admitted that India is the most vulnerable country in the world to climate change. The reasons for this are many. No country in the world has the demographic expansion which India is experiencing. Around 60 per cent of India's agriculture is rain fed and the number of rainy days has decreased, leading to a decrease in groundwater recharging. Due to climate change, India is subjected to irregular monsoons, flooding, and higher temperatures. The Himalayan glaciers are receding, which further impacts the perennial rivers of north India. Also, rising sea levels will adversely affect millions of people living along the country's 7,500 km coastline.

Thus, as India is a large country with many living in poverty, an inadequate infrastructure and lack of government planning to deal with complex weather systems lead to increased vulnerability. Social and cultural boundaries also hinder planning for mitigation and disaster relief. Climate change in South Asia may necessitate fraternity with India's traditional rivals, China and Pakistan, and a belligerent Hindu government may prove disastrous for tens of millions of climate migrants. India needs to remain secular, democratic, and cooperative with its neighbours to survive this impending crisis.

Shared Burden: Caste and Racial Subjugation

Before indentured Dalits and South Asians, millions of enslaved Africans were exploited for centuries under European colonialism. Afro-Guyanese scholar, Walter Rodney (1972), argued that Europe underdeveloped Africa and the brutality of the colonial encounter still persists. The Atlantic human bondage trade occurred from the fifteenth to the nineteenth centuries. This inhumane practice involved over 36,000 European slave voyages that forcibly removed 12 million Africans to the Americas (Segal 1995). During the treacherous middle passage across the ocean, up to 20 per cent of the enslaved died, that is, well over 2.2 million Africans (Gomez 1998). Millions more were killed and internally displaced in Africa.

Enslaved and free African labourers built the plantations, roads, canals, tunnels, ports, railroads, and cities, that is, the economic engines of the West, but their contributions are rarely acknowledged. America's position as the sole superpower in the world was built on the backs of free African labour, just like the Hindu economy was built on bonded Dalit workers in India.

Historical and current caste and racial oppression are similar and form a basis for mutual alliances. The issues of struggle and programmes taken for liberation by African-Americans and Dalits are also important to consider. Both movements share a long-standing history, have gone through many ups and downs, have faced numerous internal and external conflicts, and are searching for new programmes and ways to face them. Interestingly, during the nineteenth and twentieth centuries, the two issues were connected in the minds of American leaders who spoke out against enslavement.

The caste school of race relations[7] connected the two forms of oppression, and the term 'caste' was used in the writings and speeches of prominent opponents of enslavement, such as Frederick Douglass, William Lloyd Garrison, Horace Greeley, and Harriet Beecher Stowe. Segregated churches proved especially vulnerable to accusations of harbouring the insidious caste spirit.

---

[7] This term refers to American sociologists who used the word 'caste' to describe the separation between European Americans and African Americans in the US during the Jim Crow era and earlier. The most notable publications in this field are Warner (1936), Myrdal (1944), and Dollard (1937).

After legal enslavement was abolished in the Americas,[8] African-Americans continued to experience decades of racial oppression under Jim Crow laws. Even though blacks served in the American Civil War, World War I, and World War II, they still faced racism, segregation, and lynching by European Americans. Separate and unequal access to public facilities and resources was the norm, until the 1960s Civil Rights Movement brought in changes. However, race and caste continue to be critical factors in the lower educational achievement, income, health, and life expectancy of African-Americans and Dalits, respectively, compared to European Americans and Hindus.

One prominent civil rights leader was William Edward Burghardt Du Bois (1868–1963), who strongly protested against lynching, Jim Crow laws, and discrimination in education and employment. His cause included people of colour everywhere, particularly Africans and Asians in European colonies. Du Bois was an early proponent of pan-Africanism and helped organize several pan-African congresses to fight for the independence of African colonies from European rule.

Another powerful African-American leader in the 1920s was Marcus Mosiah Garvey, Jr (1887–1940), promoter of the Back-to-Africa movement and founder of the Universal Negro Improvement Association (UNIA). The two leaders differed significantly in the solutions they offered and this limited mutual support. Garvey denounced Du Bois's efforts to achieve equality through integration and instead, endorsed racial separatism. The elder Du Bois initially supported the concept of Garvey's Black Star Line, a shipping company that was intended to facilitate commerce within the African diaspora, however his enthusiasm soon waned.

With UNIA's rising influence, Du Bois considered Garvey's programme of racial separation implausible and a capitulation to white supremacy. It was a tacit admission that African Americans could never be equal to European Americans. More infuriating, Garvey tried to engage with the enemy, the European American supremacists, in their mutual goal of separation. Noting how popular African repatriation was with racist thinkers and politicians, Du Bois feared that Garvey threatened the gains made by his own movement. Yet, over time, Du Bois became increasingly frustrated

---

[8] In 1888, in Brazil.

with the lack of racial progress in the US and towards the end of his life, he too decided to separate and migrate to Africa, where he died.

Like Du Bois and Garvey, Ambedkar struggled deeply with the issues of separation and civil rights for Dalits. Born in the Indian heartland, Ambedkar was a true nationalist. He wanted all of India to develop, especially the rural areas. However, despite the legal and policy safeguards he struggled to enshrine in the Constitution, the lack of progress for Dalits made him consider separatism as a means to an end. Like Du Bois and Garvey, Ambedkar was also an internationalist and sought the aid of the British and the United Nations (UN) to reform casteism.

In the 1946, Ambedkar wrote to Du Bois to inquire about the National Negro Congress petition to the UN, which attempted to secure minority rights through the UN council. Ambedkar explained that he had been a 'student of the Negro problem' and that 'There is so much similarity between the position of the Untouchables and the position of the Negroes of America, that the study of the latter is not only natural but necessary.'

Du Bois (1946) responded by telling Ambedkar that he was familiar with his name and had 'every sympathy with the Untouchables of India'. Throughout his career, Ambedkar turned to the US history, particularly to the abolition era and the Reconstruction period after emancipation in 1863, for inspiration and for cautionary lessons about how a society might become intolerant and fall into disarray.

Organic Intellectuals: Ambedkar, Du Bois, and Garvey

Ambedkar, Du Bois, and Garvey were distinguished leaders who lived in the shadow of legendary predecessors. For Garvey and Du Bois, there were Paul Bogle (1820–1865), Sojourner Truth (1797–1883), Frederick Douglass (1818–1895), Harriet Tubman (1822–1913), and several others. Ambedkar looked up to Jyotirao Phule, who titled his major anti-Brahmin polemic *Slavery* (1873) and dedicated it to the Americans.

The long history of Dalit and African-American resistance was critical to Ambedkar, Du Bois, and Garvey in building their movements. Each edited and published newsletters to disseminate subaltern history and revolutionary ideas to the masses burdened by colour and caste. The three figures were organic intellectuals who held an opinion of their movement similar to that of the Italian Marxist, Antonio Gramsci, that their followers contained the embryo of a socialist state. After observing the occupation of factories by Italian workers in the 1920s, Gramsci wrote of the organic capacities of the working class: 'It was necessary to see these and other sights, in order to be convinced how limitless the latent powers of the masses are, and how they are revealed and develop swiftly as soon as the conviction takes root among the masses that they are arbiters and masters of their own destinies' (cited in Forgacs 2000). The oppressed held the key to their own future, but to attain that they must first look upon themselves with respect.

Ambedkar, Du Bois, and Garvey based their education on 'self-respect' and captivated the minds of Dalits and African-Americans in the same way that Gramsci encouraged the Italian working class by expressing to them that they were the key to the developing state. The three leaders created organizations and curricula that emphasized to Dalits and African-Americans that they were as dignified as any Hindu and European American person. They remained grounded in the reality of everyday Dalits and African-Americans and focused on creating their own parallel resources of knowledge to end their cultural exploitation.

Like Gramsci, the three men of colour operated in the shadow of Marx and each embraced various forms of social programmes, community projects, and state-sponsored aid. They created programmes for the oppressed related to the culture of collectivity and egalitarianism, which came from the pre-caste and pre-enslavement period. Du Bois taught courses on Marx and believed that capitalism was a primary cause of racism. He and Ambedkar were disappointed with mainstream socialists, who they saw as prejudiced and one-dimensional. Both remained steadfast in the need for safeguards and affirmative action since they realized that simply giving-in to private enterprise through Dalit and African-American capitalism would perpetuate inequality and likely result in elite members getting co-opted.

Like Gramsci, Du Bois and Ambedkar were rigorous sociologists and political theorists, while Garvey stressed African history. Du Bois and Ambedkar were brilliant intellectuals and prolific authors whose works remain relevant and well read. Du Bois wrote one of the first scientific treatises in the field of American sociology, he was an expert on the Reconstruction period, and developed many useful theories, such as 'the wages of whiteness' (Du Bois 1935). He worked with scholars and activists to establish the Niagara Movement and the National Association for the Advancement of Colored People (NAACP), an organization that was influential in the Civil Rights Movement for decades. As mentioned earlier, Du Bois fostered several pan-African congresses, was an ardent peace activist, and advocated for nuclear disarmament.

For Garvey, the emphasis was on self-help, mutual aid, economic development, and encouraging Africans to replace ethnic and regional identities with pan-African ones. His motto was,'One God! One Aim! One Destiny!'. Garvey and Du Bois understood that divisive issues within Africa and its diaspora limited unity and resistance to centuries of racism and colonialism. Both viewed the African diaspora as fertile ground for developing organic African intellectuals who could articulate the ideas of pan-African consciousness that could serve to unite the continent and its people worldwide.

Along with UNIA, Garvey founded the African Communities League (ACL) and the Black Star Line. The UNIA claimed four million members in 1920, and Garvey continues to be a hero in the Caribbean, especially in Jamaica. Garveyism inspired other movements, such as the Nation of Islam and Rastafari groups, that proclaim Garvey as a prophet.

Ambedkar was a great legal scholar and an active legislator who focused on labour and gender issues. Regarded as the chief architect of India's Constitution, Ambedkar crafted reservation polices in the public sector for Dalits, women, and other marginalized groups, which have led to significant changes in educational access and achievements. Perhaps Ambedkar's greatest achievement was his conversion to Buddhism and re-establishment of the religion in India among Dalits. Ambedkar's popularity has been growing in the recent years and he is considered a legendary hero by tens of millions of Dalit women, children, and men.

Women's Role in the Revolution

Ambedkar, Du Bois, and Garvey were ardent supporters of women's rights. Each viewed the role and liberation of women as vital aspects of their movement against subjugation and, therefore, created a space for females in their organizations and programmes. The symbolism and values in women's liberation songs and music formed an alternative culture for expressing joys and sorrows that were an integral part of these movements.

Du Bois, like Frederick Douglass before him, was an ardent ally of American feminists and wrote a famous essay, 'The Damnation of Women', in 1920 (Du Bois 1920). In Garvey's UNIA, women formed the backbone of the benevolent and community service functions of the organization and of its female auxiliaries, including the Black Cross Nurses crops. Ambedkar, Du Bois, and Garvey were warmly nourished by women in turn, who were instrumental in the leaders' private and public work.

Du Bois's first wife, Nina Gomer, was devastated after losing her first child to racism as European American doctors refused to see the sick infant. She remained tireless in her devotion and managed the details of their private sphere. Du Bois had serial affairs with many accomplished women, including his second wife, Shirley Graham (1896–1977). Graham embraced Malcolm X as a son, introduced him to President Kwame Nkrumah, and was helpful in his success.

Garvey's first wife, Amy Ashwood (1897–1969), served as the organization's first secretary and co-founder. His second wife, Amy Jacques (1896–1973), was one of the key political leaders, archivists, and interpreters of the Garvey movement. Amy Jacques frequently represented the movement at public meetings and events and was a regular columnist in UNIA's newspaper, *Negro World*. She was a forceful advocate of women's rights and participated in the famous Fifth Pan-African Congress held in Manchester, England, in 1945. Her 1963 book, *Garvey and Garveyism*, was partially responsible for reviving interest in the UNIA and the Garvey movement (Garvey 1963).

Garvey's movement had separate but parallel women's and men's auxiliaries, such as the Black Cross Nurses and the Universal African Legions. The UNIA had 'Ladies Divisions' under women's leadership and established women's positions on local executives and in the celebration of Women's Day. This dual-sex UNIA structure afforded women a separate sphere of influence as well as leadership roles within the hierarchy of the women's wings of the divisions.

In a similar vein, Ambedkar tried to enshrine women's rights in the political vocabulary and Constitution of India and resigned from India's Parliament to protest the blockage of his bill on women's rights. At the state level, Ambedkar played a major role in the first Maternity Benefits Act passed in India in 1929 by the Bombay legislature. At the national level, as law minister, he introduced the Hindu Code Bill, the most formidable women's rights legislative measure of modern India, in the Parliament in 1947. The Bill sought, among other reforms, to put an end to a variety of marriage systems prevailing in India and to legalize only monogamous marriages. It also sought to confer on women the right to property and adoption, which had been denied by Hindu texts and traditional laws. The Hindu Code Bill put Indian women and men on an equal level in all legal matters.

The Bill was a threat to the male status quo and Hindu patriarchy on which the traditional family structure rested and, therefore, these forces were its main opposition. A few years after his resignation, the Hindu Code Bill was split into four bills and re-introduced in the Parliament. The Bills were passed this time and became law.

Indeed, Ambedkar's focus on women's equality provides a platform for females in the Global South and Global North to work together. Women and children comprise three-quarters of the South Asian diaspora, and reproductive rights are increasingly being challenged by a resurgent Christian-right in the West and elsewhere. The 20-year sentence given to Purvi Patel for a stillbirth in the US in 2015 and the death of Savita Halappanavar in Ireland from denial of an abortion in 2012 show that the lives of NRI women are increasingly under threat. The NRI organizations can help by embracing feminist issues and mobilizing Dalit and African women to defend reproductive rights, reservations, and social services globally, in the face of austerity and religious attacks.

★ ★ ★

This chapter explores the Indian diaspora and compares the movements led by Ambedkar, Du Bois, and Garvey. People in South Asia and the diaspora are facing several existential crises, including climate change, poverty, religious conflicts, and violence against women. With the largest diaspora in the world, there is a need for pan-South Asian secular organizations and perspectives to address mutual survival interests.

By supporting secular institutions, the wealthy NRI community can play a positive role in developing pan-South Asian and

Global South connections and linkages. The NRIs can help to build an alliance between African-Americans, coloured people, Native Americans, and European American supporters in the Global North and Dalits, women, and oppressed communities in the Global South. South Asians abroad can use the examples of Ambedkar, Du Bois, Garvey, and pan-Africanism to educate and organize people in the Global South and North who are subjected to sex, caste, race, ethnic, cultural, and class exploitation. By coming together, people of colour can more effectively address mutual challenges, such as climate mitigation.

In confronting the issue of Hindu and white supremacy, both Ambedkar and Du Bois sought legal safeguards and aggressive affirmative action as solutions. Ambedkar and Garvey argued for forms of political and social separation as well. Ambedkar's framing of systemic discrimination and his solutions to ending casteism and sexism in India can also be applied to other marginalized groups around the world. In 'Annihilation of Caste' and other writings, Ambedkar called for the state to make fundamental changes to oppressive social and gender ideologies, and to set limits on the role of religious and ideological authorities.

Ambedkar argued that the state should instead focus on equality, freedom, and fraternity for all through education and affirmative action for disadvantaged groups. Ambedkar's approach has relevance for women and minorities in the Global South and North, for example, African-Americans. His ideas can also be used to address critical issues in North–South relations, such as economic imbalance, climate change, and migration.

References

Ambedkar. 1979[1936]. 'Annihilation of Caste', in Vasant Moon (compiler) *Dr. Babasaheb Ambedkar: Writings and Speeches*, Vol. 1, pp. 25–96. Bombay: Education Department, Government of Maharashtra.

———. 1979. *The Untouchables: Who Were They and Why They Became Untouchables?*, Vol. 7, Book 2. Collected Works of Dr Ambedkar. Bombay: Education Department, Government of Maharashtra.

———. 1891–1956. Letter from B. R. Ambedkar to W. E. B. Du Bois, ca. July 1946. W. E. B. Du Bois Papers (MS 312). Special Collections and University Archives, University of Massachusetts Amherst Libraries. Available at https://credo.library.umass.edu/view/full/mums312-b109-i132; last accessed on 3 May 2020.

Anand, Nupur. 2018. 'Even the World Bank is Surprised by How Much Money Indians Abroad Send Home'. *Quartz India*, 23 April. Available at https://qz.com/india/1259525/remittance-revival-indians-sent-69-billion-back-home-in-2017/; last accessed on 29 April 2020.

Bezzi, Daniela. 2020. 'Arundhati Roy: Indian Muslims Facing 'Genocidal Climate' Amid Pandemic'. *Open Democracy*, 11 June.

Brown, Carolyn Henning. 1981. 'Demographic Constraints on Caste: A Fiji Indian Example'. *American Ethnologist* 8(2): 314–28.

Campbell, Jerome. 2014. 'Non-Resident Indians Influence Their Home Country's Election from Abroad'. Neon Tommy, Annenberg Media Center, 28 May. Available at http://www.neontommy.com/news/2014/05/non-resident-indians-influence-home-country-elections-abroad.html; last accessed on 3 May 2020.

Constable, Philip. 2001. 'The Marginalization of a Dalit Martial Race in Late Nineteenth- and Early Twentieth-Century Western India'. *The Journal of Asian Studies* 60(2): 439–78.

Du Bois, W.E.B. 1920. *The Damnation of Women, ca. 1920*. W. E. B. Du Bois Papers (MS 312). Special Collections and University Archives, University of Massachusetts Amherst Libraries. Available at http://credo.library.umass.edu/view/full/mums312-b220-i012; last accessed on 3 May 2020.

———. 1935. *Black Reconstruction in America, 1860–1880*. New York: Harcourt Brace.

———. 1946. *Letter from W. E. B. Du Bois to B. R. Ambedkar, July 31, 1946*. W. E. B. Du Bois Papers (MS 312). Special Collections and University Archives, University of Massachusetts Amherst Libraries. Available at http://credo.library.umass.edu/view/full/mums312-b109-i133; last accessed on 3 May 2020.

Duttagupta, Ishani. 2014. 'Pravasi Bharatiya Divas 2014: Modi Acts as a Magnet; But Did BJP Lose an Opportunity?' *The Economic Times*, 12 January. Available at https://economictimes.indiatimes.com/news/politics-and-nation/pravasi-bharatiya-divas-2014-modi-acts-as-a-magnet-but-did-bjp-lose-an-opportunity/articleshow/28685444.cms; last accessed on 18 June 2020.

Dollard, John. 1937. *Caste and Class in a Southern Town*. New Haven: Yale University Press.

Dwyer, Colin. 2017. 'Sikh Man Shot Outside His Seattle Home, Told To "Go Back To Your Own Country"'. *National Public Radio*, 5 March. Available at https://www.npr.org/sections/thetwo-way/2017/03/05/518637650/sikh-man-shot-outside-his-seattle-home-told-to-go-back-to-your-own-country; last accessed on 18 June 2020.

Forgacs, David (ed.). 2000. *The Gramsci Reader: Selected Writings 1916–1935*. New York: New York University Press.

Garvey, Amy Jacques. 1963. *Garvey and Garveyism: Dedicated to Truth and Better Understanding Between Races*. Baltimore: Black Classic Press.

Gomez, Michael A. 1998. *Exchanging Our Country Marks: The Transformation of African Identities in the Colonial and Antebellum South*. Chapel Hill: UNC Press.

Hultzsch, E (trans.). 1925. *Inscriptions of Asoka*, Vol. I, p. 27. Government of India.

Hundal, Sunny. 2017. 'Why NRIs Are Still Important Influencers for Modi's India'. *Hindustan Times*, 12 May. Available at https://www.hindustantimes.com/columns/why-nris-are-still-important-influencers-for-modi-s-india/story-mefpcnBAesKiVCSgdp5V8L.html; last accessed on 18 June 2020.

Ilaiah, Kancha. 1996. *Why I Am Not a Hindu: A Sudra Critique of Hindutva, Philosophy, Culture, and Political Economy*. Calcutta: Samya.

———. 2018. 'Shudras Built the Indus Valley Civilization!', *Countercurrents*, 23 August. Available at https://countercurrents.org/2018/08/history-of-constructors-and-destroyers-a-discourse-on-harappa-and-rigveda/; last accessed on 15 July 2020.

India Brand Equity Foundation. 2018. 'Union Budget of India (2017–18)'. Available at https://www.ibef.org/economy/union-budget-2017-18; last accessed on 29 April 2020.

Indian Express. 2013. 'SCs, STs Form 25% of Population, says Census 2011 Data.' 1 May.

Ismail, Feras. 2017. 'Harnish Patel Fourth Indian American Killed in South Carolina in 23 Months'. *The American Bazaar*, 4 March. Available at https://www.americanbazaaronline.com/2017/03/04/harnish-patel-fourth-indian-american-killed-in-south-carolina-in-23-months423096/; last accessed on 18 June 2020.

Kerur, Bhargavi. 2007. 'Foreign Trip May Cost Udupi Pontiff Ascension'. *DNA India*, 28 November. Available at https://www.dnaindia.com/india/report-foreign-trip-may-cost-udupi-pontiff-ascension-1135925; last accessed on 23 April 2020.

Klass, Morton. 1960. *East and West Indian: Cultural Complexity in Trinidad*. New York: Columbia University Press.

Ministry of External Affairs (MEA). 2018. 'Population of Overseas Indians'. 31 December. Available at http://mea.gov.in/images/attach/NRIs-and-PIOs_1.pdf; last accessed on 18 June 2020.

Myrdal, Gunnar. 1944. *An American Dilemma*. New York: Harper & Row.

Non Resident Indians Online. 2020. 'Statistics of Indians Abroad'. Available at https://www.nriol.com/indiandiaspora/statistics-indians-abroad.asp; last accessed on 23 April 2020.

Par, R.G. n.d. 'The Fallacy of the Caste System in Mauritius'. *Lexpress*, 7 June. Available at https://www.lexpress.mu/idee/309149/fallacy-caste-system-mauritius; last accessed on 3 May 2020.

Parth, M.N. 2020. 'India Arrests Activist Anand Teltumbde over 2018 Caste Violence.' *Al Jazeera*. 14 April.

Press Trust of India. 2017. 'Indian Techie Shot Dead by American Yelling "Get Out of my Country"'. *Business Standard India*. 25 February. Available at https://www.business-standard.com/article/pti-stories/indian-techie-shot-dead-by-american-yelling-get-out-of-my-country-117022500008_1.html; last accessed on 18 June 2020.

Rodney, Walter. 1972. *How Europe Underdeveloped Africa*. UK: Bogle-L'Ouverture Publications.

Rooney, Katharine. 2019. 'India's Record-Breaking Diaspora in Numbers'. *World Economic Forum*, 20 September. Available at https://www.weforum.org/agenda/2019/09/india-has-the-world-s-biggest-diaspora-here-s-where-its-emigrants-live/; last accessed on 23 April 2020.

Seenarine, M. 1999a. 'Recasting Indian Women in Colonial Guiana', in M. Gosine and D. Narine (eds), *Sojourners to Settlers: Indian Migrants in the Caribbean and the Americas*, pp. 81–124. New York: Windsor Press.

———. 1999b. 'Indentured Indian Women in Colonial Guyana: Recruitment, Migration, Labor & Caste,' in M. Gosine and D. Narine (eds), *Sojourners to Settlers: Indian Migrants in the Caribbean and the Americas*. New York: Windsor Press.

———. 2004. *Education & Empowerment Among Dalit (Untouchable) Women in India: Voices from the Subaltern*. New York: Edwin Mellen Press.

Segal, Ronald. 1995. *The Black Diaspora: Five Centuries of the Black Experience Outside Africa*, p. 4. New York: Farrar, Straus and Giroux.

Sharma, Mihir Swarup. 2019. 'The Impact Of "Howdy, Modi" on PM, Trump and NRIs'. *NDTV*, 23 September. Available at https://www.ndtv.com/opinion/howdy-modi-what-it-means-for-pm-and-his-bond-with-nris-2105650; last accessed on 18 June 2020.

Takaki, Ronald. 1998. *Strangers from a Different Shore: A History of Asian Americans*, p. 62. Boston: Little, Brown and Company.

Telugu Association of North America (TANA). 2020. 'About TANA Foundation'. Available at https://www.tana.org/foundation/about-tana-foundation; last accessed on 18 June 2020.

Thakur, Atul and Rema Nagarajan. 2014. '80% of AAP Funds from Outside Delhi'. *The Times of India*, 4 January. Available at https://timesofindia.indiatimes.com/india/80-of-AAP-funds-from-outside-Delhi/articleshow/28074062.cms; last accessed on 18 June 2020.

The Hindu. 2007. 'Shiroor Seer Backs Puttige Swamiji', 29 November. Available at https://www.thehindu.com/todays-paper/tp-national/tp-karnataka/Shiroor-seer-backs-Puttige-swamiji/article14884868.ece; last accessed on 23 April 2020.

———. 2015. 'India's Religions by Numbers'. 26 August.

Times of India, The. 2017. 'Invest Big in Capital, Naidu to Telugu NRIs'. 9 May. Available at https://timesofindia.indiatimes.com/city/vijayawada/invest-big-in-capital-naidu-to-telugu-nris/articleshow/58588049.cms; last accessed on 18 June 2020.

Tinker, Hugh. 1993. *A New System of Slavery: The Export of Indian Labour Overseas 1830–1920*. London: Hansib Publishing.

United Nations. 2019. 'International Migrant Stock 2019'. UN Department of Economic and Social Affairs. Available at https://www.un.org/en/development/desa/population/migration/data/estimates2/estimates19.asp; last accessed on 23 April 2020.

United Nations Department of Economic and Social Affairs (UNDESA). 2018. 'World Population Prospects—Population Division'. Available at https://population.un.org/wpp/; last accessed on 17 June 2020.

US Census Bureau. 2019. 'ACS Demographic and Housing Estimates'. American Community Survey, December 2019. Available at https://data.census.gov/cedsci/table?q=united%20states&g=0100000US&hidePreview=false&tid=ACSDP5Y2018.DP05&vintage=2018&cid=DP05_0001E; last accessed on 23 April 2020.

US Department of Commerce. 1913. '1910 Census: Volume 1. Population, General Report and Analysis.' Bureau of the Census.

Warner, W. Lloyd. 1936. 'American Caste and Class', *American Journal of Sociology* XLII: 234–7.

8

Racelessness and Ambedkar's Idea of Annihilation

Post-apartheid South Africa

GOOLAM VAHED AND ASHWIN DESAI

South Africa achieved the status of a pariah nation as a result of its policy of segregation and apartheid, which was the official policy of the white-minority National Party government between 1948 and 1994. Apartheid entrenched white racial superiority in the South African society and used a host of repressive measures to ensure minority rule. Black Africans, coloureds,[1] and Indians, that is, the 'non-whites', were denied the right to vote and access to white 'spaces' that ranged from schools to public transport to jobs. Non-whites were also separated and corralled into separate racial group areas. There were differences, however, in the way they were incorporated into the broader political economy. Indians, for example, enjoyed more rights than Africans in terms of land ownership and access to semi-skilled and skilled jobs in the Transvaal and Natal (KwaZulu-Natal). Coloureds, likewise, enjoyed labour preference in Western Cape over Africans.

The antidote to this racist system for those struggling against it was to raise the spectre of non-racialism. This had a powerful effect as it contradicted the foundations of the apartheid system. This espousing of non-racialism was not only at the level of speechifying

---

[1] A term that refers to a mixed-race group.

but also, the activists sought to build this ethos into their everyday organizing. The sport of cricket, for example, was historically played separately by the different 'non-white' groups. They played against each other in what was known as interracial tournaments. However, in the 1950s, this was done away with and the 'non-whites' started playing together without any racial designations. Politically, too, the Congresses representing different racial groups came together in the 1950s to constitute the Congress Alliance. While this might not have done away with everyday racial prejudice, it did send a powerful signal to those who sought to divide and rule. Similarly, the United Democratic Front (UDF) that emerged in the 1980s as the dominant anti-apartheid internal resistance movement enshrined the principle of non-racialism.

Nelson Mandela, leader of the African National Congress (ANC) who was imprisoned for 27 years and would emerge as the country's first president in 1994, epitomized this thread by preaching against black and white domination. During the Rivonia Trial in 1964, where he was charged with terrorism, he famously stated in his defense statement: 'I have fought against white domination, and I have fought against black domination. I have cherished the ideal of a democratic and free society in which all persons will live together in harmony with equal opportunities.... It is an ideal for which I am prepared to die' (Mandela 1964). On Mandela's assumption of the office of the president, his negotiating team and cabinet reflected his desire to build on the tradition of non-racialism.

At some stage in this folding from apartheid to democracy, non-racialism was adopted by white South Africans. However, there was a curious bastardization of the idea that evolved through the long twentieth century. Non-racialism became attached to the idea of racelessness: we do not recognize race, therefore we are non-racial, and to recognize race is to be a racist; so, the historic privileges accumulated by whites (and to a lesser extent, Indians) cannot be questioned as this goes against the grain of non-racialism. Attempts to redress apartheid legacies through affirmative action policies quickly got labelled as reverse racism.

One sees racelessness tied to whiteness, what the American poet and essayist Adrienne Rich calls 'white solipsism', meaning the trend to 'think, imagine and speak as if whiteness described the world'. Rich takes pains to point out that while this way of seeing does not reflect 'the consciously held belief that one race is inherently superior to all others', white solipsism reinforces racism by its occlusions and indicates 'a tunnel vision which simply does not see non-white experience or existence as precious or significant, unless in spasmodic, impotent guilt-reflexes, which have little or no long term, continuing momentum or political usefulness' (cited in Gqola 2001: 101).

Wits University academic Melissa Steyn's (2005: 121) definition of whiteness 'as the shared social space in which the psychological, cultural, political, and economic dimensions of this privileged positionality are normalized, and rendered unremarkable' is apposite. This approach is epitomized by former South African cricket fast bowler Allan Donald, who recounted that 'the non-whites who had played international cricket for us had all been easily assimilated into our dressing room, enjoying the banter, respecting the team ethos. No problem' (Donald 1999: 217). What the 'correct demeanour' is often comes to be defined by the prevailing white culture. One is reminded of French philosopher Alain Badiou's (2001: 25) famous phrase: 'Become like me and I will respect your difference.' 'Whiteness' allows for a seeming commitment to non-racialism (or more appropriately, colour blindness) that occludes the historical and contemporary privilege of being white.

In this context, the Sri Lankan-born writer and academic Yasmin Gunaratnam's assertion that 'whiteness is naturalized and left to stand as a de-racialized (and also often a de-ethnicized) norm, with "race" being the defining property and experience of "Other" groups' (Gunaratnam 2003: 29) is apposite. This allows 'those categorized as white to ignore, deny, avoid or forget their racialized subjective and social positionings' (Gunaratnam 2003: 112).

This idea of racelessness, depoliticized and decontextualized, has an uncanny resemblance to Satish Deshpande's (2013) coining of the concept of 'castelessness' in the Indian context. Both India and South Africa have had to deal with the problem of sections of their population being treated as second-class or even third-class citizens as a result of historic caste discrimination in the one instance, and race discrimination in the other. The history of apartheid and segregation in South Africa separated whites from blacks (Africans, coloureds, and Indians), and in India, there was a caste hierarchy which structured relationships and determined work and life opportunities. Each of these countries has attempted to redress the situation by instituting certain measures: in the South

African case, it is the policy of affirmative action post 1994; and in Independent India, it is the reservation policy. The comparison is very revealing, even though there is a fundamental difference between India and South Africa. Africans constitute around four-fifths of the population of South Africa and hold the reins of power. In India, in contrast, upper-caste Hindus, who are in the minority, constitute the ruling class.

Castelessness and racelessness are, in some ways, a reaction to these redress measures.

Castelessness

Over the past century, many academics have tried to draw comparisons between race and caste. Though the concept of caste is fluid, most colonial administrators and social theorists, since the nineteenth century, have argued that it is the most fundamental component of a rigid and hierarchical Indian society (Dirks 2001). The comparison with race in the United States (US) drew obvious comparisons. 'Caste' appeared in the writings and speeches of well-known opponents of slavery, including Frederick Douglass, William Lloyd Garrison, Horace Greeley, Theodore Parker, William Seward, Gerrit Smith, and Cassius Clay (Immerwahr 2007: 277).

When the Maharaja of Baroda, Sayajirao Gaekwad, visited Chicago in 1893, he was impressed with the work of anti-race activists and imported American educators to design the education syllabus in his state. It was he who sponsored Ambedkar to study at Columbia University in New York, and not go to England, where most Indians aspired to go (Immerwahr 2007: 278). The 1930s and 1940s saw the emergence of the 'caste school of race relations'; the Dalit Panthers in the 1970s modelled themselves on the Black Panthers; and there were calls for the recognition of caste oppression at the World Conference against Racism, Racial Discrimination, and Xenophobia in 2001. One recent work to take up this comparison is Gyanendra Pandey's 2013 work, *A History of Prejudice*, which analyses race and class as they unfolded in the US and India.

One of the critiques of race as caste thesis is that it presented a static analysis of race that failed to capture the 'dynamic aspects of race relations' (Immerwahr 2007: 281).

Race and apartheid have been central to our work. How could they not be? We were both born when apartheid was at its zenith. In the early 1960s, tens of thousands of Indians were put on the move and corralled into bounded racial areas, often at the point of apartheid's bayonets. Places of worship, schools, and sporting clubs were destroyed. We went to Indian schools and our early social relations were almost entirely within the Indian community. We both lived through the heady days of the Black Consciousness Movement (BCM) that saw mainly university-based Indian students adopt the broader rubric of 'black' that included coloureds, Indians, and Africans. Also, we bore witness to the slow erosion of petty apartheid that engulfed the lives of our parents, and then the heady days of the release of Mandela and the promise of building a 'Rainbow Nation'. While the notion was fuzzy, it did beckon a society that would not be haunted by racial division and domination that marked the lives of our parents and grandparents.

In this context, how could we not be intellectually and emotionally aroused by the fluidity and congealing of race, its attachment to political and economic ends of power and privilege, and its ability to reinvent itself just as its obituary was about to be written as Mandela came to life as the president of the Republic of Non-Racialism?

Regarding caste, though there was a large Indian population in South Africa, caste was not a central concern with either of us as we were growing up or even as academics. There were divisions among Indians, but the starkest were around class, language, and regional origins in India. We ourselves began to read more systematically on caste when we came across the works of B.R. Ambedkar, albeit late in our academic writings. Mohandas K. Gandhi, Ambedkar's political and ideological rival who spent most of the years from 1893 to 1914 in South Africa, was someone we grew up with and whom we have written extensively on (Desai and Vahed 2016).

Ambedkar came to our serious attention around 2014, when his *Annihilation of Caste* was republished with an introduction by Arundhati Roy (Ambedkar 2014). This publication came at a time when we were working on our own history of *The South African Gandhi* (Desai and Vahed 2016). The republished book resulted in us reading more extensively about Ambedkar, not only to understand the ways in which he differed from Gandhi but also because some of the issues he was concerned with, in particular the upliftment of marginalized peoples, were similar to what we ourselves were grappling with in South Africa, where the shine of the 'Rainbow Nation' had been wearing off and issues of social justice and redress had become highly politicized and contentious.

Ambedkar focused intensely on social and economic justice. He saw the 'deeply entrenched social inequities and caste loyalties' in India as 'serious obstacles to democratic participation and a shared sense of citizenship and nationhood' (Arora 2013). He saw caste as a major barrier to the progress of India's 'servile classes'. He wrote that caste was 'not a physical object like a wall of bricks or a line of barbed wire which prevents the Hindus from co-mingling and which has, therefore, to be pulled down. Caste is a notion. It is a state of mind. The destruction of caste ... means a notional change' (Ambedkar 1944: 19). He argued that political change without addressing social and economic inequality was akin to 'build[ing] a palace on a dung heap' (Teltumbde 2017: 83). Ambedkar's call for the total destruction of the caste system was the reason that the Jat-Pat-Todak Mandal, an organization of Hindu social reformers, withdrew its invitation to him to address their national convention in 1936, and why his 1944 publication was titled *Annihilation of Caste*.

Ambedkar was scathing of Gandhi whose ideas, he felt, meant that:

> Common man must keep on toiling ceaselessly for a pittance and remain a brute. Gandhism, with its call of back to nature, means back to nakedness, back to squalor, back to poverty and back to ignorance for the vast majority of the people.... Class structure in Gandhism is not an accident. It is its official doctrine. (cited in Loomba 2005: 196)

In *Caste, Class and Democracy*, Ambedkar contended that British rule would be followed by the tyranny of upper-caste Indians who loathed the 'untouchables' (Ambedkar 2002). The 'servile classes' had to be given a political voice because 'self-government and democracy become real ... when the governing class loses its power to capture the power to govern' (Ambedkar 2002: 136). Ambedkar's solution was the policy of 'reservation', referred to as 'affirmative action' in other settings such as South Africa, Malaysia, and the US. This policy was implemented after Gandhi's objection to the Poona Pact of 1932, which would have given Dalits a separate electorate, similar to that of Muslims and Sikhs, and would have separated Dalits from Hindus, thus jeopardizing the numerical majority of Hindus. Ambedkar withdrew his request when Gandhi threatened to fast until death. Ambedkar would later write: 'there was nothing noble in the fast. It was a foul and filthy act ... the worst form of coercion against a helpless people' (cited in Loomba 2005: 196). The Poona Pact:

> cemented the claims of the Congress and specifically of Gandhi to represent all of India, thus helping to conceal the fact that the leadership was exclusively upper caste and the even more closely guarded 'public secret' that these castes represented a very small minority of the Hindu population. The muting of caste identities was thus a necessary precondition for the construction of a Congress 'majority'. (Deshpande 2013: 35)

Ambedkar drafted the Indian Constitution and enshrined affirmative action as an antidote to caste discrimination. The 'reservation' policy provided quotas in education, public jobs, and elected assemblies for the scheduled castes, scheduled tribes, and subsequently, the other backward class (Gang et al. 2011: 43). The result of upper-caste hegemony was that the beneficiaries of reservations were 'reduced to the status of supplicants for whom a special concession was being made by the majority that "owned" the nation. This effectively positioned the upper caste minority as the de facto owner of the nation, with the power to grant favours to this or that subgroup' (Deshpande 2013: 36). In contrast to the upper caste, members of the depressed classes were permanently marked as a 'caste-marked exception', while the upper castes existed as 'a casteless norm. Neither route leads towards the annihilation or even the diminishing of caste.... The "annihilation of caste" seem more like a disabling dream than an empowering utopia' (Deshpande 2013: 36).

The South African Context

South Africa is a country built on race, class, and gender discrimination. Historically, the white settler population and their descendants, since their arrival in the seventeenth century, have subjugated the African peoples, coloureds, and Indians, who began arriving in the country from 1860 as indentured migrants and were followed by free migrants. Most Indians were working class and lived in dire economic circumstances until the 1960s. Access to mass education changed the class composition of Indian South Africans in the subsequent decades with the emergence of a professional class consisting of doctors, lawyers, civil servants, teachers, and accountants. Class mobility meant that as apartheid fell, a large number of Indians were part of the middle class in South Africa and the propensity of those seeking university education was on the rise.

Disparities cut across all sectors of society with a clear racial hierarchy: whites at the top, followed by Indians, coloureds, and Africans, in that order. Apartheid had touched every aspect of people's lives and affirmative action was seen as a proactive policy aimed at addressing and correcting past injustices, to level the playing fields going forward. It was applied in every sector of the society—from education to employment and even in national sporting teams—in the pursuit of transforming the society. This was done through such legislation as the Employment Equity Act (EEA) and Black Economic Empowerment (BEE), the aim being to reflect the demographics of the country and address the gross economic disparities in the country. Initially, the beneficiaries of EEA were intended to be women, people with disabilities, and blacks, with this latter category including Africans, coloureds, and Indians.

South Africa is now a 'non-racial' society, but all South Africans have to mark a box stating their race on identity documents, when filling out Census forms and even when applying for jobs, research funding, and seeking admissions to educational institutions. Sociologist Gerhard Maré argues that this reinforces racial identities:

> No one wants to define what each of the four races is, and how they are to be recognised.... So the [classification] ... remains hidden, locked into the race thinking of those engaged in classification. And here lies the rub. We all participate in keeping this system of classification operational, we are all expected to be its minions, because we can draw on the 'standards'... already familiar to us—in this case, the very criteria set by apartheid. (Maré 2014: 101)

Another South African academic, Christi van der Westhuizen, takes a different view of those mooting for a raceless society. She gets brilliantly to the nub of this approach in her 2017 book on white Afrikaner women in post-apartheid South Africa. She shows that their identity creates a number of:

> sometimes contradictory, pairings ... of good whites, good blacks, bad whites, bad blacks. These permutations make available positions that allow Afrikaans whites to redirect [the] moral stain of racism to *all* sides, or to culturally re-encode racism to remove race altogether, while paradoxically proclaiming white supremacy. The next options consist of reversals. First, the moral reversal of the apartheid and post-apartheid orders so as to cast aspersions over both the struggle against apartheid and the democratic era. Second, to shrug off apartheid as a moral burden carried by white people and to reassign it to black people, as a 'chip on the shoulder'. A related innovation of whiteness is to commandeer black people to exonerate white people from apartheid guilt, while claiming white innocence, based on white ignorance in relation to apartheid. Finally, racist paternalism ('our blacks') is used to claim white innocence on the basis of phantasmatic social affinity between black and white. (van der Westhuizen 2017: 194)

This discourse:

> embraces the neo-liberal modes of depoliticisation, decontextualisation and desocialisation of subjects to deny their structural contingencies and to maintain unequal power relations. Black people only surface from generalised elision if they are 'good blacks' who take individual responsibility for lost 'opportunities' that are the result of apartheid oppression. Apartheid as systematised oppression becomes depoliticised as 'difficult times' or the 'wrong time'. (van der Westhuizen 2017: 197)

The idea of racelessness has, in recent times, been taken up by sections of Indian South Africans whenever the issue of their privileged status is raised.

Indian South Africans

Studies in the post-apartheid era suggest that Indians are prospering economically. For example, the headline in a local Durban-based newspaper, *Daily News*, dated 11 August 2016, read: 'Economists: Indians Benefited from Apartheid' (Nxumalo and Mngoma 2016). The article stated that a study by economist Siphamandla Mkhwanazi found that in the period 1996–2014, the

Indian population in South Africa saw the fastest growth in per capita income. Economist Bonke Dumisa also contended that corporate and multinational businesses were promoting Indians in the corporate world and not black African people. He warned that this was 'a sensitive issue that must be discussed; however, people don't want to discuss it' (Nxumalo and Mngoma 2016). Another economist, Dawie Roodt, stated that Indians should not be beneficiaries of affirmative action because 'the number with qualifications has skyrocketed and unemployment is falling. It is a sweet time for Indians' (Nxumalo and Mngoma 2016).

This report sparked anger among Indians. In a letter to a local newspaper, Les Govender, for example, described the report as 'utter nonsense':

> The misguided responses ... will only serve to stir up interracial tension while most South Africans are working towards social cohesion. It is shocking that Dumisa is quoted as saying that after 1994 the 'Indian population was more advantaged than other races'. Surely he knows that since 1994 our children have been sidelined for admissions to tertiary education institutions because of the quota system and that Indians across the board are being discriminated against on the basis of affirmative action. Research will also confirm the reality that thousands of Indians live in abject poverty.... Educational qualifications were not handed out to Indians by the apartheid government. Indians worked hard, made personal sacrifices and persevered in our quest to improve our lives. We were able to overcome our plight as so called 'second-class citizens' by prioritising education as the key to economic and social upliftment. When no schools were provided for Indians, our forefathers contributed funds from their meagre earnings to build state-aided schools.... By saying that 'even though we were all oppressed, we were not equally oppressed', Dumisa is acknowledging the oppression that Indians faced. It makes me wonder why Indians are now begrudged their success even after facing such oppression. This issue must be confronted openly and in an objective manner with a view to emulating Indians for the benefit of all South Africans. (*Natal Mercury* 2016)

Whilst it is true that statistics do not account for the Indian working class that has suffered during the transition, Govender's response shows the conundrum of Indian South Africans who explain their economic success as the outcome of hard work. When this success is focused upon to show that the discrimination faced by Indians was not the same as that of Africans, they become defensive. The reality is that Indians as 'middlemen' were differentially incorporated into the apartheid system, enjoying access to land and schooling which was denied to Africans.

In a subsequent interview with the *Post Newspaper* (2016), which is geared for an Indian ethnic market, this is precisely the point that Dumisa made:

> The apartheid regime oppressed all the 'non-white' race groups. There were, however, four official classifications; you had whites as the 'first class' citizens with all the privileges; there was a second category, which was rather fuzzy; then there were Indians and coloureds as 'third class' citizens seriously oppressed, but with some exceptions here and there. Then, there were black Africans as 'fourth class' citizens with a few extra oppressive measures designed specifically for them, and this included Bantu Education ... which was specifically designed for the 'Bantu to know his place'.

Thus, when South Africa moved into its post-apartheid period in 1994, the different groups were not starting from the same position.

> The black African population group had more hurdles to jump to be able to compete equally with people of other races. In golf terms, this is called 'the handicap'. The apartheid extra-oppressive measures thus ensured the black African group had more disadvantages than the other race groups.... We cannot redress past imbalances if we are deliberately in denial about the historical reality thereof.... How do we improve the economic superstructure if we are in denial about the factual historical foundations? (*Post Newspaper* 2016)

Dumisa's points are telling in terms of the historically differential incorporation of Indians and Africans into the political economy. There are two prongs to the rise of the Indian professional class: the merchant-class children who went to university and moved out of family businesses; and those from the working class, especially the townships of Chatsworth and Phoenix, who were the first generation of their families to enter tertiary institutions. Education was key to entrenching inequality and privilege.

As Africans and Indians became urbanized in the 1930s and 1940s, they competed for social space in Durban. The competition was uneven. Indians had a permanent presence in the city, whereas the Africans did not as the Native (Black) Urban Areas Act of 1923 regulated their movement. Influx control laws gave local councils the power to remove 'surplus' Africans, which in practice meant anyone not employed. An amendment in 1937 gave Africans 14 days to find employment or to return to their 'Reserves' (later 'Homelands'). The Native Laws Amendment Act of 1952 amended Section 10 of the Group Areas Act. It permitted Africans to be permanent residents in urban areas only if they had been born in the city and had lived there continuously for more than 15 years, or were employed continuously for at least 15 years, or who had worked continuously for the same employer for more than 10 years. All other Africans faced forcible removal. The Act also prohibited Africans from moving to any area where it was unlikely they would find employment and 'agitators' could be deported 'from any area without recourse to the courts.' Indians could own land in the city, Africans could not, and Indians dominated the transport and the small business sector.

Crucially too, under apartheid, the Bantu Education Act of 1953 took away control of education from missionaries and placed it under direct government control. The separate and grossly unequal education system was designed to train African students to be 'hewers of wood and drawers of water' for the white-dominated economy. The then Minster of Native Affairs, Hendrik Verwoerd, told parliament that there was no space for Africans in the white society 'above certain forms of labour.... It is of no avail for him to receive training which has its aim in the absorption of the European Community, where he cannot be absorbed.' Mission education, he felt, had 'misled him by showing him the greener pastures of European Society where he is not allowed to graze' (South African History Online 2011). Africans were to be confined to a life of menial work at the service of the white man. On the other hand, higher education facilities provided a means of economic upliftment for Indians who were needed in the local economy.

'Indian-speak' of being hardworking evokes a stereotype that has existed since the time of Gandhi, who was prone to talk about the productive Indian and the 'lazy' native. When the white Natal municipal authority was debating the Natal Municipal Corporation Bill in 1905, which would have required persons belonging to 'uncivilized races' to register, Gandhi wrote: 'one can understand the necessity of registration of Kaffirs who will not work, but why should registration be required for indentured Indians who have become free, and for their descendants about whom the general complaint is that they work too much?' (GoI 1999).

In another article titled, 'The Relative Value of the Natives and the Indians in Natal', Gandhi referred to a speech by Reverend John Dube of the Ohlange Institute in Inanda, who stated that Africans had the capacity for improvement if given the opportunity by whites, and suggested: 'A little judicious extra taxation would do no harm; in the majority of cases it compels the native to work for at least a few days a year.' On the other hand, the Indian stood 'in striking contrast with the native. While the native has been of little benefit to the State, it owes its prosperity largely to the Indians. While native loafers abound on every side, that species of humanity is almost unknown among Indians here' (Gandhi 1905).

One of the ironies of Gandhi's argument about the lazy native is that Indian indentured labourers had to be imported precisely because the Zulu Kingdom had not been defeated; they had access to land, and refused to work under brutal conditions for white colonists. As Belich (2009: 382) puts it: 'What whites wanted from blacks was labour under unreasonable conditions—tight control to the point of semi-slavery, and wages so low they were sometimes only a tenth of those earned by white workers. Blacks were naturally reluctant to accept this, leading to a white mythology of black indolence.' It was only through violent land dispossession and layers of taxation that they were forced to labour on terms set by the colonists. These historical differences are not accounted for in Indian discussions about affirmative action and employment equity, which aim to achieve permanent societal transformation by enforcing certain measures on educational institutions and employers. The post-apartheid state continues to use apartheid categories as a basis for affirmative action—black African, Indian/ Asian, coloured, and white. Initially, coloureds and Indians were spoken of under the umbrella term 'black', but black Africans now refers to the group that was most oppressed under apartheid, and therefore the one that is seen as being most in need of redress.

Race to Educate

Education provides a good example of how this plays out since it is one of the immediate concerns of many middle-class Indian parents and is annually in the spotlight when one student or another is denied a place at university, especially in medical schools, despite excelling academically. There are two sides to this question. The most obvious is the prioritization of historically racially under-represented groups, but the other is class based, for in practice, within each 'race' group, learners from poorly resourced schools are forced to compete with learners from highly resourced ones for limited places reserved for each race group. Students have been going to extremes to beat the system. There are instances of students changing their race (from Indian to coloured, for example) to gain an advantage, or even paying for places at university. The current system continues to favour rich Indians, for not only are they better positioned to gain university access as a result of being able to attend better schools, or even buy places, but there are hundreds of Indian South African students studying medicine in places like China, Mauritius, and India.

At the University of KwaZulu-Natal (UKZN), in 2014, for example, the university went back on its offer of a place at its medical school to an applicant after learning that she was Indian. The family had not stipulated their race on the original application because, as the father explained: 'We don't subscribe to a racist outlook so when forms stipulate race my family always leaves that out' (Anthony 2014). However, the student was given admission to a pharmacy course. A similar incident had taken place almost a decade earlier at the University of Cape Town (UCT) Medical School.

In a 2005 case, an Indian student named Sunira took UCT to court for not giving her a seat in the medical school. The UCT's 'purported admissions policy' discriminated against Indians by accepting that all African and coloured students who applied to UCT were considered to be 'educationally disadvantaged' even if they had attended private schools. Indian students, on the other hand, were not regarded as having received a disadvantaged education under apartheid. High Court Justice Rosheni Allie stated that while the admission policy appeared to be discriminatory, the question was whether 'the discrimination is reasonable, justifiable and necessary to redress the past inequalities' (Maughan 2005). She ruled that a conclusion that UCT's admission policy amounted to an infringement of Sunira's rights could not be sustained. 'The objective reality', she went on, 'is that students educated at schools previously set aside for African people, are more disadvantaged than others.' The case was dismissed with hefty legal costs. However, the judgment did not deal with the issue of discrimination between African, coloured, and Indian people who all had privileged educational backgrounds by virtue of attending private schools (Maughan 2005).

While every year there are complaints from Indians about being denied admission at medical schools across the country, the overall demographics do not paint such a bleak picture, despite the fact that the racial composition of students has changed dramatically and the entrance criteria are considerably higher for whites and Indians than they are for Africans and coloureds. Indians also fare well when the statistics are computed across the country. Of the 1,170 students in first-year medicine in 1991, 72 per cent were white, 16 per cent African, 10 per cent Indian, and 3 per cent coloureds. In 2006, out of a total of 1,447 first-year medical students, 46.5 per cent were black African, 14.1 per cent Indian, 9.7 per cent coloured, and 29.7 per cent white. Thus, the percentage of Indian students had actually increased (Myburgh 2007).

Statistics, however, are of little consolation to those Indians whose children perform considerably better academically than African children (for a variety of socio-economic reasons) but still cannot get admissions in medical schools and other health science programmes. To them, the system is unjust. The perception that affirmative action is unfairly affecting them is very powerful. A common everyday refrain is that Indians were not white enough in the past and are not black enough now. Attorney Arshana Shyam Nirhoo, who emigrated to the US, said that her decision to leave South Africa was due to her concern that affirmative action policies were favouring Africans to the detriment of Indians. She was concerned about the future professional prospects of her four children. As she pointed out in 2012:

> The minority groups in South Africa have become too complacent. Perhaps it's fear of reprisals against them, or they lack the courage and confidence to stand up against injustice. Whatever it is, it does not bode well for the future of Indians in this country. It is disappointing that they have forgotten that their forefathers were also part of the struggle against apartheid, and therefore their children should not be subjected to additional discrimination by being rejected at tertiary institutions as a result of their skin color. (Shah 2012)

Anand Jayrajh, executive member of the 1860 Indentured Labourers Foundation, Verulam, and occasional writer for the *Post*

Newspaper, wrote in 2017, when Indians globally were commemorating the end of indenture:

> Racial segregation was supposed to have been buried, yet the Indian still encounters discrimination and feels marginalised as a minority group. Even after over two decades of freedom, relics of the apartheid system are still invoked in order to marginalise many who have excelled in the academic field, but are nevertheless barred from enrolling at tertiary institutions in the guise of affirmative action.... The Indian youth was not responsible for and not even born during apartheid. Yet, when Indians qualify—with exceptional results—and apply for vocational employment, they are still discriminated against on the basis of the colour of their brown skin. Thus, the struggle continues, albeit on a different front and in a different form from that engaged against the old-style apartheid. (Anand 2017)

Many Indians bemoan the fact that the category 'black' has been disaggregated to exclude Indians and coloureds, and also simultaneously deny that they were advantaged during apartheid compared to Africans. Indians (and whites) mostly argue for open and even playing fields, where the brightest get admissions at universities and the best qualified are given job opportunities; in other words, 'merit-based' selection. However, as Deshpande (2013: 39) points out in the Indian context, 'we lack detailed accounts of processes and modalities, the concrete ways in which an upper caste identity secretes and synergises the dispositions and embodied competences that add up to that abstract term: "merit".' The problem with this line of argument is that people suffer from amnesia, failing to question the status quo and how the South African society arrived where it is. The various components that make up the citizenry of the country did not start in the same block.

Some Final Reflections

The sentiments of Indians regarding the application of affirmative action policies show the different perceptions of race among South Africans. For many Africans, race is the primary, even the only, resource available to them to get access to jobs, promotions at work, and educational opportunities in a context of uneven playing fields. For most Indians, in contrast, race is a barrier to equal opportunities and even playing fields. They see affirmative action and employment equity as reverse racism or reverse discrimination. Deshpande makes a similar argument with regard to India, where, he points out, higher-caste Hindus oppose reservations:

> Having encashed its traditional caste-capital and converted it into modern forms of capital like property, higher educational credentials and strongholds in lucrative professions, this section believes itself to be 'caste-less' today. Not only is there no dialogue possible between the two sides, they are trapped in a perverse relationship where each is compelled to unravel the arguments knitted by the other. (Deshpande 2013: 32)

It is much the same in South Africa where whites, and to a lesser extent Indians, were better placed at the time of non-racial democracy, due to the relative advantages they enjoyed during the apartheid era, and now want all forms of racial redress to be done away with. The reality is that the commanding heights of the economy are still in the hands of the whites. Indians are dominant in the professions relative to Africans. Meanwhile, lower down, the causal brutality of everyday life, replete with its own interior violence from rape to summary executions of suspected thieves, relives the horrors of apartheid.

Maré, amongst others, bemoans the fact that persistence of race classification on Census forms and other documentation creates and fixes identity, especially when it involves those who were born after the advent of non-racial democracy ('born-frees') and never actually experienced apartheid, but have a racial identity imposed on them. He writes that 'race belonging cannot be avoided. The individual is trapped in the already classified body, burdened with the allocated attributes of his or her category' (Maré 2014: 89).

Maré has a point that reinforcing racial identity may harm the project of creating a universal South African citizen and a society based on individuality and universality. We would make two points in response though. The first is that the Census is about more than just fixing identity. It can be used for social justice programmes as well as knowledge on the basis of which social policy can be formulated. Second, despite the heady promise of the Mandela era, race boundaries in the post-apartheid period are increasingly reinforced as South Africans struggle over scarce jobs, admissions for higher education, and government tenders. It is not the categorization that is creating race tensions but the continuation of apartheid geography and economic inequality.

The question of affirmative action will continue to vex Indian South Africans. There is no doubt, as Maré points out, that one of the ironies of this situation is that at the same time that South Africa is seeking to move away from race-based identities, such policies reinforce them. Calls for an end to race categories are not altruistic but self-serving. For most Africans, race-based redress is necessary, while it is the minorities, already in positions of economic power, who may see race as divisive. Race is rooted in the politics of everyday African life and is not something that most use as an instrument to further their life chances.

We would argue though that affirmative action based only on race is a misnomer. Through sheer numbers, Africans will come to dominate in universities and work. More doctors, engineers, and accountants will be produced relative to other racial groups. Indian South Africans with economic muscle will send their children overseas to study, for example, ensuring that they will be able to maintain their class position. Some means has to be found to implement a system of economic empowerment that favours the disadvantaged and is more likely to empower the poor, but is not solely based on race.

Indians and whites want to leave race behind, believing that they are now 'raceless', just as the upper castes in India believe that they are now 'casteless' (Deshpande and John 2010: 41). What has happened in South Africa is that many Indians, privileged relative to Africans in the apartheid period, have cashed in on those benefits and no longer need any protection or special privileges. They have, to quote Deshpande and John (2010: 41) in the Indian case, 'acquired all the resources that guaranteed them the "legitimate" advantages of inherited wealth, expensive education and abundant connections among their own kind'. Those Indians and whites that rely on family rather than race for social capital are eager for a race-blind society that does not question class privilege.

The way that the transition to democracy has played out in South Africa is that those who have either inherited privilege (whites) or have been able to use their relative advantage (Indians) vis-à-vis other racial groups disenfranchised during apartheid have sought to use the language of non-racialism as a basis for racelessness.

The poor on the other hand, and we have seen this with the Indian poor and black African poor, are attaching themselves more closely to apartheid racial identities—the Indian poor do this to insulate themselves from what they see as a threat, to what little they have, from black Africans. Black Africans are using the language of racial chauvinism to demand greater benefits. Deshpande points to similar trends in India.

It is in this context that we seek to use Ambedkar's notion of annihilation; that is, a programme to destroy race and caste, and in the process, attack the conditions that allow these identities to be used as anchors and catapults of privilege, rather than use these identities as a way to secure crumbs. The struggle is to find a way in which the Indian and black African poor are able to act with each other and not in competition with each other: in other words, to confront the idea of racelessness with militant non-racialism that sees class and race privilege as its target and annihilation.

References

Ambedkar, B.R. 1944[1936]. *Annihilation of Caste: With a Reply to Mahatma Gandhi*, 3rd edition. Jalandhar: Bheem Patrika Publications. Available at https://www.sbibengalcouncil.com/Annihilation-of-caste.pdf.

———. 2002. *The Essential Writings of B.R. Ambedkar*, pp. 132–48. Oxford India Paperbacks. New Delhi: Oxford University Press.

———. 2014. 'Introduction' by Arundhati Roy. *Annihilation of Caste: The Annotated Critical Edition*, in S. Anand (ed.). New Delhi: Navayana.

Anand Jayrajh. 2017. 'Those Who Stayed Thrived, and Made It Their Home', p. 16. *Post Newspaper*, 8–12 November.

Anthony, Lauran. 2014. 'Med School Rejects Student over Race', *IOL*, 19 February. Available at https://www.iol.co.za/news/south-africa/kwazulu-natal/med-school-rejects-student-over-race-1649737; last accessed on 30 November 2017.

Arora, Namit. 2013. 'Caste Iron'. *The Caravan: A Journal of Politics and Culture*, 1 November. Available at http://www.caravanmagazine.in/perspectives/caste-iron; last accessed on 25 September 2013.

Badiou, Alain. 2001. *Ethics: An Essay on the Understanding of Evil*. London and New York: Verso.

Belich, James. 2009. 'Replenishing the Earth: The Settler Revolution and the Rise of the Anglo-World, 1783–1939'. Oxford: Oxford University Press.

Desai, Ashwin and Goolam Vahed. 2016. *The South African Gandhi: Stretcher-Bearer of Empire*. Stanford and New Delhi: Stanford University Press and Navayana.

Deshpande, Satish. 2013. 'Caste and Castelessness: Towards a Biography of the "General Category"'. *Economic and Political Weekly* 48(15): 32–9.

Deshpande, Satish and Mary E. John. 2010. 'The Politics of Not Counting Caste'. *Economic and Political Weekly* 45(25): 39–42.

Dirks, Nicholas B. 2001. *Castes of Mind: Colonialism and the Making of Modern India*. Princeton: Princeton University Press.

Donald, A. 1999. *White Lightning*. London: Collins Willow.

Gandhi. 1905. 'The Relative Value of the Natives and the Indians in Natal', *Indian Opinion*, 9 September.

Gang, Ira N., Kunal Sen, and Myeong-Su Yun. 2011. 'Was the Mandal Commission Right?: Differences in Living Standards between Social Groups'. *Economic and Political Weekly* 46(39): 43–51.

Government of India (GoI). 1999. 'Editorial'. *The Collected Works of Mahatma Gandhi* (eBook), Vol. 4, p. 351. New Delhi.

Gqola, P. 2001. 'Defining People: Analysing Power, Language and Representation in Metaphors of the New South Africa'. *Transformation* 47: 94–106.

Gunaratnam, Yasmin. 2003. *Researching Race and Ethnicity: Methods, Knowledge and Power*. London: Sage.

Immerwahr, Daniel. 2007. 'Caste or Colony?: Indianizing Race in the United States'. *Modern Intellectual History* 4(2): 275–301.

Loomba, Ania. 2005. *Colonialism/Postcolonialism*, 2nd edition. London: Routledge.

Mandela, Nelson. 1964. 'I am Prepared to Die' (Speech), 20 April. *YouTube*. Available at https://www.youtube.com/watch?v=gQvlxnWELHM; last accessed on 18 May 2020.

Maré, Gerhard. 2014. *Declassified: Moving Beyond the Dead End of Race in South Africa*. Johannesburg: Jacana.

Maughan, Karyn. 2005. 'Indian Couple to Pay UCT's Legal Fees', *IOL*, 7 March. Available at https://www.iol.co.za/news/south-africa/indian-couple-to-pay-ucts-legal-fees-235661; last accessed on 24 December 2017.

Myburgh, James. 2007. 'Our Medical School Quotas: How Race Influences Admittance to Study Medicine', *Politicsweb*, 20 March. Available at http://www.politicsweb.co.za/news-and-analysis/on-medical-school-quotas; last accessed on 12 December 2012.

Natal Mercury, The. 2016. 'Opinion: Letter to the Editor', p. 7. 22 August.

Nxumalo, Mphathi and Nosipho Mngoma. 2016. 'Economists: Indians Benefited from Apartheid', *Daily News*, 11 August. Available at https://www.iol.co.za/dailynews/news/economists-indians-benefited-from-apartheid-2056013; last accessed on 20 February 2018.

Pandey, Gyanendra. 2013. *A History of Prejudice: Race, Caste, and Difference in India and the United States*. Cambridge: Cambridge University Press.

Post Newspaper. 2016. Available at https://www.facebook.com/postnewspaper/posts/1085440248170360, 18 August; last accessed on 18 May 2020.

Shah, Archana. 2012. 'People in Peril: Indians in South Africa', *Khabar*. Available at http://www.khabar.com/magazine/cover-story/people_in_peril_indians_in_south_africa; last accessed on 22 December 2017.

South African History Online. 2011. 'Apartheid Legislation 1850s–1970s'. Available at https://www.sahistory.org.za/article/apartheid-legislation-1850s-1970s; last accessed on 19 May 2020.

Steyn, M.2005. 'White Talk: White South Africans and the Management of Diasporic Whiteness', in A. Lopez (ed.), *Postcolonial Whiteness*, pp. 119–35. New York: State University of New York Press.

Teltumbde, Anand. 2017. *Dalits: Past, Present and Future*. New Delhi: Routledge India.

van der Westhuizen, Christi. 2017. *Sitting Pretty: White Afrikaans Women in Postapartheid South Africa*. Pietermaritzburg: University of KwaZulu-Natal Press.

9

Common Struggles?

Why There Has Not Been More Cooperation between African-Americans and Dalits

KEVIN BROWN AND LALIT KHANDARE

Kevin Brown has facilitated several academic journeys of American scholars, familiar with the African-American experience of racial subordination in the United States (US), to India. As part of those journeys, he has participated in over a dozen major conferences and workshops that compared those experiences to the Dalit experience of oppression in India. These discussions have occurred at leading academic institutions in India, such as the A.N. Sinha Institute of Social Science in Patna, Bihar; Indian Institute of Dalit Studies in New Delhi; Jindal Global Law School in Sonepat, Haryana; Mahatma Gandhi Kashi Vidyapith University in Varanasi, Uttar Pradesh; National Law School of India in Bengaluru, Karnataka; Tata Institute of Social Sciences in Mumbai and the University of Mumbai, Maharashtra. He has also attended several meetings with groups of various activists and intellectuals concerned with Dalit liberation in Bengaluru, Hyderabad, Ahmedabad, Mumbai, and New Delhi. Finally, Brown has spoken at celebrations for Ambedkar's birthday in London, New York, Mumbai, and New Delhi. One striking commonality in all of these events is that someone invariably raises the following question: Why do more African-American scholars not visit India to explore the common struggle of the Dalits or to interact with intellectuals concerned with efforts to overcome the oppression that Dalits encounter? Dalits, arguably, are the most oppressed group in all of human history, and given the extensive African-American history of subordination and oppression, with their concomitant resistance to it, this question is fair.

Beyond providing aid to Africa, the motherland, the gaze of African-American activists and intellectuals, who looked internationally, has traditionally been driven by the same desire that motivated their struggles within the US: to overcome the racial oppression inflicted by white supremacy. One of the first comparisons of the African-American experience to oppression of groups other than in Africa occurred before the Civil War. Black and white sympathizers compared the treatment of African-Americans to the caste system in the Indian subcontinent. Beginning in the early decades of the twentieth century, however, a new transnationalism drew connections between the discrimination that African-Americans faced domestically with that suffered by other people of colour throughout the world as a result of western colonialism and imperialism. This perspective was built upon the concept of the world of people of colour fighting against white supremacy. It was against the backdrop of the growing embrace of this colour cosmopolitanism by black activists and intellectuals that their attention increasingly turned to more detailed and sophisticated comparisons to the struggles of the Indian freedom fighters[1] against colonial control by the British. As Nico Slate (2012: 8) stated, it was 'at the height of empire and white supremacy, at a time when many African Americans and Indians found little in common, that forward-thinking individuals laid the groundwork for more inclusive conceptions of belonging and resistance'. Some of the founding leaders of the Indian anti-colonial freedom movement came to the US and interacted with black intellectuals, such as Booker T. Washington, W.E.B. Du Bois, and later, Benjamin Mays and Walter White. African-American activists had previously viewed their struggle as that of a nation within a nation. This concept made it easier to compare their liberation efforts to colonial struggles against European powers, particularly those in India and Africa. For example, Du Bois (1986: 514) stated that when he exhorted blacks to support India's anti-colonial struggle, 'Remember that we

---

[1] The term 'Indian freedom fighter' refers to activists who were fighting against British colonial rule in India.

American Negroes are the bound colony of the United States just as India is of England.'

After Indian Independence, the view of the African-American struggle as part of a global struggle against white supremacy continued to influence the African-American views on international events as they came to understand the colonial struggles on the African continent against European powers. Over 35 African nations had managed to gain independence by the late 1970s, but the liberation struggles of blacks in southern Africa against the white minority rule provided further justifications for the continued international focus of the African-American perspective on the global fight against white supremacy. Even today, the African-American view continues to centre on a struggle against white supremacy, which, conversely, lessens the attention that black scholars pay to intra-national liberation struggles of subordinated groups whose oppression is not rooted in white supremacy, like the Dalits. However, the world is now 70 years removed from India's Independence and it has been nearly 25 years since the establishment of majority rule in South Africa. While the African-American struggle is one against subordination and oppression rooted in white supremacy, it is also an intra-national struggle against oppression and subordination. Analogizing the African-American struggle to that of other oppressed groups struggling against subordination within their own countries could produce additional useful information on and additional insights into the African-American struggle.

The first section will discuss the long-standing African-American cultural outlook and the use of the caste analogy. This analogy remained the dominant comparison of oppression of blacks to oppression on the Indian subcontinent from the 1830s to the 1920s. The next section examines the development of comparisons between African-American and Indian freedom fighters' struggles and the interactions between leading intellectuals and activists of both groups. The third section discusses the period post 1947, after India got independence. The global emphasis of African-Americans refocused on the anti-colonial struggles against white supremacy in the form of European colonialism on the African continent. By 1970, almost all African nations got independence, however, Zimbabwe, Namibia, and South Africa were still victimized by white supremacy in the form of minority rule. The African-American international attention throughout the 1970s and 1980s was drawn to the racial struggle against the continuation of white minority rule in southern Africa.

African-American Cultural Outlook and First Analogies to the Indian Caste System

Without question, the central feature of the African-American experience has been the treatment of blacks as involuntary members of a historically oppressed racial group. The subordinate position of blacks has long been justified by rationales generated by the dominant white community based upon its presumed superiority and the presumed inferiority of blacks. However, against the background of 400 years of racial domination, the descendants of Africa's sons and daughters forcibly delivered to the US soil, and non-blacks sympathetic to their cause, formulated a counter-discourse to the belief that blacks are the paradigmatic inferior group in the US. The development of this cultural outlook was limited by, and responsive to, the racial oppression imposed on the African-American community, and it was based on an understanding that black people were oppressed, not inferior. Thus, the African-American system of belief is based upon the collective struggle of black people in the US against white supremacy. This perspective provides an antithetical interpretation of the behaviours, attitudes, and experiences of African-Americans to that derived from America's traditional culture.

On the eve of the American Civil War (1861–5), 92.3 per cent of blacks resided in the states that legalized slavery (Bureau of the Census 1979) and 93.7 per cent of them were slaves (Gibson and Jung 2002). Although the states in the north of the US had abolished slavery, northerners did not necessarily believe in racial equality. The extent of discrimination that blacks endured in the North varied from state to state, but they were traditionally situated at the bottom of a racial social system by custom, if not explicitly by law. Blacks were systematically separated from whites or excluded from railway cars, stagecoaches, and steamboats (Gibson and Jung 2002). They were segregated into secluded and remote corners of theatres, lecture halls, and, if they existed, schools. Blacks could not enter most hotels, restaurants, or resorts, except as servants, and they prayed in separate pews and partook of the Christian sacrament of the Eucharist after whites. Free blacks were also denied political equality in the North and the border states (Grofman et al. 1992; Woodward 2002).

Abolitionists in the US, including Frederick Douglass, William Lloyd Garrison, Harriet Beecher Stowe, and Charles Sumner, analogized the treatment of blacks to the Indian caste system (Immerwahr 2007). The caste system was principally understood in the US as a hierarchical system of social division in which membership in an endogamous group was hereditary and permanent. From the perspective of those concerned about the black struggle against racial oppression, invoking the caste system was an effort to improve the chances for success. The caste system was a cultural system that was in direct conflict with the commitment to individualism and equality at the core of American culture. Thus, the comparison of blacks' circumstances to the Indian caste system allowed those who believed in racial equality to not only critique slavery in the South but also criticize the northern racist attitudes towards blacks by arguing that the US was imposing a caste system that American core values had to reject as unjust.

Abraham Lincoln was elected president in 1860; he was from the newly formed Republican Party, which was created to oppose the spread of slavery. His election precipitated an effort by southern states to leave the Union and, hence, was the initial cause of the American Civil War.

After Union forces won the Civil War, three amendments were added to the Constitution to grant and expand the legal rights of blacks, including providing black males with the franchise. To amplify those rights, the Congress enacted five major civil rights measures before 1876. Further, in order to protect the rights of the freed slaves, the Union continued to maintain a significant military presence in the southern states. These constitutional amendments and federal legislation represented the legal view of the 1860s that legislation was necessary to disestablish the effects of the US racial caste system (Calabresi and Leibowitz 2013). However, after the disputed presidential election of 1876, the two major political parties reached a compromise that allowed the Republican candidate to assume the presidency, but led to the withdrawal of federal troops from the South.

Without federal troops to protect the rights of newly freed blacks, southern state legislatures began to systematically eliminate the ability of black males to exercise their franchise. As black males were being purged from the voter rolls, southern legislatures began to adopt segregation statutes. Legal segregation spread in the South and the US Supreme Court, in its 1896 decision in the case of *Plessy* v. *Ferguson*,[2] upheld a Louisiana statute that mandated the separation of whites from people of colour on railroad cars, provided the accommodations were equal. In upholding the statute, the US Supreme Court concluded that the doctrine of 'separate but equal' did not violate the equal protection clause of the Fourteenth Amendment to the US Constitution. Justice Harlan wrote separately to castigate his brethren for their decision. While dissenting, Harlan drew on the analogy of caste. In perhaps the most famous passage from any opinion of a US Supreme Court justice, Harlan stated that 'in the view of the constitution, in the eye of the law, there is in this country no superior, dominant, ruling class of citizens. *There is no caste here.* Our Constitution is color-blind and neither knows nor tolerates classes among citizens. In respect of civil rights all citizens are equal before the law.'[3]

Comparisons during India's Struggle for Independence

The first South Asians immigrated to the US in the early 1850s. Their numbers increased slowly through the nineteenth century, but then accelerated. Though some South Asians sought to be classified as white, their efforts were ultimately rebuffed. Due to their status as foreigners, in some instances, the South Asians were treated better than the blacks. However, as African-Americans increasingly observed the treatment of South Asians by whites in the US, they noted that generally, South Asians encountered the same racial prejudice.

Rudimentary comparisons of the African-American struggle to situations in South Asia also increased significantly in the first few

---

[2] *Plessy* v. *Ferguson*, 163 U.S. 537 (1896).

[3] *Plessy* v. *Ferguson*, 163 U.S. 559 (1896; Harlan, J., dissenting); emphasis added. Even Justice Thurgood Marshall uses the caste-based language to describe the purposes of the Fourteenth Amendment. In *Kadrmas* v. *Dickinson*, Marshall states: 'the intent of the framers of the Fourteenth Amendment was to abolish caste legislation.' See *Kadrmas* v. *Dickinson Public Schools*, 487 U.S. 450, 469 (1988; Marshall, J., dissenting).

decades of the twentieth century. Several developments led African-American intellectuals and activists to analogize their struggle against white supremacy in the US to the Indian freedom fighters' struggle against white supremacy in the form of colonialism in the Indian subcontinent by the British.[4] This analogy became part of the African-American view that its community not only suffered in America as a result of white supremacy but also its struggles were part of an international struggle of people of colour in a white-dominated world. Thus, African-Americans also needed to work towards a comprehensive solution to centuries of worldwide oppression.

Increasing Number of South Asian Encounters: The Impact of White Supremacy in the US

As mentioned earlier, South Asians came to the US as early as the 1850s, but their numbers remained very small throughout the nineteenth century (Ramnath 2005). According to the 1900 Census, there were only 2,050 South Asian residents in the US (Mazumdar 1989). Generally speaking, they were upper-caste students, businessmen, and professionals. As conditions worsened for South Asians in Canada, more of them migrated to the US. By 1910, there were between 5,000 and 10,000 South Asians in the country (Mazumdar 1989: 50). Most resided in California, and a majority were Sikhs, with about a third being Hindus (Mazumdar 1989).[5] Some also resided in the northeast and midwest and became part of working-class neighbourhoods from New York to Baltimore to Detroit (Bald 2013). However, American media and federal and state agencies referred to all South Asians as Hindus. It is also important to note that Americans drew a distinction between the Chinese and Japanese, whom they considered Mongolians, and South Asians (Takaki 1989: 294–5).

As the numbers of South Asians in America increased after the turn of the twentieth century, one complication existed regarding any possible solidarity movement between them and the African Americans. It, typically, does not take long for immigrants to the

---

[4] For two excellent books covering this period, see Horne (2009) and Slate (2012).

[5] The US Census Bureau added a Hindu race category to the 1920 Census. See Pew Research Center (2015).

US to realize that there is a racial hierarchy with whites at the top and blacks at the bottom. Thus, many immigrants of colour attempt to distance themselves from the African-Americans. Nevertheless, they find it impossible to be accepted as white. This was also true for many South Asian immigrants. Many of them did not associate with African-Americans, but instead maintained a discreet distance.

Some South Asians sought the protection of white privilege by following Friedrich Max Mueller's theory that, thousands of years ago, white Aryans from Central Asia had invaded India and subjugated the native Dravidian people who, Mueller concluded, were descendants of Africans (Banks 1998).[6] Thus, as per Mueller's theory, upper-caste Hindus were of the same racial stock as whites in the US. Using this theory, some South Asians asserted that since they were descendants of Aryans, they were actually white (Banks 1998). These efforts often played out in the legal system whenever the question of citizenship came up.

The US Congress's first restrictive immigration measure, the Naturalization Act of 1790, limited citizenship in the US to 'free white persons'.[7] From 1909 to 1923, there were a series of naturalization cases brought up by South Asians who asserted that they were Caucasian and, hence, eligible for citizenship by naturalization. According to Taunya Banks (1998), a superficial review of these cases indicates that the courts were confused about how to handle the racial status of South Asians and granted their petitions initially.[8] The US Supreme Court, however, delivered the final word in its 1923 decision in *U.S. v. Bhagat Singh Thind*.[9] Thind was a

---

[6] One of India's foremost historians, Romila Thapar, discusses these theories in 'The Aryan Question Revisited' (Thapar 1999).

[7] See Lopez (1996: 42–6; citing Naturalization Act, Ch. 3, 1 Stat. 103 [1790]). After the Civil War, the Congress amended this Act to expand coverage to those of African nativity or African descent (Lopez 1996: 43–4; citing Naturalization Act, Ch. 255, § 7, 16 Stat. 254 [1870]).

[8] Also, in 1974, when the federal government put together its first draft of definitions for race and ethnicity to be used by all federal agencies, it originally included persons having origins from the Indian subcontinent in its definition of 'whites'. The final version, however, included them in the definitions of Asians. For a discussion of this, see Brown (2014).

[9] *U.S. v. Bhagat Singh Thind*, 261 U.S. 204 (1923).

light-skinned Sikh born in Punjab. He was also a former sergeant in the US Army[10] who received an honourable discharge.[11] Thind asserted that as a Caucasian, he was entitled to naturalized citizenship. The Supreme Court rejected his argument, noting that while attempting to determine what the original framers of the 1790 statute meant by the words 'white persons', the basis should be its usage in common, ordinary speech and not scientific classification. Thus, '[i]t may be true that the blond Scandinavian and the grown Hindu have a common ancestor in the dim reaches of antiquity, but the average man knows perfectly well that there are unmistakable and profound differences between them to-day.'[12] The *Thind* case ultimately ended any legal pretence that South Asians could be considered white in the US. Thus, for legal purposes, they were treated as people of colour.

As the number of South Asians in America increased, African-Americans were able to see that the American society often discriminated against them for having darker skin in the same ways that they discriminated against the blacks. For example, the Governor of California from 1917 to 1923, William Stephens, stated that 'the Hindu ... is the most undesirable immigrant in the state. His lack of personal cleanliness, his low morals and his blind adherence to theories and teachings [so] entirely repugnant to American principles makes him unfit for association with American people' (Horne 2009: 33). As a result, African-Americans became increasingly aware of the reality that, in the US, people from the Indian subcontinent were also oppressed by white supremacy (Bald 2013).[13] This could not help but further the sense that blacks and South Asians were allies in a collective struggle against white supremacy.

---

[10] In *re Bhagat Singh Thind*, 268 F. 683 (1920, District Court of Oregon).

[11] Thind would eventually achieve citizenship under the Nye-Lea Act of 1935, which created a path to citizenship for any veteran of World War I who was not eligible for citizenship because he was not a free white person or of African descent. See Coulson (2015: 5).

[12] *U.S. v. Bhagat Singh Thind*, 261 US 209 (1923).

[13] See, generally, Bald (2013) discussing the experiences of Bengali seamen in the US and how they tended to live in integrated neighbourhoods with blacks, Puerto Ricans, and other minorities.

Special Emphasis on the Influence of Lala Lajpat Rai on Black Intellectuals

Out of the numerous South Asians who visited the US, one deserves a special mention. Seeking American support for the Indian Independence movement, Indian intellectual and freedom fighter Lala Lajpat Rai, known as 'The Lion of Punjab', visited the US in 1905 and, again, from December 1914 to December 1919 (Horne 2009: 68; also see Balaji 2015). Rai, who was also a lawyer and president of the Bar Association of India, founded the India Home Rule League of America to advocate self-rule for India (Balaji 2015). Touring the country, Rai made a point of studying the racial situation. He became personally acquainted with Booker T. Washington, John Hope (the first African-descended president of Morehouse College and later, Atlanta University), and Mary Ovington (Rai 1919[1916]).[14] He also developed a close friendship with the legendary black intellectual W.E.B. Du Bois, primarily based on the notion of Indian Independence and black equality.[15] Up to the point of meeting Rai, Du Bois had not devoted much attention to the anti-colonial struggles on the Indian subcontinent (Balaji 2015). Du Bois was a central figure in terms of fostering an international perspective on the African-American struggle. He would later be known as the 'Father of Pan Africanism' (Contee 1969). Du Bois organized the Second Pan-African Congress in Paris in 1919, which presented an anti-colonialism petition to the Versailles Peace Conference that settled the issues related to the conclusion of World War I. The petition sought the right of self-determination against European colonialism for the world's various people of colour. Rai's friendship with Du Bois was so close that Du Bois dedicated his 1928 novel, *Dark Princess*, to Rai, which was about a love story between an Indian princess and an African-American man (Balaji 2015). Du Bois would go on to become one of the strongest supporters of close relations between India and African-Americans. He even came to believe that the rights of blacks in America could only be protected when done in

---

[14] Lala Lajpat Rai (1919[1916]) thanked all of them in the 'Preface' of his book.

[15] For a recent discussion on the connections of Rai with Du Bois and its impact on Rai, see Sinha (2015).

common cause with colonized and subordinated people of colour in the Third World (Richardson 2015).

Rai published a book on his travels in 1916, *The United States of America: A Hindu's Impression and a Study*, and a second book in 1928, *Unhappy India* (Prashad 2000).[16] Rai's writings, like those of many later Indian freedom fighters, viewed the African-American struggle from two different vantage points. In one way, Indian freedom fighters and African-Americans were allies in a common global struggle of people of colour against white supremacy, but, in a contrasting way, the treatment of blacks in the US could also function as an effective rebuttal to criticisms of caste discrimination, especially based on 'untouchability', practised in the Indian subcontinent. By critiquing the treatment of blacks in the US, Indian freedom fighters could argue that America, and by extension Britain, had no standing to justifiably critique the Indian caste system on moral grounds. In addition, the British also sought to christianize India.[17] Pointing out the discriminatory treatment that African-Americans suffered in the US was an effective rebuttal to the argument that Christianity was a more compassionate religion than Hinduism. If blacks were treated badly in Christian nations, how could Christians righteously critique India's religiously rooted caste system?

Rai accepted Mueller's Aryan conquest theory. He went so far as to suggest that the same considerations and causes for caste in India could be found at the bottom of the racial 'caste' feelings in the US, noting that the parallels to the worst aspects of the laws of Manu exist in American life. For instance, it is often difficult to tell the caste of a Hindu based on their colour, and Rai noted the same was true of race in the US. When Rai visited the US, the one-drop rule was the predominant means used to determine the race of a person. Under this rule, merely one drop of black blood made a person black (Mencke 1979). Thomas Dixon Jr, author of *The Clansman*,[18] discussed the accepted dogma of one drop of black

---

[16] Vijay Prasad (2000) referred to this as 'Afro-Asian Traffic'. Rai's later book was primarily written to refute American author Katherine Mayo's book, *Mother India* (Mayo 1927). Mayo's book was very critical of Indians and asserted that British rule was a tremendous benefit.

[17] For a recent discussion of these efforts, see Brown (2018).

[18] See Dixon and Wintz (2015). This book was made into the infamous 1915 movie, *The Birth of a Nation*. The movie, portraying African-Americans

blood in his 1902 best-selling fictional novel, *The Leopard's Spots* (Dixon and Wintz 2015). In explicating the convention, he wrote, 'One drop of Negro blood ... kinks the hair, flattens the nose, thickens the lip, puts out the light of intellect, and lights the fires of brutal passions' (Dixon and Wintz 2015: 242). There were a significant number of blacks who were fair enough to look white but, because of the one-drop rule, were treated the same as 'the blackest black, having no white blood at all' (Brown 2014). Rai noted that interracial marriage and dining in the US, just like inter-caste marriage and dining in India, were forbidden. As in India, segregation and discrimination functioned with regard to legal rights, education, and even religion. When applied to Dalits, the caste system forbade them from lucrative occupations; and segregation functioned the same way for blacks in the US. Blacks also received more severe punishments than whites for the same criminal offences, and this punishment was often meted out by mobs instead of courts of justice. Caste Hindus mobs would also punish Dalits for violating caste-based restrictions.

Rai concluded that slavery in America was worse than any institution developed in Asia and that blacks were still suffering from oppression. He went on to note that even under segregation, some aspects of the American treatment of blacks were worse than those inflicted upon Dalits due to caste in India (Rai 1928: 110–13). In pointing out that lynching was the worst form of race prejudice in the US, which often the 'best elements of the community' take part in, Rai (1928: 104) quoted extensively from the National Association for the Advancement of Colored People's (NAACP) magazine, *The Crisis*, founded by Du Bois.[19] Like many Indian freedom fighters, Rai also expressed his unmitigated condemnation of untouchability:

> I condemn untouchability in the strongest terms possible as an absolutely in-defensible, inhuman and barbarous institution, unworthy of Hinduism and the Hindus. It is a blot on what is otherwise one of the noblest of cultures—if not the noblest and most humane culture—the genius of man has evolved during the whole history of the race. (Rai 1928: 139–40)

in an extremely negative light, concluded that providing blacks with equal rights was a mistake, and depicted the Ku Klux Klan as the saviours of white society. The movie helped to revitalize the Ku Klux Klan.

[19] Du Bois was its principal editor from 1910 until 1934.

Ghadar Party Conspiracy and the African-American Community

Coinciding with Rai's second visit to the US was the trial of members of the Ghadar Party conspiracy. For many Americans, this brought the Indian cause for independence to the forefront. The Ghadar Party conspiracy was the most prominent of the attempts to initiate a pan-Indian rebellion against British control of the Indian subcontinent during World War I, at least with the US connections. Ghadar Party discouraged discussion about religion and identified itself as democratic and egalitarian in outlook, across caste, religion, or regional differences. It also got support from Indian organizations across the US and globally (Sohi 2014). Punjabi Sikhs in California were the primary members of the party. A large number of Ghadar Party members had returned to India by 1915, mostly to Punjab. The Ghadar Party attempted to spark an uprising against the British in India. The uprising failed, and mass arrests of Ghadar Party members ensued in Punjab and the Central Provinces of India. American intelligence officials also arrested several important Ghadar Party members in the US and put them on trial in San Francisco. These trials, which took place from November 1917 to April 1918, were the largest and most expensive trials in the US to that point in time (Sohi 2014).

The Ghadar Party conspiracy eventually became a subject of debate in the African-American community. For example, *The Crisis* magazine voiced its support for the Indian freedom fighters. Commenting on the Ghadar Party conspiracy, the magazine indicated that the NAACP found the result unjust because Indians were struggling to free their country from a foreign power. A 1921 edition of the pro-communist African-American magazine, *The Crusader* (September 1920),[20] similarly commented on the Ghadar Party conspiracy, saying: 'it is essential to the early success of our cause that the Negro seek cooperation with the Indian nationalists ... and all other peoples participating in the common struggle for liberty and especially with those peoples whose struggle is against the great enslaver of the darker races—England' (*The Crusader*, August 1921, cited in Horne 2009: 45).

---

[20] *The Crusader* was founded as a black communist magazine by Cyril Briggs, who had worked for the *Amsterdam News*. It published articles calling for African nationalism and was anti-colonial.

Idea of Nation within a Nation

As early as the 1850s, black nationalist Martin Delany described the situation of blacks in the US as that of 'a nation within a nation' (Delany 1993: 209). However, Du Bois was the primary person who publicized this notion to black America. In his words:

> The so called Negro group ... while it is in no sense absolutely set off physically from its fellow Americans, has nevertheless a strong, hereditary cultural unity born of slavery, common suffering, prolonged proscription, and curtailment of political and civil rights.... Prolonged policies of segregation and discrimination have involuntarily welded the mass almost into a nation within a nation. (Du Bois 1947: 362–3)[21]

The idea of the black community as a nation within a nation made the comparison of African-Americans to other people of colour suffering from colonialism, whether in Asia or Africa, more appropriate. Specifically, it made the colonial struggle by Indian freedom fighters against the British empire an apt analogy to the African-American struggle. Indians and African-Americans were both categorized by the British and their American cousins as the 'darker races', which led the groups to 'engineer one of the most creative and politically significant redefinitions of racial borders ... the invention of the colored world' (Bald 2013: 65). African-Americans would extend this idea to the colonial struggles occurring in Africa.

Relationship between the Indian Freedom Fighters and Leaders of the African-American Community

No single individual had a greater impact in shaping the black community's understanding of the Indian Independence movement than Mohandas K. Gandhi. During Gandhi's South African advocacy for the rights of South Asians, he distanced this struggle for equality from that of the black Africans. Gandhi characterized

---

[21] As more and more blacks from the South moved to the North after 1910, Harlem in New York City became an important centre for black intellectual development. The Harlem Renaissance also took place in the 1920s. After World War I, New York City was a deeply divided and a very unequal city. Contemporary observers would refer to Harlem as a city within a city. See Bald (2013: 162).

Africans as uncivilized, troublesome, dirty, and living like animals. He protested bitterly against a British effort to construct housing that would have integrated the Indian indentured servants with the blacks, and spoke of the purity of the races and the need to ensure that it was maintained (Krishna 2014). However, there was a progressive change in Gandhi's opinion of blacks. In India, Gandhi became an admirer of African-American educator Booker T. Washington. The educational philosophy of Washington stressed upon the acquisition of skills and knowledge that could be used to generate gainful employment and financial independence for black people. Gandhi's 'immense respect for [Washington's] ideas ... was an early factor in helping him gradually transcend his earlier racist views' (Burnett 2008). By the mid-1920s, Gandhi too was analogizing the South Asian situation under colonialism with that of the blacks under segregation (Slate 2012: 124).

In the words of Daniel Immerwahr (2007: 292), 'sending prominent blacks over to India became a sort of cottage industry in the 1930s and 1940s.'[22] Like Rai and other Indian freedom fighters, Gandhi's objections to untouchability were known by the black media. Gandhi's willingness to perform chores normally only done by Dalits, his adoption of a Dalit daughter, and his referring to Dalits as 'Harijans' were aspects of his that were admired by the black community. Thus, by the 1930s it was common for the African-American journals and newspapers to refer to Gandhi as one of the foremost sages and seers of human history. Therefore, attempting to arrange a meeting with him was high on the wishlist of these black leaders. One of the earliest visits by an African-American to India was the four-month visit led by Reverend Howard Thurman in 1936.[23] Thurman was a professor of religion at both the historically black Morehouse College and Howard University during his career. Thurman's former student, James Farmer, would go on to help establish the Congress of Racial Equality (CORE), which was based on Gandhi's philosophy of non-violence or *satyagraha* (Thurman 1969).

Thurman travelled to India on a pilgrimage of friendship as a guest of the Student Christian Movement of India, Burma, and Ceylon, with Reverend Edward Carroll and both of their wives. Carroll was a graduate of Morgan State University, another historically black

---

[22] Bayard Rustin and William Stuart Nelson also journeyed to India during this time.

[23] For Thurman's account of the trip, see Thurman (1979: 103–36).

university, and the Yale Divinity School. The group spoke with Indians about Jim Crow and the discrimination faced by African-Americans in the US. During their visit to India, they spent time in Madras (now Chennai), Calcutta (now Kolkata), and Darjeeling. At Bardoli, the group became the first African-Americans to meet Gandhi face-to-face and this further forged a connection between the two groups (Chandan 2017). Gandhi gave a warm welcome to the group that was described by his secretary thus: 'This is the first time in all the years that we have been working together that I've ever seen him come out to greet a visitor so warmly' (Immerwahr 2007: 292). During the visit, Thurman and Gandhi talked about many issues, including the situation of the Dalits in India. For Gandhi, in Hinduism's ideal form, the caste system was a non-competitive and non-oppressive functional division of labour that did not imply hierarchy. Thus, Gandhi felt that the proper path for South Asians was to reform Hinduism, not to destroy the caste system. In describing his meeting with Gandhi, Thurman noted that Gandhi told him he used the term 'Harijans', meaning 'children of God', to refer to the Dalits because he wanted to create in the minds of caste Hindus an acute contradiction that could only be resolved by transforming their attitude towards Dalits (Thurman 1979). According to Homer Jack, the Thurmans were so impressed with Gandhi that they asked him to come to the US 'not for White America, but for the Negroes', pleading, '[W]e have many a problem that cries for solution, and we need you badly' (Jack 1969: 219).

Channing Tobias, a future NAACP chairman, and Benjamin Mays travelled to India with 13 official delegates from the US on a visit that departed in late 1936. At the time, Mays was the dean of the School of Religion at Howard University. He would go on to serve as the president of Morehouse College from 1940 to 1967. During that time, Mays taught and mentored many influential African-American activists, including Martin Luther King Jr, Julian Bond, and Maynard Jackson. Indeed, Mays would eventually go on to give King's eulogy (Chandola 1992). During their trip to India, Mays and Tobias also spoke with Gandhi about non-violence and how the African-Americans could learn from him about dismantling oppression (Horne 2009; Jack 1969: 219). In his autobiography, *Born to Rebel*, Mays pointed out the striking similarities between the Anglo-Indian oppression and the African-American oppression, leading him to believe that 'the war against discrimination in the United States has been and must be waged by all Negroes—black, white, tan—together' (Mays 2011: 153). Mays also raised the question of the treatment of Dalits with Gandhi during their talk. He came to believe that as bad as untouchability was, it would likely be abolished before segregation was legally abolished in the US.

With the outbreak of hostilities in World War II, the relationship between leaders in the African-American community and Indian freedom fighters intensified. For example, A. Phillip Randolph asserted that blacks should support Indian Independence because it was intimately connected to the black cause in the US (Mays 2011).[24] Also, Japan actively attempted to recruit members of the Indian freedom fighters movement arguing for an alliance of people of colour. Simultaneously, the executive director of the NAACP, Walter White, sought to use this opportunity to press American politicians to form an alliance with the Indian freedom fighters (Slate 2012: 127–33). As White saw it, with America joining the Allies in the fight against Hitler's Germany, they were waging a war against Aryan supremacy; however, the US practised white supremacy in the form of segregation of blacks, and the British practised Anglo supremacy in the form of colonialism in India. In order to address this hypocrisy, White envisioned an American mission sent by President Roosevelt to the British to help push for Indian Independence. The mission would include an African-American representative, and Roosevelt would take a sweeping stand against discrimination based on colour in the US. The mission would then urge Indian Independence after the War as a way for the British to take a stand against Anglo supremacy. White shared this plan with several black leaders in the US, including Du Bois, Randolph, Roy Wilkens, and William Hastie, as well as eminent author Peal S. Buck and 1940 Republican Party presidential nominee, Wendell Willkie. White sent a copy of his proposal to President Roosevelt; while unable to convince the Roosevelt administration to send such a delegation, White's plan did further the notion of a link between the Indian freedom fighters and African-American struggles.

---

[24] Randolph had organized the first predominately black labour union, the Brotherhood of Sleeping Car Porters. His continuous agitation helped to convince President Roosevelt to issue an executive order in 1941 that banned race discrimination in the defence industries during World War II. He also successfully pressured President Harry S. Truman to issue the Executive Order 9981 in 1948 that ended segregation in the armed forces.

Renowned black activist Paul Robeson also analogized the Indian national struggle to that of the African-Americans as he argued that the formation of an Indian national government was the best path to assuring that India would not be unduly influenced by Japan (Horne 2009: 169). Robeson had met Jawaharlal Nehru and his sister, Vijaya Lakshmi Pandit, in London back in the 1930s and they developed a close friendship. Also, when Nehru came to the US in 1949, he had dinner at Walter White's home. White and Ralph Bunche, who served as chair of the Department of Political Science at Howard University and was the first African-American to win the Nobel Peace Prize, arranged a private meeting for Nehru, where he met with a group of prominent black leaders in New York City (Slate 2012: 178–80).

Lack of Cooperation and Connection with Dalit's Struggles

By the end of World War II, African-American activists and intellectuals understood that the common opinion of white America viewed people from the Indian subcontinent as people of colour, not white. Even though the foreign status of those from South Asia might shield them from some aspects of discrimination in the US, they predominately experienced oppression by white supremacy in a way similar to blacks. Additionally, those black activists and scholars who viewed segregation as part of the African-American struggle against white supremacy were aware of the analogy to the Indian freedom fighters struggle against white supremacy in the form of British colonialism. Thus, many African-Americans activists and intellectuals came to believe that a common cause existed between them and those on the Indian subcontinent.

As for the Dalit's struggle against caste-based discrimination, Gandhi and other Indian freedom fighters had consistently voiced their objections against untouchability to the black community. The black community viewed the Indian freedom fighters not only as fighting to end British occupation, but also to abolish untouchability. In addition, the view of the African-American activists and intellectuals that their struggle was part of an international fight of people of colour against white supremacy obscured their understanding of how deeply rooted in the culture on the Indian subcontinent were the discriminatory cultural practices that Dalits encountered. Indeed, active support of African-American leaders for the Dalit liberation struggle might also have run the risk of infringing upon the African-American/Indian freedom fighters alliance. African-American activists and intellectuals may not have been able to tell whether the African-American situation in the US was better than that of the Dalits in India; however, what seems apparent is that most of them would have generally felt that the Dalits had a significant advantage in their struggle because the Indian freedom fighters had committed to work to end discrimination based upon untouchability.[25] Also, there would be little doubt about this commitment after the Indian Independence, given the extensive provisions that were written into the Indian Constitution to improve the conditions of Dalits. Thus, for African-Americans, the commitment that Dalits had was one which they did not have from the white leaders of the US. This favourable position of the Dalits, due to the enlightened nature of the Indian freedom fighters, was a strong impression, evident by the well-known fact of the influence of Gandhi on the non-violent approach of Reverend Martin Luther King Jr (King et al. 1992).

International Perspective of African-Americans after India's Independence

By the end of World War II, the African-American international perspective understood that its struggle against white supremacy in the US was also part of an international struggle of people of

---

[25] As a side note, Kevin Brown understands this sentiment of African-Americans leaders who met the Indian freedom fighters. In October 2012, Brown led a group of 13 American academics familiar with the African-American struggle on a three-week journey through India that included stops in Mumbai, Varanasi, and New Delhi. They participated in a number of conferences, workshops, and meetings with activists and intellectuals concerned about the oppression of Dalits. Their very last meeting was a 90-minute sit-down discussion with the president of the Indian National Congress party, Rahul Gandhi. He started the discussion by saying, 'You must understand oppression from the perspective of the oppressed group.' The group found this statement particularly enlightening. The rest of the conversation left them with the same positive feeling that many African-American leaders had had after meeting leaders of India's freedom fighters. They wanted Rahul Gandhi to visit America and talk to white Americans about the need to understand the African-American struggles.

colour in a white-dominated world. At that time, the only independent and majority-ruled black African nations were Ethiopia and Liberia. Like India's struggle for independence against the United Kingdom, the template of viewing the African-American struggle from an international perspective as one of a global struggle against white supremacy would apply to the colonial struggles against European powers on the African continent. Indeed, these comparisons would have resonated even more strongly with the African-Americans since they were focusing on the struggles of their distant relatives.

In 1957, Ghana became only the third independent sub-Saharan African nation. Shortly after the monumental African-American victory in the Montgomery Bus Boycott led by Reverend King, several leaders of the black Civil Rights Movement, including King, Congressmen Adam Clayton Powell and Charles Diggs, Horace Mann Bond, Bunche, Mordecai Johnson, and Randolph, attended Ghana's independence celebration. They were the invited guests of Ghana's first president, Kwame Nkrumah (King et al. 1992). The appearance of so many members of the black civil rights establishment was a tangible proof of the bond between the African-American civil rights struggle and the African decolonization movements (Richardson 2015: 170–1). King (1961: 118) would later point out that: 'The liberation struggle in Africa [was] the greatest single international influence on American Negro students.' He would also note that the anti-colonial struggle was faring better than the fight for civil rights in the US.

The number of independent black countries in Africa continued to increase throughout the 1960s and 1970s. By the late 1970s, 35 sub-Saharan African countries had gained independence from European colonial rule.[26] However, there were still ongoing liberation struggles by native black Africans in southern Africa against the white minority governments that controlled Zimbabwe, Namibia,

---

[26] Ghana (1957); Guinea (1958); Chad, Benin, Nigeria, Ivory Coast, Madagascar, Central African Republic, Mali, Niger, Senegal, Burkina Faso, Mauritania, Togo, Zaire, Somalia, Congo, Gabon, Cameroon (1960); Sierra Leone (1961); South Africa (under minority rule until 1995); Burundi, Rwanda, Uganda (1962); Kenya, Tanzania (1963); Malawi, Zambia (1964); Gambia (1965); Botswana, Lesotho (1966); Equatorial Guinea, Mauritius, Swaziland (1968); Guinea-Bissau (1969). See 'Indigenous People of Africa and America', available at http://ipoaa.com/african_independence.htm.

and South Africa. As the attention of African-American scholars and activists turned increasingly towards the liberation struggles in southern Africa, the same view of a fight against white supremacy by people of colour still applied. This also reinforced the belief that, in an international context, African-American struggles were part of a global struggle of people of colour against white supremacy.

★ ★ ★

The answer to the question, 'why more African-American activists and intellectuals do not come to India to learn about the Dalit struggle', may have its genesis in the Indian freedom fighters' struggle for independence from the British colonial control. The African-American struggle is best understood as the historical struggle of blacks against the manifestations of white supremacy in the US. However, starting in the first few decades of the twentieth century, activists and intellectuals of the African-American community found common ground with the Indian freedom fighters. In the process of their struggle, African-Americans developed an understanding of their situation as that of a nation within a nation. This concept helped African-American activists and intellectuals analogize their struggle against white supremacy in the US to the Indian freedom fighters' struggle against white supremacy in the form of British colonial control. This analogy not only helped to further interactions between the leaders and activists of these two groups, but it also helped to cement the view of African-Americans that when they consider their struggle in an international context, they should view it as part of a larger global struggle of people of colour against white supremacy. After the founding of the Republic of India, African-Americans were able to draw similar analogies between their struggle and the colonial struggles on the African continent that eventually led to the independence of more than 35 African nations over the next three decades. The international view of the African-American struggle as part of a larger global struggle against white supremacy also applied to the struggles by native blacks in southern Africa against white-minority rule that took place in the latter decades of the twentieth century.

Considering the African-American struggle in an international context as part of a larger global struggle against white supremacy increases the difficulty of African-Americans finding common ground with Dalits. That is because this perspective obscures the ability of African-American activists and intellectuals to comprehend the full measure of the Dalit struggle against caste-based oppression in India, as it is rooted in the Hindu religion and not white supremacy. While the African-American struggle is one against white supremacy, it is also an intra-national struggle against oppression, like that of the Dalits. As mentioned earlier, the world is now 70 years from the founding of the Republic of India and almost 25 years from the institution of majority rule in South Africa. The passage of this time has revealed that leaders of independent countries have very different agendas and concerns compared to those struggling against colonial control of foreign invaders. As such, the analogy of African-Americans as a nation within a nation may no longer be as relevant as it was during the colonial struggle. Thus, the African-American community can learn a tremendous amount about its own struggle by comparing and contrasting it with the intra-national struggles of other groups against their oppression, such as the Dalits, even if their oppression is not rooted in white supremacy.

References

Balaji, M. 2015. 'Globalizing Black History Month: Professor and the Punjabi Lion'. *Huffington Post*, 23 February. Available at https://www.huffingtonpost.com/murali-balaji/globalizing-black-history_b_6737948.html; last accessed on 30 November 2019.

Bald, V. 2013. *Bengali Harlem and the Lost Histories of South Asian America*. Cambridge, MA: Harvard University Press.

Banks, T.L. 1998. 'Both Edges of the Margin: Blacks and Asians in Mississippi Masala, Barriers to Coalition Building'. *Asian American Law Journal* 5(7). Available at http://scholarship.law.berkeley.edu/aalj/vol5/iss1/2; last accessed on 30 November 2019.

Brown, K.D. 2014. *Because of Our Success: The Changing Racial and Ethnic Ancestry of Blacks on Affirmative Action*. Durham, NC: Carolina Academic Press.

Brown, S.J. 2018. 'Providential Empire?: The Established Church of England and the Nineteenth-Century British Empire in India'. *Studies in Church History* 54: 225–59.

Bureau of the Census. 1979. *The Social and Economic Status of the Black Population in the United States: An Historical View, 1790–1978*. Current Population Reports, Special Studies, Series P-23, No. 80, US Department of Commerce, Washington, DC.

Burnett, L. 2008. 'Gandhi's Connections with Booker T. Washington, W.E.B. Du Bois, and Marcus Garvey'. *The Cross-Cultural Solidarity History Education Project*. Available at http://crossculturalsolidarity.com/gandhis-connections-with-booker-t-washington-w-e-b-du-bois-and-marcus-garvey/; last accessed on 30 November 2019.

Calabresi, S.G. and L.C. Leibowitz. 2013. 'Monopolies and the Constitution: A History of Crony Capitalism'. *Harvard Journal of Law and Public Policy* 36(3): 983–1097.

Chandola, M.V. 1992. 'Affirmative Action in India and the United States: The Untouchable and Black Experience'. *Indiana International and Comparative Law Review* 3: 101–33.

Chandan, S. 2017. '"The Strongest Bond of Fraternity": Social, Political and Artistic Links between India and African Americans Before and After India's Independence'. *Brown Girl Magazine*, 23 August. Available at https://www.browngirlmagazine.com/2017/08/the-strongest-bond-of-fraternity-social-political-and-artistic-links-between-india-and-african-americans-before-and-after-indias-independence/; last accessed on 30 November 2019.

Contee, C.G. 1969. 'The Emergence of Du Bois as an African Nationalist'. *The Journal of Negro History* 54(1): 48–63.

Coulson, Doug. 2015. 'British Imperialism, the Indian Independence Movement, and the Racial Eligibility Provisions of the Naturalization Act: United States v. Thind Revisited'. *Georgetown Journal of Law and Modern Critical Race Perspective* 7(1): 1–42.

Delany, M.R. 1993. *The Condition, Elevation, Emigration, and Destiny of the Colored People of the United States*. Baltimore, MD: Black Classic Press.

Dixon, T. and T. Wintz. 2015. *The Clansman: An Historical Romance of the Ku Klux Klan*. New York, NY: Routledge.

Du Bois, W.E.B. 1947. 'Three Centuries of Discrimination'. *The Crisis* 54 (December): 362–3.

———. 1986. *Newspaper Columns by W.E.B. Du Bois*, Vol. 1 (compiled by H. Apthekar). White Plains, NY: Kraus-Thomson Organization.

Gibson, C. and K. Jung. 2002. 'Table 4: South Region—Race and Hispanic Origin: 1790 to 1990', in *Historical Census Statistics on Population Totals by Race, 1790 to 1990, and by Hispanic Origin, 1970 to 1990, for the United States, Regions, Divisions, and States*. Working Paper Series No. 56. Washington, DC: United States Census Bureau.

Grofman, B., L. Handley, and R.G. Niemi. 1992. *Minority Representation and the Quest for Voting Equality*. New York, NY: Cambridge University Press.

Horne, G. 2009. *The End of Empires: African Americans and India*. Philadelphia, PA: Temple University Press.

Immerwahr, D. 2007. 'Caste or Colony?: Indianizing Race in the United States'. *Modern Intellectual History* 4(2): 275–301.

Jack, H. 1969. 'Gandhi and Martin Luther King', in Norman Cousins (ed.). *Profiles of Gandhi: America Remembers a World Leader*, pp. 219–22. Delhi: Indian Book Co.

King, Jr, M.L. 1961. 'The Time for Freedom has Come', Section SM, p. 25. *The New York Times*, 10 September. Available at https://www.nytimes.com/1961/09/10/archives/the-time-for-freedom-has-come-this-belief-dr-king-asserts.html; last accessed on 19 June 2020.

King, M.L., C. Carson, S. Carson, and T.H. Armstrong. 1992. *The Papers of Martin Luther King, Jr., Volume VI: Advocate of the Social Gospel, September 1948–March 1963*. Berkeley: University of California Press.

Krishna, S. 2014. 'A Postcolonial Racial/Spatial Order: Gandhi, Ambedkar, and the Construction of the International', in A. Anievas, N. Manchanda, and R. Shilliam (eds). *Race and Racism in International Relations: Confronting the Global Colour Line*, pp. 151–68. New York, NY: Routledge.

Lopez, I.H. 1996. *White by Law: The Legal Construction of Race*, pp. 42–6. New York, NY: New York University Press.

Mayo, K. 1927. *Mother India*. New York, NY: Blue Ribbon Books.

Mays, B.E. 2011. *Born to Rebel: An Autobiography*. Athens, GA: University of Georgia Press.

Mazumdar, S. 1989. 'Racist Responses to Racism: The Aryan Myth and South Asians in the United States'. *Comparative Studies of South Asia, Africa and the Middle East* 9(1): 47–55.

Mencke, J.G. 1979. *Mulattoes and Race Mixture: American Attitudes and Images, 1865–1918*. Ann Arbor, MI: UMI Research Press.

Pew Research Center. 2015. 'What Census Calls Us: A Historical Timeline'. 10 June. Available at http://www.pewsocialtrends.org/interactives/multiracial-timeline/.

Prashad, V. 2000. 'Afro-Dalits of the Earth, Unite!'. *African Studies Review* 43(1): 189–201.

Rai, L.L. 1919[1916]. *The United States of America: A Hindu's Impressions and a Study*, 2nd edition. Calcutta: R. Chatterjee.

———. 1928. *Unhappy India*. Calcutta: Banna Publishing Company.

Ramnath, M. 2005. 'Two Revolutions: The Ghadar Movement and India's Radical Diaspora, 1913–1918'. *Radical History Review* 92(1): 7–30.

Richardson, III, H.J. 2015. 'From Birmingham's Jail to beyond the Riverside Church: Martin Luther King's Global Authority'. *Howard Law Journal* 59(1): 169–96.

Sinha, B. 2015. 'Dissensus, Education and Lala Lajpat Rai's Encounter with WEB Du Bois'. *South Asian History and Culture* 6(4): 462–76.

Slate, N. 2012. *Colored Cosmopolitanism: The Shared Struggle for Freedom in the United States and India*. Boston, MA: Harvard University Press.

Sohi, S. 2014. *Echoes of Mutiny: Race, Surveillance, and Indian Anticolonialism in North America*. New York, NY: Oxford University Press.

Takaki, R. 1989. *Strangers from a Different Shore: A History of Asian Americans*. Columbus, GA: Little, Brown and Company.

Thapar, Romila. 1999. 'The Aryan Question Revisited'. Transcript of lecture delivered at the Academic Staff College, Jawaharlal Nehru University, 11 October. Available at http://members.tripod.com/ascjnu/aryan.html; accessed on 18 February 2008.

Thurman, H. 1969. 'A Plea from Black America', in Norman Cousins (ed.). *Profiles of Gandhi: America Remembers a World Leader*, pp. 43–45. Delhi: Indian Book Co.

———. 1979. *With Head and Heart: The Autobiography of Howard Thurman*. New York, NY: Houghton Mifflin Harcourt.

Woodward, C.V. 2002. *The Strange Career of Jim Crow*. New York, NY: Oxford University Press.

10

Can Ambedkar Speak to Africa?*
Colour, Caste, and Class Struggles in Contemporary South Africa

GOOLAM VAHED

Young activists in Africa are reading Frantz Fanon, Thomas Sankara, Stephen Bantu Biko, and a host of writers who point to the pitfalls and possibilities of political and economic freedom in Africa. There is a deep sense that the post-colonial governments that arose in the wake of the anti-colonial movement failed in their quest to break the shackles of Western imperialism. A growing body of work has pointed to the machinations of a comprador bourgeoisie that acts in alliance with Western interests and against those of the poor and downtrodden in their home countries. As Phyllis Taoua (2018: 8) has argued, while nationalist leaders in the mid-twentieth century Africa were successful in convincing their colonial masters that freedom was synonymous with national liberation, 'national liberation did not deliver meaningful freedom to the majority of people in Africa'.

In South Africa, the euphoria of the post-1994 Nelson Mandela years has been steadily replaced by militant protests that cut across

---

* This chapter draws in part from an essay co-authored by Ashwin Desai and Goolam Vahed, 'Can Ambedkar Speak to Africa?: Colour, Caste and Class Struggles in Contemporary South Africa', in Suraj Yengde and Anand Teltumbde (eds), *The Radical in Ambedkar: Critical Reflections*, New Delhi: Allen Lane, 2018, pp. 17–31. Published with permission from Penguin Random House India.

workplaces, townships, and universities. Colonial icons have had their statues smashed and the credentials of liberation heroes have been questioned. As Andy Clarno (2019) asks:

> In 1994, the South African apartheid regime was overturned and black South Africans gained formal equality under the law.... The democratization of the state was a remarkable achievement.... Yet 25 years after the end of apartheid, the lives of working-class black people remain extremely precarious in South Africa. With high rates of permanent unemployment, a severe shortage of decent housing, a devastating HIV/AIDS epidemic, perpetual landlessness, and state violence, the black working class has been denied the promises of liberation. What went wrong?

It is within the context of this intellectual and political ferment that Ashwin Desai and I re-examined Mohandas K. Gandhi's years in South Africa in *The South African Gandhi: Stretcher-Bearer of Empire* (Desai and Vahed 2016), in which we revealed Gandhi's identification with the Empire and his disregard of Africans during his stay in South Africa. As one can imagine, the book solicited a variety of responses, some supportive and others extremely angry (see Vahed 2017). Gandhi, after all, was inducted into South African liberation history as an icon by none other than Mandela himself, with his life in Africa captured by the phrase, 'India gave us a Mohandas, we gave them a Mahatma'.

As a militant struggle against what some have labelled the transition from racial apartheid to class apartheid in South Africa gathered momentum (see Saul and Bond 2014)—in the process generating xenophobic and racial, especially Afro-Indian, tensions, adding a new dimension to the already ambivalent relationship between the Africans and Indians in Africa (see Desai and Vahed 2017)—it became clear that this was a politics that Gandhi could not speak to. Were there others in the Indian liberation movement who could relate to both the historical fight of the downtrodden and their present struggles? Could the struggles of the poor and oppressed in India help suture Afro-Indian relations on a continent Indian South Africans call home?

During the course of researching the book on Gandhi, Desai and I read more widely about the Indian political thought. It became clear that Gandhi's contemporaries and ideological rivals, such as M.N. Roy, Bhagat Singh, J.P. Narayan, Ram Chandra, and above all,

B.R. Ambedkar were barely known to the South African masses, including the diasporic Indian population. This was understandable given that in over two decades that Gandhi spent in South Africa, he maintained links with leading Indian South African anti-apartheid activists, such as Yusuf Dadoo and Monty Naicker, and his son Manilal Gandhi and his family had made South Africa home. However, as pointed out by Maclean and Elam (2015: 6), anti-colonial revolutionary thought in late colonial South Asia was not the monopoly of Gandhi but 'the product of a global network of Indians' that included Sikhs, socialists, atheists, scholars, syndicalists, swamis, students, and even Soviet sympathizers. While Gandhi has been portrayed as a 'revolutionary' in many senses, Maclean and Elam (2015: 7), in fact, contend that 'in the long history of Indian historiography, he often represents the position *against* which "revolutionaries" were defined'.

Ambedkar's writings resonated with us. Just as Fanon insisted that race, and not just class, be central to any analysis of African/colonial society, similarly Ambedkar insisted on the poverty of work that ignored the role of Brahmins/caste in the Indian society. This, together with Ambedkar's social location as a Dalit and his prescient critique of the Indian National Congress (INC), spoke powerfully to the contemporary politics of those in South Africa who sought to smash the icons of colonialism and prosecute a radical anti-imperial struggle out of the dung-heap, to steal Ambedkar's phrase, of post-colonial dead ends, hoping to eradicate recent forms of suppression, such as neoliberalism and commodification.

Thus, Ambedkar's work was particularly relevant in the African context. *Annihilation of Caste* (Ambedkar 1945) is a case in point. In South Africa, the form and nature of Indian indenture meant that caste was punctured and trespassed both in marriage and in everyday social relations. The setting in Natal made it difficult to transplant the conventional caste system. Employers did not recognize caste, age, or religious distinctions, and all workers had to do the same work under the same rules. Caste did not disappear altogether, but it was marked by many sites of transgression.

Even as we move into the twenty-first century, Ambedkar's ideas of caste continue to have relevance because new forms of social inclusion and exclusion, based around class, caste, religion, and language, are emerging among Indians in South Africa, tied in part to the rise of Narendra Modi and his Hindu nationalist

Bharatiya Janata Party (BJP) in India, which has an allure for many Hindus in the diaspora, as well as the rise of global Islamic movements, which are imposing a 'Muslim' identity on Muslim South Africans, whether by choice or not (see Desai and Vahed 2019: 157–82; Kumar 2012).

'A Plea to the Foreigner'

Ambedkar's writings certainly speak to us at the present conjuncture in South Africa. Chapter IX of *What Congress and Gandhi Have Done to the Untouchables* (Ambedkar 1946), titled 'A Plea to the Foreigner', is especially relevant. Protests over the past few years by a new generation of activists confronting South Africa's social, economic, and political inequities, and global racism and neoliberalism, provide, among other things, a critique of the Gandhian link. However, the danger in the South African context is that this critique is evolving into an insular African nationalism, rather than a global anti-imperial politics (see Desai and Vahed 2017).

Ambedkar (1946: Chapter IX, Section I) argued in his work that most foreigners sided with the INC in the Indian struggle for independence, attributing this to the 'propaganda' of the Indian press which 'does not give publicity to any news, which is inconsistent with the Congress prestige or the Congress ideology'. Newspapers survive on funding, and those started by the Dalits did not get support in the form of advertising revenue from businesses or the government, making it difficult for them to survive. 'Will Congress' "Fight for Freedom" Make India Free?', he asked (Ambedkar 1946). As discussed later, parallels can be drawn with the South African transition where white capital and the Western countries threw their lot behind the African National Congress (ANC).

Ambedkar (1946: Chapter IX, Section II) was concerned that Congress, 'far from planning for democracy is planning to resuscitate the ancient form of Hindu polity of a hereditary governing class ruling a hereditary servile class'. He made a distinction between the freedom of India and the freedom of the people of India. One did not guarantee the other. According to Ambedkar (1946: Chapter IX, Section X), 'the Fight for Freedom led by the governing class is, from the point of view of the servile classes, a selfish, if not a sham, struggle' since the governing class was 'struggling for freedom to rule the servile classes' (Ambedkar 1946).

For Ambedkar, the governing class comprised 'principally of the Brahmins ... whose allies had formerly included the Kshatriyas (warrior class) but now had support from the Banias (trading class)' (Ambedkar 1946). He considered the change

> quite inevitable. In these days of commerce, money is more important than [the] sword.... That is one reason for this change in party alignment. The second reason is the need for money to run the political machine. Money can come only from and is in fact coming from the Bania. If the Bania is financing the Congress it is because he has realised—and Mr. Gandhi has taught him—that money invested in politics gives large dividends. (Ambedkar 1946)

Ambedkar saw a 'continuous struggle for power' between the ruling and 'servile' classes of society. The servile class suffered from an 'inferiority complex' and regarded the 'governing class as their natural leaders and themselves volunteer[ed] to elect members of the governing classes as their rulers'. He further argued that 'self-government and democracy become real not when a constitution based on adult suffrage comes into existence but when the governing class loses its power to capture the power to govern.' The transition in India was not making 'India safe for democracy' but freeing' the tyrant to practise his tyrannies' (Ambedkar 1946: Chapter IX, Section III).

Ambedkar did not join the INC. He regarded 'deeply entrenched social inequities and caste loyalties' as 'serious obstacles to democratic participation and a shared sense of citizenship and nationhood' (Arora 2013). On caste, he wrote that it 'was not a physical object like a wall of bricks or a line of barbed wire which prevents the Hindus from co-mingling and which has, therefore, to be pulled down. Caste is a notion. It is a state of mind' (Ambedkar 1945: 58). This had a parallel in South Africa in the form of a medical student, Steve Biko, who, in the late 1960s, launched the Black Consciousness Movement (BCM), which essentially called on black South Africans to shed their inferior mentality and reliance on white liberals, and awaken to their self-worth in order to free themselves from white oppression. Black, in his definition, included Indians, coloureds, and Africans (see Biko 1996).

Ambedkar was frustrated with the slow progress in addressing Dalit concerns. In his critique of Gandhi, he wrote:

> Under Gandhism the common man must keep on toiling ceaselessly for a pittance and remain a brute. Gandhism, with its call of back to

nature, means back to nakedness, back to squalor, back to poverty and back to ignorance for the vast majority of the people.... Class structure in Gandhism is not an accident. It is its official doctrine. (cited in Loomba 2005: 196)

How analogous is this to recent developments in South Africa?

The Negotiated Settlement in South Africa

The 1980s in South Africa was a period of persistent internal resistance to apartheid that ran the gamut from education to workers to service delivery protests across South Africa's townships. As the resistance refused to be crushed, the apartheid government began a series of secret meetings with Nelson Mandela, then still a prisoner of the regime. Alongside this, sparked by white capital's meetings with the banned ANC, the ruling National Party (NP) engaged in talks with the ANC in exile. On the ANC's side, there was a realization that as much as the regime was on the back foot, it was nowhere close to defeat. The ANC's supplier of arms, the Soviet Union, was crumbling and front-line African states that had supported the party, such as Mozambique, Lesotho, Angola, and Zimbabwe, were facing destabilization by the apartheid regime and were also keen to see a deal (see Price 1991).

The ANC was not only open to negotiations, it was also keen to be seen as the predominant negotiating partner. Its strength in negotiations would be enhanced if it could produce a stable political environment. One of the challenges it faced was the internal resistance movement led by the United Democratic Front (UDF), formed in 1983, which, while swearing allegiance to the ANC, had its own leadership and was radicalized by the end of the 1980s. It was a mass-based movement whose constituents often acted on their own without consulting the top leadership (see Seekings 2000).

The UDF's death knell was sounded by the fact that the ANC could not countenance an independent politics born in the cauldron of struggle as it sought to show, during the negotiation process, that it could deliver stability, especially as it made major compromises on the armed struggle and, more crucially, on economic policy. As the ANC struggled with multiple challenges during the transition, it was determined that there would be no political impulses from anti-apartheid forces acting outside its controlling gaze. As ANC and South African Communist Party (SACP) stalwart Rusty Bernstein put it, 'when mass popular resistance revived again inside the country led by the UDF, it led the ANC to see the UDF as an undesirable factor in the struggle for power and to undermine it as a rival focus for mass mobilisation' (quoted in Saul and Bond 2014: 90).

With the release of Mandela, the environment was dominated by the ANC discourse of negotiation and compromise. In the course of the transition, the ANC elbowed aside all other opposition, especially that coming from quarters seeking a more radical outcome to the transition from apartheid, absorbing the UDF, while the Congress of South African Trade Unions (COSATU) and even the SACP entered into an alliance with the ANC as its junior partners (Bond 2005).

More than two decades into post-apartheid South Africa, the negotiated settlement is showing tension at the seams. It is the statues that are victimized. The removal of statues is not an end in itself; the aim is much more significant and extends to the nature of the transition in South Africa and, more generally, to decolonization. The statues of long-dead men, such as Rhodes and Gandhi, are significant in moments of crisis. As Katherine Verdery (1999: 5) tells us: 'Desecrating a statue partakes of the larger history of iconoclasm. Tearing it down not only removes that specific body from the landscape, as if to excise it from history, but also proves that because it can be torn down, no god protects it.... The person it symbolizes dissolves into an ordinary, time-bound person.'

Conversely, as Rahul Rao (2016), a lecturer in politics at the SOAS University of London, UK, points out:

> If tearing down statues offers one form of iconographic decolonisation, the Dalit movement in India has pursued the very different strategy of building statues, principally of the great Dalit leader and architect of the Indian Constitution, B.R. Ambedkar. Ambedkar statues can be seen everywhere in India, typically depicting the man wearing a suit, holding a copy of the Constitution, and pointing the way forward with an outstretched hand. Every element of this portraiture means something. The suit brings to mind the Columbia—and LSE—educated Ambedkar's willingness to embrace Enlightenment ideas that might have been European in their provenance, with none of the hesitation that a more nativist post colonialism might evince. The Constitution reminds us of the debt that all Indians owe this

man who remains the preeminent Dalit icon even as he transcends caste. The outstretched finger is a prophetic gesture leading his people out of caste bondage on a journey that was as political as it was spiritual: Ambedkar's conversion to Buddhism towards the end of his life itself powerfully symbolised his view of the inadequacies of both caste Hindu reform efforts and the promise of a purely secular enlightenment. But crucially, Ambedkar statues are not 'just' symbols: their construction also functions as a claim over space in a sociopolitical context in which a central element of Dalit oppression has been their exclusion by caste Hindus from public spaces of the village such as temples and wells. (Rao 2016)

Deconstructing Icons: Cecil John Rhodes

In March 2015, students at the University of Cape Town (UCT), South Africa, demanded the removal of Cecil John Rhodes's statue. He was denounced as a racist, imperialist, and the pioneer of a repressive system that saw black workers dragooned into a migrant labour system. A UCT student representative council member, Ramabina Mahapa, claimed that they wanted the statue removed because it 'represented what Rhodes stood for: racism and white supremacy' (Masondo 2015). The protesting students garnered massive support through a social media campaign called #RhodesMustFall (Masondo 2015). The cause of this unrest was a man who once butchered his way across the Limpopo and turned the area into his personal fiefdom, aptly named Rhodesia. Rhodes's desire for dominance was insatiable, dreaming of a line of imperial march from Cape to Cairo. During the anti-apartheid struggle in South Africa, Rhodes was denounced and pilloried by black South Africans as a representation of colonial pillage. So, any defence of Rhodes was likely to be muted.

However, there was one sticky issue. None other than Nelson Mandela, the first president of non-racial South Africa, rescued Rhodes, dusted him off, and gave him legitimacy by inaugurating The Mandela Rhodes Foundation. It followed the typical template of many post-1990 deals: the Rhodes Foundation had the money and Mandela the prestige, and together they could help needy black students get to the University of Oxford, UK, so the argument went. Mandela gave Rhodes a new lease of life when he agreed to add his name to the Rhodes Foundation. At the inauguration of The Mandela Rhodes Foundation in 2003, Mandela said: 'I am sure that Cecil John Rhodes would have given his approval to this effort to make the South African economy of the early 21st century appropriate and fit for its time' (*Sowetan* [26 August 2003] cited in Desai 2015). Mandela used the same occasion to strongly condemn activists who suggested that white-run corporations should pay reparations to apartheid survivors.

However, the protest against Rhodes runs much deeper than simply a demand for the removal of his statue. After the abolition of apartheid in 1994, the Truth and Reconciliation Commission (TRC) was established to highlight crimes against humanity in South Africa during the apartheid period. This time frame precluded the crimes of people such as Rhodes. Big business too was not required to properly bear witness to its long record of dispossession and exploitation.

Instead, the TRC gave multinational corporations, such as Anglo American and the Rupert empires, a platform to dishonestly claim their long opposition to apartheid. While the TRC recommended a once-off 1 per cent corporate tax to raise money for victims of apartheid, the then Thabo Mbeki government rejected this on the grounds that the financial markets would interpret such a measure as anti-business (Klein 2011). In proposing The Mandela Rhodes Foundation, Mandela stated that 'the bringing together of these two names represents a symbolic moment in the closing of the historic circle; drawing together the legacies of reconciliation and leadership and those of entrepreneurship and education' (Berkeley Center 2013). According to Njabulo Ndebele, chair of The Mandela Rhodes Foundation, the foundation represented:

> a gesture of reconciliation between two historic moments: the moral ambiguities in the historical triumphs of colonialism and the transformative mandate of a modern democratic South Africa. The two names side by side engender unflagging energy, because the tension in their interaction is ultimately irresolvable as a constant spur to reflection on the possibilities, and the difficulties, of people living together in history. (Berkeley Center 2013)

How quickly these words have come to be seen as quirky and quaint, of belonging to a time long past.

By raising the spectre of Rhodes, students at the UCT were actually beginning to critique the contours and boundaries of the negotiated settlement itself, which had kept intact the structures of white capitalist domination. Amit Chaudhuri (2016) makes the poignant observation:

> From its start in South Africa, Rhodes Must Fall announced that it intended to address this unequal vision of the world as it manifests itself within universities—declaring itself 'a collective movement of students and staff members mobilising for direct action against the reality of institutional racism at the University of Cape Town. The chief focus of this movement is to create avenues for REAL transformation that students and staff alike have been calling for.'

The Rhodes statue was removed from the UCT but the movement spread to the University of Oxford where his statue stands at Oriel College. The university has thus far resisted removing it. These movements are not only about removing Rhodes' statue, but also what he stood for, institutional racism, and to decolonize the education system.

For the past few years, students across South African campuses have been calling for a radical restructuring of the education system to incorporate 'free quality decolonized education'. The protests have, at times, been violent and bloody. By decolonized education, UCT student Athabile Nonxuba explained, they wanted an education in which the curriculum did not dehumanize black students; stopped undermining the thinking of Africans; was taught by decolonized African people; advanced the interests of Africans rather than Eurocentric interests; stopped valorizing the work of European thinkers like Karl Marx and instead introduced the ideas of Africans; and introduced African languages (Evans 2016).

With a new post-apartheid generation of young South Africans straining to have their voices heard, nostalgia for the struggle is not high on their list of priorities. In addition, 26 years have now passed and with former president (Jacob Zuma) persistently accused of corruption and talk of 'state capture' by a single family, the Guptas, who arrived from India in the 1990s, and with many South Africans buckling under financial pressure resulting from the global coronavirus pandemic, the ANC is fast losing its aura as a party of liberation.

Mandela and White Capital

Following the protests around Rhodes, the critique of the 'Mandela moment' had come thick and fast in South Africa, both from the inside and outside. The ANC duly swept to power in 1994 and with the world watching, Nelson Mandela was inaugurated as the first black president of a democratic South Africa. It was expected that democracy would bring its own dividends, to be shared fairly among all South Africa's people. However, as time would show, the ANC embraced a severely damaging neoliberal economic logic. John Saul, who had invested so much of his academic and activist life in the Southern African project, wrote:

> A tragedy is being enacted in South Africa, as much a metaphor for our times as Rwanda and Yugoslavia and, even if not so immediately searing of the spirit, it is perhaps a more revealing one. For in the teeth of high expectations arising from the successful struggle against a malignant apartheid state, a very large percentage of the population—among them many of the most desperately poor in the world—are being sacrificed on the altar of the neo-liberal logic of global capitalism.... The most startling thing I personally discovered about the New South Africa is just how easy it has become to find oneself considered an ultraleftist! (Saul 2001: 1)

The ANC government failed to deliver on an accelerated redistributive programme. Some former ANC members, such as Julius Malema, leader of the Economic Freedom Fighters (EFF) political party, argued that the writing was on the wall from the very beginning. At the University of Oxford in 2015, Malema stated:

> The deviation from the Freedom Charter was the beginning of selling out of the revolution. When Mandela returned from prison he got separated from Winnie Mandela and went to stay in a house of a rich white man ... he was looked after by the Oppenheimers. Mandela used to attend those club meetings of those white men who owned the South African economy. The Nelson we celebrate now is a stage-managed Mandela who compromised the principles of the revolution, which are captured in the Freedom Charter. (Areff 2015)

There is much resonance between young Africans' demands and Ambedkar's ideas. Ambedkar called, among other things, for state socialism, a policy of reservations, an end to institutional oppression, and the restoration of human dignity. Meanwhile, nationalization of the mines and land redistribution are key cries of young black activists. The land question has been at the heart of the debates about post-apartheid South Africa, with many activist groups calling for the large-scale redistribution of land to transform the economy and reduce poverty (see Ntsebeza and Hall 2007).

In *States and Minorities: What Are Their Rights and How to Secure Them in the Constitution of Free India*, Ambedkar (1947) speaks of a model of economic development that he described as 'state socialism', calling for state ownership of land, free education, state planning of the economy, and state provision of healthcare. On the question of landownership and violence, he wrote in 'Buddha or Karl Marx':

> As to violence there are many people who seem to shiver at the very thought of it. But this is only a sentiment. Violence cannot be altogether dispensed with. Even in non-communist countries a murderer is hanged. Does not hanging amount to violence? If a murderer can be killed, because he has killed a citizen, if a soldier can be killed in war because he belongs to a hostile nation why cannot a property owner be killed if his ownership leads to misery for the rest of humanity? There is no reason to make an exception in favour of the property owner, why one should regard private property as sacrosanct? (Ambedkar 1955)

As Clarno wrote recently:

> The ANC government adopted a neoliberal economic strategy promoting free trade, export-oriented industry, and the privatization of state-owned businesses and municipal services. This has given rise to a small black elite, but the old white elite continues to own the vast majority of land and wealth in the country. In the words of Achille Mbembe, 'This is the only country on Earth in which a revolution took place which resulted in not one single former oppressor losing anything.' Meanwhile, the lives of poor and working-class black South Africans are as precarious as ever. Post-apartheid South Africa is now regarded as the most unequal country in the world. In recent years, South Africa has been the site of constant struggles as working-class black communities fight for access to land and housing, water and electricity, health care and education, and a living wage. Renewing a Mozambiquan rallying cry, social movements in post-apartheid South Africa insist that 'A luta continua' ('The struggle continues'). (Clarno 2019)

The agreements laid down during the negotiations between the ANC and the Nationalists have meant that the promises made around creating a better life for all have been stymied in favour of the few.

Parallels can be drawn with Ambedkar's analysis of India. As Arora (2013) points out, Ambedkar, 'more than any other leader of that movement, which would come to define all of independent India's heroes, understood that India's deeply entrenched social inequities and caste loyalties were serious obstacles to democratic participation and a shared sense of citizenship and nationhood'. When he resigned from Nehru's cabinet in October 1951, Ambedkar stated that he had done so because the government's focus was excessively on economic rather than social development. According to Ambedkar, 'to leave inequality between class and class, sex and sex, which is the soul of Hindu society untouched and to go passing legislation relating to economic problems is to make a farce of our Constitution and to build a palace on a dung heap' (Teltumbde 2017: 83).

Ambedkar's words of 1951, as well his 'plea to foreigners', strike a chord in contemporary South Africa where the commanding heights of the economy remain in white hands.

The Present

South Africans are living in difficult times, witnesses to the attempted reclamation and ownership of history by younger black Africans, seeking to come to terms with the racist legacy of colonial warlords like Cecil John Rhodes, confronted by the unfulfilled promises of political transformation; as of April 2020, South Africa, like India and many other countries across the world, is in a complete lockdown over the coronavirus pandemic that has spread across the world. This epic tragedy has infected millions across the world, claimed the lives of thousands, and destroyed economies globally. As always, the poor are paying a disproportionate price. In India, the coronavirus tragedy followed violent protests in December 2019 against what was seen as an anti-Muslim Citizenship Amendment Bill (CAB), in which many lives were lost.

Ambedkar, I would argue, speaks to these times. The anger that he displayed, both in his actions and writings against caste and other inequalities, has mostly gone under the radar of intellectuals and activists. Ambedkar would likely have approved of protests over education in South Africa and the CAB in India, for he believed in the 'insurrectionary duties of the citizen, one that he begins to articulate with unprecedented clarity in *Annihilation of Castes*.

Indeed, the treatise forges a galvanizing relationship between the ethics of revolutionary annihilation and the creative energies of the people, between a people's immeasurable force and their spiritual capacity to constitute themselves anew' (Kumar 2015: 7).

The fallout from the coronavirus pandemic will force people across the globe to break with what was before and constitute both ourselves and our worlds afresh. Will it be a world in which we carry our caste, race, ethnic, and other prejudices as well as class privileges with us, or will we help to shape a new world shorn of crass consumerism and prejudices?

In the South African context, the ANC was long mired in corruption. What is encouraging for observers is the outing of Jacob Zuma as president in 2018 and the appointment of the Zondo Commission to investigate 'state capture', as well as new forms of opposition to the party's class apartheid. In the early post-apartheid years, there was hope that an independent left would provide a clear alternative to the ANC but that optimism faded when the SAPC and the major trade union movement, COSATU, chose to remain within the tripartite alliance. The populist countrywide civic uprisings over service delivery have been ephemeral. Arguably, more significant in recent times has been the #FeesMustFall movement among university students who succeeded in their demand for free (but not yet decolonized) university education.

For a while, it appeared that at the heart of the new uprisings would be an ideology that attacked class privilege, cutting across racial boundaries. That appears to have taken a turn towards racial nationalism. In response to charges of corruption, when he was president, Jacob Zuma sought to make increasing appeals to a crude racial nationalism, while opening doors to transnational capital, to deflect criticism of the ANC's policies. This is not as blatant under the new president, Cyril Ramaphosa, but is played out in real life in the way that affirmative action policies, for example, are reserved for Africans (see Alexander 2007). More worrying for minorities is that the EFF party, led by former ANC Youth League member Julius Malema and seen by Indians as being racist and anti-Indian, is winning most support among the young (see Hans 2017). The spectre of the Indian as a foreigner is raised every now and then. As Marè (2014: 118) related:

> In 2012, in a kind of inclusive chauvinism, rioters in Rustenberg threatened 'Indian' South African shopkeepers with violence and

taunts, calling them *amakwerekwere*, a term previously reserved for foreigners of African origin. Around the country, people of Asian and Indian descent, including those who have lived here for generations [and who are South African citizens], confront such sentiments—as do foreigners from across the continent and beyond.

This racial nationalism has a parallel with India, where 'there has been a steady process of what the eminent historian Romila Thapar has called "syndicated Hinduism". This has entailed the more or less systematic consolidation of an ever-widening Hindu self-consciousness across castes' (Vanaik 2014: 60). As Jonah Blank (2019) put it, Hindutva is:

> an ideology that seeks to reformulate Hinduism into something that most practitioners' grandparents would barely understand. Religions change—that's as timeless as time. But the transformation currently under way in Hinduism is among the most significant in modern history.... For many today, religion is less a matter of what you *believe*, or even what you *do*, than of who you *are*.... Hinduism not a theology, but an identity. The stakes here are not faith or practice—the issues are those of identity: *We're being outbred by minorities. We're being laughed at by the world. We're overrun with immigrants—and you know what kind. We're second-class citizens in our own nation. Make India Great Again.*

What kind of politics will emerge out of these fallen statutes, embryonic student and community movements, protests against discriminatory immigration legislation, or even the coronavirus pandemic? Will it be an anti-imperialist, anti-racist global movement from below? Or will racial and religious nationalists win the argument? One of the impulses of *Annihilation of Caste* is the 'need to posit a revolutionary subject through the general mobilisation of the multitude. The reclamation of authentic belief, the right to truth, and the ability to mobilise a shared and general will, Ambedkar insists, are inseparable from one another; together they constitute a people's movement towards free and revolutionary democracy' (Kumar 2015: 7).

The politics that Ambedkar envisaged is emerging on the streets and in the classrooms of Cape Town and Accra, and Delhi and beyond—a politics of the 'wretched of the earth' currently under siege because some leaders have taken advantage of the coronavirus pandemic to introduce measures which are giving rise to surveillance states and authoritarian societies. Though there are differences between South Africa and India, Ambedkar's teachings and political ideas have great relevance at the present time, and it is incumbent on Indian and other intellectuals and activists to make them more widely known.

References

Alexander, Neville. 2007. 'Affirmative Action and the Perpetuation of Racial Identities in Post-Apartheid South Africa', *Transformation: Critical Perspectives on Southern Africa* 63: 92–105.

Ambedkar, B.R. 1945. *Annihilation of Caste: With a Reply to Mahatma Gandhi*, 3rd edition. Amritsar: Ambedkar School of Thoughts, Katra Janfan Singh. Available at https://archive.org/stream/in.ernet.dli.2015.71655/2015.71655.Annihilation-Of-Caste-With-A-Reply-To-Mhatma-Gandhi_djvu.txt.

———. 1946. *What Congress and Gandhi Have Done to the Untouchables*. Bombay: Thacker. Available at http://www.ambedkar.org/ambcd/41A.What%20Congress%20and%20Gandhi%20Preface.htm; last accessed on 3 December 2016.

———. 1947 *States and Minorities: What Are Their Rights and How to Secure them in the Constitution of Free India*, Memorandum on the Safeguards for the Scheduled Castes submitted to the Constituent Assembly on behalf of the Scheduled Castes Federation. Available at http://www.ambedkar.org/ambcd/10A.%20Statesand%20Minorities%20Preface.htm.

———. 1955. 'Buddha or Karl Marx'. Published posthumously. Available at http://www.ambedkar.org/ambcd/20.Buddha%20or%20Karl%20Marx.htm; last accessed on 18 July 2017.

Areff, Ahmed. 2015. 'Rich White Men Made Mandela Turn against the Revolution—Malema'. *News 24*, 26 November. Available at http://www.news24.com/SouthAfrica/News/rich-white-men-made-mandela-turn-against-the-revolution-malema-20151126; last accessed on 28 September 2016.

Arora, Namit. 2013. 'Caste Iron', *The Caravan: A Journal of Politics and Culture*, 1 November. Available at http://www.caravanmagazine.in/perspectives/caste-iron; last accessed on 25 September 2017.

Berkeley Center. 2013. 'A Discussion with Professor Njabulo S. Ndebele, Chair of the Mandela–Rhodes Foundation'. 29 October. Available at https://berkleycenter.georgetown.edu/interviews/a-discussion-with-professor-njabulo-s-ndebele-chair-of-the-mandela-rhodes-foundation; last accessed on 7 October 2016.

Biko, Steve. 1996. *I Write What I Like*. Johannesburg: Ravan Press.

Blank, Jonah. 2019. 'How Hinduism became a Political Weapon in India'. *The Atlantic*, 24 May. Available at https://www.theatlantic.com/international/archive/2019/05/hindu-nationalism-narendra-modi-india-election/590053/; last accessed on 7 April 2020.

Bond, Patrick. 2005. *Elite Transition: From Apartheid to Neoliberalism in South Africa*. Scottsville: University of KwaZulu-Natal Press.

Chaudhuri, Amit. 2016. 'The Real Meaning of Rhodes Must Fall'. *The Guardian*, 16 March. Available at https://www.theguardian.com/uk-news/2016/mar/16/the-real-meaning-of-rhodes-must-fall; last accessed on 7 October 2016.

Clarno, Andy. 2019. 'Neolibralism after Apartheid: From South Africa to Palestine/Israel'. *Marxist Sociology* Blog, 31 January. Available at https://marxistsociology.org/2019/01/neoliberalism-after-apartheid-lessons-for-palestine-from-south-africa/; last accessed on 6 April 2020.

Desai, Ashwin. 2015. 'Relief Must Be More than Symbolic', *The Star*, 6 April. Available at https://www.iol.co.za/the-star/relief-must-be-more-than-symbolic-1841238; last accessed on 3 September 2017.

Desai, Ashwin and Goolam Vahed. 2016. *The South African Gandhi. Stretcher-Bearer of Empire*. Stanford and Delhi: Stanford University Press and Navayana.

———. 2017. 'Stuck in the Middle: Indians in South Africa's Rainbow', *South Asian Diaspora* 9(2): 147–62.

———. 2019. *A History of the Present: A Biography of Indian South Africans, 1994–2019*. New Delhi: Oxford University Press.

Evans, Annit. 2016. 'What Is Decolonized Education?' *News24*, 25 September. Available at http://www.news24.com/SouthAfrica/News/what-is-decolonised-education-20160925; last accessed on 3 October 2016.

Hans, Bongani. 2017. '#EFFTurns4: Malema Attack Enrages Indians'. *IOL*, 29 July. Available at https://www.iol.co.za/news/politics/effturns4-malema-attack-enrages-indians-10546442; last accessed on 29 October 2017.

Klein, Naomi. 2011. 'Democracy Born in Chains'. 13 February. Available at http://www.naomiklein.org/articles/2011/02/democracy-born-chains#endnote3; last accessed on 9 October 2016.

Kumar, Aishwary. 2015. *Radical Equality: Ambedkar, Gandhi and the Risk of Democracy*. Stanford: Stanford University Press.

Kumar, Pratap. 2012. 'Place of Subcaste (Jati) Identity in the Discourse on Caste: Examination of Caste in the Diaspora', *South Asian Diaspora* 4(2): 1–14.

Loomba, Ania. 2005. *Colonialism/Postcolonialism*, 2nd edition. London: Routledge.

Maclean, Kama and J. Daniel Elam. 2015. 'Reading Revolutionaries: Texts, Acts, and the Afterlives of Political Action in Late Colonial South Asia: Who Is a Revolutionary?', in K. Maclean and J.D. Elam (eds), *Revolutionary Lives in South Asia: Acts and Afterlives of Anticolonial Political Action*, pp. 1–11. London: Routledge.

Marè, G. 2014. *Declassified: Moving Beyond the Dead End of Race in South Africa*. Johannesburg: Jacana.

Masondo, Sipho. 2015. 'Rhodes Must Fall Campaign Gains Momentum at UCT'. *News24*, 23 March. Available at http://www.news24.com/SouthAfrica/News/Rhodes-Must-Fall-campaign-gains-momentum-at-UCT-20150323; last accessed on 1 October 2016.

Ntsebeza, Lungisile and Ruth Hall (eds). 2007. *The Land Question in South Africa: The Challenge of Transformation and Redistribution*. Cape Town: HSRC Press.

Price, Robert M. 1991. *The Apartheid State in Crisis: Political Transformation of South Africa, 1975–1990*. Oxford: Oxford University Press.

Rao, Rahul. 2016. 'On Statues'. *The Disorder of Things*, 2 April. Available at https://thedisorderofthings.com/2016/04/02/on-statues/; last accessed on 19 July 2017.

Saul, John. 2001. 'Cry for the Beloved Country: The Post-apartheid Denouement', *Monthly Review* 52(8): 1–51.

Saul, John and Patrick Bond. 2014. *South Africa: The Present as History: From Mrs Piles to Mandela and Marikana*. New York: Boydell & Brewer.

Seekings, Jeremy. 2000. *The UDF: A History of the United Democratic Front in South Africa, 1983–1991*. Cape Town: David Philip.

Taoua, Phyllis. 2018. *African Freedom: How Africa Responded to Independence*. Cambridge: Cambridge University Press.

Teltumbde, Anand. 2017. *Dalits: Past, Present and Future*. New Delhi: Routledge India.

Vahed, Goolam. 2017. 'The Past in the Present: Writing the South African Gandhi', *Journal of Labor and Society* 20(1): 107–27.

Vanaik, Achin. 2014. 'India's Landmark Election', in Leo Panitch and Greg Albo (eds), *Transforming Classes: Socialist Register 2015*, pp. 54–72. London: Merlin Press.

Verdery, Katherine. 1999. *The Political Lives of Dead Bodies*. Columbia: Columbia University Press.

Index

#RhodesMustFall, 236

Adi Dharmi movements, 119–21
Adityanath, Yogi, 167
Adivasis, 162, 164
Adoption Act, 102
affirmative action policies, 189–91, 193, 196, 198–201
African-American capitalism, 175
African-Americans, 172–4, 211–12, 217
  comparison with Indian struggle for independence, 210–23
  cultural outlook, 208–10
  sentiment of African-Americans leaders, 223n25
  struggle, from an international perspective, 223–5
  struggle against oppression and subordination, 206–7, 214–15, 220–21
African Communities League (ACL), 176
African National Congress (ANC), 185, 240–1, 243
Aiyyangar, Ananthasayanam, 148
Alma-Ata Declaration, 1978, 20

Ambedkar, B.R., 3, 158–61, 174–6, 232
  abolishment of slavery of women under patriarchal systems, 101
  alternatives to patriarchal norms, 100–3, 113
  analysis of India, 242
  annihilation, notion of, 189–90, 202
  Annihilation of Caste, 116, 188–9, 232, 242, 244
  'A Plea to the Foreigner', 233–5
  Bahishkrit Bharat, 116, 137
  Caste, Class and Democracy, 189
  on caste system, 141
  on community's progress, 117
  conversion to Buddhism, 150, 176
  feminist philosophy of, 91, 103–14
  on gender equality and social justice, 70–1, 92, 113
  hermeneutics, 149–51
  idea of pollution, 111
  ideas of caste, 232
  Maternity Bill, 102, 113

model of economic
  development, 241
Mooknayak, 116, 137
patriarchal norms, critique of,
  92–100
perception of women's issues,
  70
reservation polices, 176
*The Rise and Fall of Hindu
  Women*, 117, 149–50
on social and economic justice,
  189
social order, critique of, 138
on socio-economic and political
  status of women, 69
on women empowerment, 69,
  83
on women's education, 101–2
on women's health, 20
women's rights, 176–8
on women's subjugation, 141–4,
  149
Ambedkarite feminism/feminist
  thought, xxxii, xxxiv, xxxvii
Ambedkarite movement in
  Karnataka, 119–20
anaemia, 72, 76, 81
Anglo supremacy, 221
anti-caste movements, 161
apartheid, 184–5, 231
arranged marriages, 116
Aryan conquest theory, 215
Aryan supremacy, 221

Barve Committee Report, 6
Beijing Conference on Women,
  70–1
Bharatiya Jana Sangh, 148
Bharatiya Janata Party (BJP), 233
Bhim Sena, 119
Bhore Committee, 20
Black Africans, 184, 193–4, 196,
  198, 202, 218, 224, 242

black Civil Rights Movement, 224
black community as a nation, 218
Black Consciousness Movement
  (BCM), 188, 234
Black Cross Nurses, 177
Black Economic Empowerment
  (BEE), 191
black feminists, 109
Black feminist thought, xxxvii
Black Panthers, 187
Black Star Line, 176
Bogle, Paul, 174
bonded labour abolition policies,
  in independent India, 62–6
Brahmanical
  order, 150
  taboos, 163
Brahmanized feminism, 140
Brahmin superiority, 140
Brihanmumbai Municipal
  Corporation (BMC), 5
Buddhism, 150, 159, 161, 176

caste and racial subjugation, 172–4
caste-based
  discrimination, xxxii, 7
  in India, 186–7
  oppression, xxxii, 110
caste endogamy, 116
caste-induced social hierarchy, 9
castelessness, 186–90
caste purity, 142–3
caste system, in India, xxxi, 41,
  47–8, 70, 111, 116–17, 138,
  141–2, 147, 150, 161
Chakravarti, Uma, 92, 110
Chandalas, 160
Chandra, Ram, 231
Chandragutti Incident, 1986, 120
Charvaka school of materialism,
  161
Chilakurti case, 1991, 139
child marriage, xxxiii

Child Marriage Restraint Act, 1929, 149
Civil Rights Movement, 1960s, 173
community-based sensitization, xxxvi
conducive environment for women workers, framework for, 9
conjugal rights, 146
coronavirus pandemic, 242–3
creolization, 168
custodial deaths, 106

Dalit Feminist Theory, xxxi
Dalit Panthers, 187
Dalit(s), xxxvi, 10, 157–159, 162
    Ambedkar's concern for people's health, 20–2
    artisans, 47
    capitalism, 40, 175
    caste and racial subjugation, 172–4
    Christians, 164
    cultures, 160, 169
    experience of oppression in India, 205, 222
    feminism, 41, 92, 112
    as Harijans, 219–20
    indentured, 164
    issues of separation and civil rights for, 174
    liberation struggle, 222–3
    literature, 41
    poor, 42
    resistance, 158
    as sanitation workers, 3
Dalit Sangharsha Samiti (DSS), 120
Dalit Voice, 120
Dalit women, xxxii–xxxiii, 9
    in agricultural labour, 41
    in agricultural relations, study of, 43–4
        access to additional sources of income, 63–4
        approach to overcome shame, 63–6
        difference between stigmatizing working conditions and personalized shaming, 59
        experience of stigma and shame, 41–6, 50–6, 61
        Marxist way to overcome, 63
        personalized shaming, responses to, 58–60
        response to shame, 46–7
        state action, 47–50
        stigmatizing working conditions, responses to, 57–8
        susceptibility to exposure of stigma and shame, 56–7
    forms of stigma and shame, xxxv
    in Karnataka, 160
        contemporary practices of discrimination, 132–3
        data sources and methodology, 118–19
        education, access to, 125–6
        employment, access to, 127–8
        population distribution, 121–4
        prevalence of underage marriage, 130–2
        status, 125–8
    marginalization of, 108
    'triple oppression' of, 120
    violence against, 110
Dayabhaga law, 145–7
Deshpande, Satish, 186, 199–201
Devi, Bhanwari, xxxiii, 108
dignity
    of sanitation workers, 4–6
    of women, 5, 10, 22–3, 43–4, 49, 64, 66, 95, 100, 105

Index

Directive Principles of the State Policy, 117
Divorce and Maintenance Act, 102–3
Dixon Jr, Thomas
 The Clansman, 215
 The Leopard's Spots, 216
Douglass, Frederick, 172, 174
Dowry Prohibition Act, 1961, 149
Du Bois, William Edward Burghardt, 157, 173–9, 206, 214, 218, 221

education and employment, relation between, 128–30
effective female literacy rate (ELR), 76
Employment Equity Act (EEA), 191
Employment of Manual Scavengers and Construction of Dry Latrines (Prohibition) Act, 1993, 3, 21
 prohibitions, 4
endogamy, xxxi, 141, 168
Equal Remuneration Act, 1976, 149

Family Courts Act, 1984, 149
female foeticide and infanticide, 77–80
female sex workers, 104–5
female subjectivity, in colonial India, xxxvi
feminist epistemology, Ambedkar's, xxxvi

Gaekwad, Sayajirao, 187
Gandhi, Mohandas K., 188–9, 218–20, 231, 234–5
 philosophy of non-violence or *satyagraha*, 219
Garvey, Jr, Marcus Mosiah, 157, 173–9
Geetha, V., 92, 111–12

gender equality and women empowerment, study
 Ambedkar's view, 70–1
 data source, 71–2
 discriminatory practices towards girl child, 77–80
 male child preference, 77–80
 methodology, 72–3
 resource allocation and vulnerability in outcomes, 80–1
 state-level programmes and policies, 84–5
 variables included in study, 73–7, 89–90
 women's autonomy and economic empowerment interlinkages, 81–5
gender justice, xxxi–xxxii, xxxvii–xxxviii
 Ambedkarite approaches to, xxxv–xxxvii
gender-sensitive labour laws, 117
Ghadar Party conspiracy, 217
girl child, discriminatory practices towards, 77–80
Gramsci, Antonio, 175
Guru, Gopal, 92, 108–9

Hindu caste system, 117
Hindu Code Bill, 70, 92, 100–4, 117, 145, 147–9, 178
Hinduism, 159
Hindu Mahasabha, 148
Hindu Marriage Bill, 144
Hindu Succession Act (HSA), 102, 104
honour killings, xxxii, 106

Immigration and Nationality Act of 1965, 165
Immoral Traffic (Prevention) Act, 1956, 149

indentured labourers, 164
Indian academia, feminist issues in, 104
Indian-Americans, 165
Indian South Africans, 192–6, 200–1
Indian struggle for Independence, 210–23
indigenous capitalism, 47
Indo-Trinidad villages, 169
infant mortality rate (IMR), 75
inter-caste marriage, 116
International Conference on Population and Development (ICPD), 70
interracial tournaments, 185
Intestate Succession Bill, 144

jati, 162
Jat-Pat-Todak Mandal, 189
Jim Crow laws, 173
Joseph Bhore Committee Report, 21
judicial separation, 146

Karnataka SC population, 121–4
 Balgai, 122
 coastal region, 121
 composition, 122–3
 Edgai, 122
 percentage and growth of, 122
 in rural region, 121
 rural *vs* urban, 121
 sex ratio, 123–4
 women, 123–4

latrine facilities, availability and types of, 4–5, 5n1
legal
 age for marriage, in India, 131
 enslavement, 173
lesbian suicides, 106
Lingayat movement, 162
lower-caste women, xxxii, 140

Mahabharata, critique of, 92, 96–7, 113, 149
Mahad Satyagraha, 1927, 117
Mahapa, Ramabina, 236
Mahila Samakhya Karnataka (MSK) programme, 120–1
Malcolm X, 177
male child preference, 77–80
Malkani Committees Reports, 6, 8
malnutrition, 76, 83
Mandela, Nelson, 185, 188, 230, 238–41
Mandela Rhodes Foundation, 237–8
Manorama, Ruth, 120–1
manual scavenging, 4–5, 7, 10, 22
 employment of scavengers, 21
Manusmriti, 69
 critique of, 69, 92, 97–100, 150
Maré, Gerhard, 191, 200, 243
Marriage Act, 102
Maternity Act, 102–103
Mays, Benjamin, 206, 220–1
Menon, Nivedita, 92, 104–6
Mica Mines Labour Welfare Fund Bill, 20
middle-class Hindus, 164
Ministry for Overseas Indian Affairs, 166
missing girls, 74, 88–9
Mitakshra rule of law, 145
Montgomery Bus Boycott, 224

National Association for the Advancement of Colored People (NAACP), 176, 216–17
National Campaign on Dalit Human Rights (NCDHR), 106
National Commission for Women Act, 1990, 149
National Federation of Dalit Women (NFDW), 106, 121
National Negro Congress, 174
National Policy for the Empowerment of Women, 71

Naturalization Act of 1790, 212
Niagara Movement, 176
non-racialism, 184–5, 201
non-resident Indians (NRIs), 163–5, 179
   awareness of caste, 169
   conservatism among, 166–7
   in defining policies, 166
   foreign interference, 167
   funding of political parties, 166–7
   influence in politics, 166
   informal relations of superiority–inferiority, 168
   investments, 165–6
   religion, 168
   remittances to India, 165

Omvedt, Gail, 117
othering, 105

Paik, Shailaja, 138
pan-Africanism, 173
Pandit, Vijaya Lakshmi, 222
patriarchy
   Brahmanical, xxxii–xxxiv, 110, 112, 140
   Dalit, 111–12
   graded, 110
   in India, xxxi, 91
      alternatives to patriarchal norms, 100–3, 113
      Brahmanical nature, xxxii–xxxiv, 110, 112, 140
      critique of, 92–100
      order of privilege and deprivation, 110
   Kayastha, 112
   Kunbi, 112
   Mahar, 112
   Muslim patriarchy, 112
   Rajput, 112
   Other Backward Class patriarchy, 112

Penal Code, 1861, 48
personalized shaming, 58–60
Phule, Jyotirao, xxxiv, 174
poverty and dignity, study on, 43
Pratiloma marriages, 143–4
Priyadarsin, Devanampriya, 159–60
property rights, 145–6, 148
Protection of Human Right Act, 1993, 149
Protection of Women from Domestic Violence Act, 2005, 149
pure and impure bodies, 138–41

race discrimination in South Africa, 186–7
   related to Education, 196–9
racelessness, 186
racial
   identity, 200
   justice, xxxvii, xxxviii–xl
   nationalism, 244
   oppression of African-Americans, 157
   separation programme, 173
Rai, Lala Lajpat, 214–17
Ramayana, critique of, 92–5, 113, 149
Rao, Anupama, 140
Rashtriya Swasthya Bima Yojana (RSBY), 21–22
Rau Committee, 144, 146
Rege, Sharmila, 92, 103, 107, 109–11, 139
religious prostitution, 107
reservation policy, 187
Rhodes, Cecil John, 236–9, 242
Rich, Adrienne, 185
Right to Information (RTI) Act in 2006, 5
Rivonia Trial, 1964, 185
Roosevelt, Franklin D., 221
Roy, Arundhati, 188

sacramental marriage, 147
Safai Kamgar Vikas Sangh (SKVS), 5

sanitation work, factors for
    continuance in, 18–20, 39
sanitation workers, xxxv, 3
    awareness and utilization of
        benefits, 18, 39
    common names, 7
    composition of, 11
    deprivation and disadvantage of
        women workers, 8–10
    dignity of, 4–6
    educational attainment,
        13, 34
    gender differentials, 29–30,
        32–5, 37–8
    health conditions, 17, 36
    manhole workers, official
        deaths of, 5–6
    multi-city study, method and
        material, 10
    nature of illness and treatment
        seeking, 17–18, 37–8
    problems and experience of
        discrimination, 13–17
    protection of, 4
    rehabilitation of, 4, 21
    safety at workplace and safe
        working conditions, 11–13
    sewer workers, official deaths
        of, 28
    use of protective gear/
        equipment, 31–3
    vulnerability of, 6–8
Sati (Prevention) Act, 1987, 149
Satrohan, 158
Scheduled Castes (SCs), 40
    body mass index (BMI) among
        women of reproductive age
        group, 131–2
    child mortality rate, 131–2, 136
    health deprivation and adverse
        health outcomes, 131–2
    infant mortality rate, 131–2,
        136
    in Karnataka, 121–4

percentage of male and female
    SC students attending
    college, 135
under-five mortality rate,
    131–2
self-stigma, 60
sex preference, in India, 77–80
sex ratio (SR), 73–4
sex work, 104–5, 107
Shiromani Akali Dal (SAD), 166
Shyamsundar, B., 119
Silicon Valley, 165
Singh, Bhagat, 231
Sinha, Chitra, 147
Slate, Nico, 206
slavery, 47–8, 187, 216
Slavery Abolition Act, 1843, 48, 62
slavery-based production relations,
    61
social
    discrimination, 7
    divide, contributing factors, 7
    exclusion of vulnerable
        populations, 7
    identity-based disparities, 22–3
    stigmatization, 60
South Africa, 230, 242–5
    apartheid and segregation in,
        184–6, 231
    negotiated settlement in, 235–7
    non-racialism/racelessness,
        184–5, 190–2
South Asian diaspora, 157, 168,
    210
    Ambedkar's relevance to Indian
        diaspora, 169–71
    in America, 165
    identity, 167
stigma–shame nexus, 42–3
    institutional shaming, 60
    prevalence of, 60
    self-stigma, 60
    social stigmatization, 60
stigmatized individual or group, 42

stigmatizing working conditions, 57–8
Stridhana, 146
Student Christian Movement of India, 219
Swachh Bharat Abhiyan (SBA), 8, 22
  number of toilets constructed, 22
  objective of, 22
  success of scheme, 22

Telugu Association of North America, 166
Telugu Desam Party (TDP), 166
Thapar, Romila, 244
Thurman, Reverend Howard, 219–20
Tirupati Temple, 163
Total Sanitation Campaign (TSC), 8
Trinidad Legislative Council, 169

United Democratic Front (UDF), 185
Universal African Legions, 177
Universal Negro Improvement Association (UNIA), 173, 176
University of Cape Town (UCT) Medical School, 197
University of KwaZulu-Natal (UKZN), 197
  purported admissions policy, 197
untouchables, 20, 40, 46–7, 63, 122, 151, 170, 189
upper-caste women, xxxii, 110
U.S. v. Bhagat Singh Thind, 212–13
US India Political Action Committee, 167

Valmiki community, 7
varna, 144, 150, 162

Washington, Booker T., 206, 219
White, Walter, 222
whiteness, 185–6
white
  privilege, 212
  solipsism, 185–6
  supremacy, 211–13
Wilkens, Roy, 221
women
  empowerment. *See also* gender equality and women empowerment, study
    Ambedkar's view on, 69–71, 83
    components, 118
    UN concept of, 118
  mine workers, 20
  sanitation workers
    deprivation and disadvantage of, 8–10
    estimate of numbers, 8
    nature of illness and treatment seeking, 17–18
    underprivileged conditions, 9–10
Women's Development Project, xxxiii
women's
  rights, 176–8
  history of, 144
  subjugation, 141–4
work-induced health hazards, 9

Yellamma cult, 120

Zuma, Jacob, 243

Editor and Contributors

Editor

Aakash Singh Rathore is the author of *Ambedkar's Preamble: A Secret History of the Constitution of India* (2020) and a regular contributor to the *Indian Express* and *Outlook* magazine. Rathore has taught at Jawaharlal Nehru University (JNU), University of Delhi, and Jindal Global University, India; Rutgers University and University of Pennsylvania, USA; University of Toronto, Canada; Humboldt University of Berlin, Germany; and Libera Università Internazionale degli Studi Sociali (LUISS) Guido Carli, Italy.

His twenty previous books range in theme from political philosophy, law, and religion to literature, sports, and wine. These include *Hegel's India: A Reinterpretation, with Texts* (2017) and *B.R. Ambedkar's The Buddha and His Dhamma: A Critical Edition* (2011). He is also the author of the forthcoming book, *B.R. Ambedkar: A Biography*.

Contributors

Sanghmitra S. Acharya is a professor at the Centre of Social Medicine and Community Health, School of Social Sciences, Jawaharlal Nehru University (JNU), New Delhi. She has published extensively in peer-reviewed journals on issues of health and social exclusion, with focus on youth in development, gender in urban spaces, and northeast India. She has 3 books and about 30 articles to her credit. Her recent work includes a co-edited book titled

Marginalization in Globalizing Delhi: Issues of Land, Livelihoods and Health (2017; with Sucharita Sen, Milap Punia, and Sunita Reddy). Her current work is on social discrimination in healthcare access among sanitation workers.

Sunaina Arya is co-editor of *Dalit Feminist Theory: A Reader* (2020; with Aakash Singh Rathore) and a PhD candidate at the Centre for Philosophy, JNU, New Delhi, completing a dissertation on feminist philosophy from a Dalit perspective. She earned her MPhil and MA from the same centre. She received an honourable mention in the Bluestone Rising Scholar Prize (2019) by Brandeis University, Massachusetts, USA. She is part of Global Dalit Changemakers, an initiative of the India China Institute, The New School, New York, USA. She was also awarded Rajiv Gandhi National Fellowship and Senior Research Fellowship by UGC for doctoral research. She has organized and presented research papers at several national and international conferences, seminars, and workshops. She is currently co-editing a special issue of *CASTE: A Global Journal on Social Exclusion*.

Kevin Brown is the Richard S. Melvin Professor of Law at Indiana University Maurer School of Law, and the emeritus director of the Hudson & Holland Scholars Program, Indiana University, Bloomington, USA. He teaches torts, law and education, race and law, and international comparative inequality. His research interest lies primarily in the areas of race, law, and education. Brown has published over 70 articles or comments on issues such as school desegregation, affirmative action, African-American immersion schools, and increasing school choice. Some of his publications include *Race, Law and Education in the Post-desegregation Era* (2005) and *Because of Our Success: The Changing Racial and Ethnic Ancestry of Blacks on Affirmative Action* (2014).

Ashwin Desai is a professor at the Department of Sociology, the University of Johannesburg, South Africa. His research interests include sports, political economy, and social policy. His latest work on the close relationship between politics and cricket in South Africa, *Reverse Sweep: A Story of South-African Cricket since Apartheid*, was published in 2017. He has co-authored the book, *The South African Gandhi: Stretcher-Bearer of Empire* (2015; with Goolam Vahed).

Lalit Khandare is an assistant professor at Pacific University, Oregon, USA. He serves on the Council of Global Social Issues and the Council on Social Work Education (CSWE). He teaches the courses research methods and thesis, program evaluation, and beyond the cycle of violence. He is engaged in research and publication in the area of housing and urban redevelopment, homelessness, public health, domestic violence, and social inclusion. He has presented his work at various conferences in USA, UK, India, Peru, and Germany. Some of his noteworthy research presentations were at CSWE, the UK Parliament, World Bank, Berlin Urban Roundtable, and Oxford University Poverty and Human Development Initiative.

Mushtaq Ahmad Malla is currently assistant professor and the head of the Department of Social Work in Government Degree College, Beerwah, Jammu & Kashmir, India. Prior to this he was working with ActionAid International as the state head for Jammu & Kashmir, India. He has also served as an assistant professor at the National Law School of India University (NLSIU), Bangalore, India, teaching public policy, and as a senior research fellow at the Institute of Rural Management Anand (IRMA), Gujarat, India. He completed his PhD from Jamia Millia Islamia, New Delhi, and MSc in social policy from the London School of Economics and Political Science, UK. His work and research are mainly focused on social protection, poverty and dignity, political economy, collective livelihoods, and minorities in South Asia.

Mala Mukherjee is an assistant professor at the Indian Institute of Dalit Studies (IIDS), New Delhi, since 2013. She completed her PhD in geography, with specialization in population studies, from JNU, New Delhi. In her doctoral thesis titled, 'Urban Deprivation and Vulnerability in Kolkata Metropolis: A Case Study of Low Income Households', she has focused on social discrimination in the urban sphere. She has published research papers in national and international journals and attended various conferences in India as well as abroad. Her research areas include urban deprivation, social exclusion, political inequality, and caste and gender intersectionality. She recently completed an Indian Council of Social Science Research project on 'North East Women in Delhi: Discrimination and Vulnerabilities'.

Komal Rajak is a doctoral candidate at the Department of Political Science, University of Delhi, India. She has presented and published research papers on caste and gender issues. She is an Ambedkarite activist who looks at feminist discourse through an Ambedkarian perspective.

Rajesh Raushan is an assistant professor at IIDS, New Delhi, India. His research interests include inequality, demographic techniques, public health, vulnerable groups, gender, human development, and multi-level modelling. He has authored the book *Child Health in India: Caste and Neighbourhood Effect* (2020). Raushan has published more than 30 research papers in peer-reviewed journals, and edited books, working papers, both national and international.

Moses Seenarine is a well-known academic author who is a Caribbean Dalit, born in Guyana, South America, six generations removed from South Asia. He has authored the book *Education and Empowerment among Dalit (Untouchable) Women in India* (2004). Seenarine's article on caste systems around the world was translated and published in Japan, and his work on women and caste in India has been cited by the Food and Agriculture Organization, United Nations Educational, Scientific and Cultural Organization, Human Rights Watch, Anti-Slavery International, the Institute for the Study of Labor, World Council of Churches, and several others.

N. Sukumar teaches political science at the Department of Political Science, the University of Delhi, India. He has researched and published widely on Ambedkarite politics, social exclusion, and human rights. He is actively involved with Ambedkarite movements and is a visiting faculty at many institutions. He blogs frequently at roundtableindia.co.in.

Goolam Vahed is a professor of history at the University of KwaZulu-Natal, South Africa. He has written on various aspects of the history of Indians and Muslims in South Africa, and on cricket. His most recent works include: *Chota Motala: A Biography of Political Activism in the KwaZulu-Natal Midlands* (2018) and *A History of the Present: A Biography of Indian South Africans, 1994–2019* (2019; with Ashwin Desai).